Light of Knowledge

LIGHT OF KNOWLEDGE

Essays on the Interplay of Knowledge, Time, and Space

Dharma Publishing

Dimensions of Thought I and II
Mastery of Mind
Visions of Knowledge
Light of Knowledge

Library of Congress Cataloging-in-Publication Data

Light of knowledge: essays on the interplay of knowledge, time,
 and space / [edited by Jack Petranker].
       p.   cm. - (Perspectives on Time, space, and knowledge)
    Includes bibliographical references.
    ISBN 0-89800-287-7
    1. Space and time--Psyhological aspects.   2. Space and time.
 3. Knowledge, Theory of.   I. Petranker, Jack.   II. Series.
 BF467.L54   1997   97-24726
 121--dc21   CIP

Cover: Photomicrograph of thiosulfate. Copyright © Corel Corp.

Typeset in Adobe Trump Mediaeval and Helvetica Light.
Printed and bound by Dharma Press, Berkeley, CA.

9   8   7   6   5   4   3   2   1

For all who belong
to knowledge and are bound to
time and space—whoever,
whenever, wherever
. . . forever

CONTENTS

ABBREVIATIONS

The following works in the *Time, Space, and Knowledge* series or the *Perspectives on Time, Space, and Knowledge* series, listed in order of publication date, have been abbreviated as indicated. All are published by Dharma Publishing. Note that the abbreviation "TSK" is sometimes also used in this volume to refer to the Time, Space, and Knowledge vision. It should be clear from context which usage is intended.

Works by Tarthang Tulku

TSK	*Time, Space, and Knowledge: A New Vision of Reality.* 1977.
LOK	*Love of Knowledge.* 1985.
KTS	*Knowledge of Time and Space.* 1990.
VOK	*Visions of Knowledge: Liberation of the Modern Mind.* 1993.

DTS   *Dynamics of Time and Space:*
           Transcending Limits on Knowledge. 1994.

Other Works

DOT   *Dimensions of Thought: Explorations in*
           Time, Space, and Knowledge (2 volumes).
           Eds. Ralph Moon and Steve Randall. 1980.

MOM   *Mastery of Mind.* 1993.

FOREWORD

Tarthang Tulku

The continuing interest in the TSK vision shown by this volume is very encouraging. I hope these essays lead readers to explore their own time and space, relying on the insights that knowledge makes available. Toward that end, I offer these TSK reflections on the significance of time, space, and knowledge in our lives.

Space Engineering

Each of us has a body that appears in the physical world. Since standard logic says that only what exists can appear, it seems our bodies must exist. Whatever exists seems to trace back to a source that also exists. Then what is the source of our bodies?

On the physical level, we might answer by pointing to the constitution of matter. Quarks and leptons are thought to comprise atoms, atoms in turn form molecules, and molecules interact to produce our bodies and allow them to operate. When we focus on these interactions, we realize that they depend on space, for unless atoms and molecules all somehow occupied the 'same' space, how could they interact?

When we view our bodies as living organisms, new dimensions of space interaction present themselves. The knowledge that instructs our cells in how to function is woven into the spatial configurations of DNA, whose strands are passed on from parent to child in a temporal lineage that traces to the earliest human beings. Shaped by their genetic heritage, the features of our body as it appears in space recapitulate the entire evolution of life on this planet: infinitely intricate patterns of knowledge transmitted through time. In allowing for such a display, space 'engineers' appearance in degrees of complexity far beyond our ability to comprehend.

At a level more fundamental than causal connections, space engineering seems to be the source of all appearance. When the edge of each entity resolves into the edge of space; when a microscope reveals nested layers of space within each solid 'thing', is appearance ultimately different from space? If we insist that substance must be 'more' than space, is not the source of this 'more' another instance of space engineering?

Coming and Going

As living, embodied beings, we are also experiencers, acting and reacting to what time presents. But what of the one who has the experience, who takes hold of events? Is that one—our separate self—also only an experience? Once an arrow falls to earth, its prior flight through the air is simply gone—vanished. If the events that constitute our lives likewise vanish once they have played themselves out, can they really support our claim to have or be a fixed identity? Though it seems strange to imagine, perhaps we are more truly no one, coming from no place and going nowhere—a shifting configuration of events, not bound to continuity in any way.

The sense that we arise, persist, and pass away seems to be based on a particular way of interpreting experience. As time presents events and space exhibits appearance, we superimpose on the stream of happenings sets of connections and interlocking stories. We relate each entity and each event to others, then react to our own constructs with judgments and emotions. Such a "relative knowledge" seems natural to us: our trusted guide for making sense of what is so.

What is the source of relative knowledge? Before the reaction is the presentation, and beneath the account is the experience. As we trace back, examining one 'layer' of manifestation after another, we reach a point where nothing manifests at all—a field of blankness. Here relative knowledge falls silent, and a new possibility for knowing presents itself. Time and space, the silent partners in each experience, grant knowledge access.

For a knowledge shaped by the stillness of space and time, the distinctions that relative knowledge relies on lose their power and significance. Space gives no name to the difference between your present being and your life in the womb. Time refuses to discriminate good and bad, pleasant and unpleasant. Reactions, judgments, and namings arise as so many additional events—part of the fluid space-time patterning of what appears.

Because it no longer makes distinctions, a space-time knowledge might not seem like knowledge at all. But that judgment comes from distinction-making mind, which only knows the nameable. Space-time knowledge is active differently: not only in the knowing of appearance, but also in the time and space of appearing itself. It encompasses the knowing that knows how to know. In all our namings of the knowing capacity— mind, consciousness, rational, irrational, subconscious, awareness, intuition—we have left unspoken this more fundamental knowledge of the whole.

For anyone tired of the obsessive wanting and grasping of ordinary understanding, space-time knowledge offers healing therapy. Why pursue a far-off goal, when there is nowhere to go? Why long for what is missing, when our sense of being separate has no substance? In space-time knowledgeability, beginnings and endings are the dance of knowledge in space; borders and obstructions the fabrications of space engineering. 'My space' and 'your space', 'coming and going', 'living and dying'! Merging with space in unforced intimacy, Great Knowledge sees only moves in a remarkable game.

Stream of Stories

If we find ourselves inspired by the prospect of such a way of seeing and being, we may have missed the point. We are the ones who rely on relative knowledge, and relative knowledge has no use for the silence of space-time knowledgeability. The one who sees with space eyes would be a different being, being differently.

Still, 'difference' remains relative. Perhaps Great Knowledge differs from relative knowledge only because we are accustomed to seeing differences. When the petals of a blossom open, shall we look to the subtle variations among them, or to the flower's timeless grace? Perhaps we are free to choose.

For instance, below the surface of appearance, language and the inputs of the senses set up partitions and proclaim them solid. Looking at how this ongoing fabrication unfolds, we discover our own role to be that of bystander. We are like television viewers absorbed in the daily news, nodding in agreement as the anchorman signs off: "And that's the way it is!"

How is the transmission created and presented? Who is the reporter and what are his sources? Who hired him? Who sponsors the broadcast? Staying with these questions is not easy, for the reporter who tells the story demands our response and our engagement—insists that we affirm. The very rhythms in which relative knowledge plays back what has been recorded invite our agreement and compel our commitment. Yet if we resist such pressures, the steady surface stream of stories begins to look like an ongoing attempt to establish a stable and reliable reality. What is the hidden cost of pursuing this goal? Are we restricting the range of what can be experienced? Are we stripping away the power of knowledge—dulling its penetrating clarity?

Perhaps we could justify paying a high price for certainty, but our strategy seems doomed to failure, for time does not play along. As the stream of stories unfolds, unanticipated changes undermine their accuracy. Battered by the flux of experience, the structures we erect first grow deformed, and then collapse.

Could we do it differently? Could we look *through* the structures that time conducts into being to acknowledge the magic of space engineering? Instead of relying on the mind that mind itself has read it into operation, could we expand the operation of mind into the depths of innovation? Could we accept that whatever happens could happen differently—each emerging moment a complete surprise?

Opening the Gate

As long as we claim to be the owners of knowledge, we affirm a structure that binds us to not knowing and uncertainty. Taking our position 'here', we confirm the unknown 'there'. The interpretations we impose freeze space-openness into place. Time becomes an external force, rushing past too quickly for us to free appearance into something lighter and more alive. Listening attentively for the silent source of what we affirm, we may hear a murmured message in the background, proclaiming that limits are inevitable.

Suppose we heard the muttered limits on our knowing as the falling silent of our saying. Could we imagine that within that silence, knowledge speaks—not to offer a new interpretation, but to free interpretations from the solidity of their claiming? As interpretation floated to the surface of appearance, could knowledge conduct time into the newly open depths of space? Freed from the linear order of relative knowledge, could past and future join with present? As the triple gate of time swung open, would space vastness emerge, inform ing all appearance and awakening a natural creativity ?

The urge to interfere with such an awakening—to tell ourselves the gate is open, or pause to marvel at the power of being present—would be strong. But if we sensed this shift occurring, we would still be free to choose. Time may conduct the structures of doing and doer, of being and 'being the one who', but that does not compel us to insist on identity. Space may present a scenery for seeming, but that does not require us to ignore the space that surrounds, contains and express-es every manifestation. Instead of manufacturing into narrative the flickering play of what presents itself, can we enter the space surround? Can we surrender our attachment to what time and language conduct?

Beneath the structure of each story, we can trace the fact of minding—a 'certain take' on the knowing capacity. But what if we are not the minding mind? Suppose instead we are the body of operation behind the operation of the ordinary body—the center of the process, the open of the relative. Can we let it be so?

Enjoyment of Availability

Though space does not depart from stillness, a space momentum seems to operate, sustaining interpretation as it constructs the present panorama. Once we take hold of what takes form in this way, its asserted truth becomes almost tangible. My anger is *real*, my perception is *real*. But why agree to let the outcome of the prevailing space-time dynamic bind us? Are the prevailing models so comprehensive—the life they offer so fulfilling? Have cultures throughout the world been foolish or deluded to affirm the truth of the miraculous, beyond all human constructs?

For all the changes that unfold through time, human experience is marked by a certain sameness, rooted in the insistence by relative knowledge that the structures set in place by language and dualistic ways of thinking must be maintained. Through all of recorded history, human beings have felt isolation and known dissatisfaction, struggled with feelings of incompleteness and sought with limited success to fulfill their desires. The future seems likely to hold more of the same: playing out the standard vision and acting out the old adventures.

The forms of knowledge we pursue today make it difficult to see this sameness. Trained to focus on what is new, we are fascinated with change and disgusted by boredom. Yet this predisposition has its positive side, for it opens our minds to new knowledge. Our deep, abiding curiosity lays the foundation for a more fundamental wonderment. If we can learn to ask questions at a different level, our fascination with new knowledge can lead to a new vision of what knowledge can be.

TSK reminds us that the limits relative knowledge reveals and affirms are also an ongoing exhibition: mounted by knowledge, accommodated by space, and presented by time. Our most repetitive projections and definitions still work feats of boundless artistry, expressions of the time-space-knowledge interplay. Inseparable from our limits, unaffected by views or theories, Great Time, Great Space, and Great Knowledge are available.

The mind seems compelled to assign meanings—to offer answers to the question, "Why?" TSK does not reject such meanings, but sees them as provisional. This suggests we could discover other meanings, but that alternative only encourages us to continue in our role as the agents of a distanced knowledge, cut off from the embodied aliveness of time and space. Instead, TSK points to the structure of relative knowledge itself, reminding us that the knowledge *embodied* in the relative is inseparable from space and time. When we know the provisional status of the investigator, the constructed status of the known, and the dynamic of the inquiry, we recognize this to be so.

Charisma of Knowledge

As partners with time and space and knowledge, we are free to unfold that partnership into intimacy. We can expand the openness of space until it encompasses the entire universe; condense the dynamic of time until no one moment stands separate from the whole. Perhaps we are not the ones who bring this about; perhaps it is time that does the expanding and condensing. Yet even if our claim to ownership is mistaken, the mistake is part of the display. 'Right' and 'wrong' are secondary.

Relative knowledge makes its separate points and holds on tightly to the structures it has pointed out. Once the points are set up, we bounce back and forth among them. It can be a rocky ride. Yet this frenetic energy can become our accommodating vehicle. Bouncing back and forth, we are dancing the rhythms of an all-pervading melody, surfing the waves of an ever cresting ocean. As knowledge-holders, we remain close to the vision of this happening.

To shift toward ths different way of knowing and being, we need a paradigm: a certain angle for the mind to take to be productive in this unaccustomed minding. One way is to anchor ourselves in the new, ready to experiment. Then we can report back that the vision is available, that we need not settle for fixed juxtapositions and solid objects with sealed identities. Still, this way is transitional. In the end we can open *any* form of thought and find the richness of appearance in *each* reflection. Within each limit, infinity is available; within restriction, unending abundance. Best of friends, mind and knowledge walk hand in hand through a space no longer empty or isolating, but rich and suffused with love.

We can embrace this perfect being, this blessing of knowledge. Perhaps we can surprise ourselves, looking with a sidelong glance as the interpreter interprets itself. Within this 'founding' story, we can turn from the patterns the mind establishes to read out mind at work. We can see and manifest the charisma of knowledge, active in time and space. The vast amazement that this is possible is already the realization that it is so.

If we begin very lightly, exploring our ways of embodying and making sense, the speculation may arise: "My own space is not separate." As this suspicion deepens, it leads us into space itself, and we realize: *Knowledge is not what the knower knows.* As each point opens, we no longer have to cling to the specifics of what is so. We may arrive at 'nothing going on'—no territories, no intentions, no understanding TSK. Are words still necessary? Well then: natural . . . magical . . . uncreate . . . . Beyond even tears.

Beauty of Fullness

As the carriers of knowledge through time, human beings have a responsibility to uphold what has been known in the past and to ask what can be known in the future; to explore the shape of knowledge and enact its gentle discipline; to expand and refine the scope of inquiry. Yet our commitment to being the one who knows prevents us from fulfilling that responsibility, for it keeps us from knowing the mind and its way of minding. Living in the world set up when mind reads out the read-outs of mind, we hear the separate echo, forgetting to hear within the echo the originating sound.

TSK invites us to integrate knowledge with the natural creativity of mind, so that 'knowing' and 'being known' become inseparable. When we no longer insist on carving the dimensions of knowledge into distinct and separate realms, on pounding everything into shape, we come to a way of being not bound to 'have-to be' and 'ought-to be', 'want-to be' and 'cannot be'. We arrive at the parenthood of knowledge.

In a world where the inner beauty of knowledge shines forth and the edge of appearance is pervasive, what role might we play? Like a great artist, we could reveal the meaning of Great Knowledge, the great benefactor. Like the great compassionate ones, we could manifest the freedom of Great Space as the truth of Great Love. As inspiration led the mind toward transformation, we could integrate experience into the fullness of Great Time, and discover at the center of our hearts the fullness of human being.

If knowledge spoke to us directly, would it urge us to make use of this present opportunity? As we listened, could we truly hear, gently awakening our natural receptivity to know? Could we respond? Could we embody Great Knowledge as the secret body of each thought . . . perception . . . quality . . . experience?

What alternative do we have? What intelligence is available? Figuring is triggering, but that not need not be our stopping point. If we pull out just one thread, the whole tapestry may vanish, revealing the hidden depth of innovation at the heart of the matter. Is it so? Can the magic of mind be all?

Tarthang Tulku
Odiyan, California
Buddha's Birthday, 1997

PREFACE

The crisis in knowledge, simmering now for many decades, is today close to boiling over. Scientific knowledge continues to grow, adding to its remarkable accomplishments, yet each advance brings with it unanticipated problems. Information expands exponentially, and with it our power to predict and to manipulate, but at the same time there is a growing sense that things are out of control, headed in unhealthy directions that we are powerless to stop. On the one hand, global progress; on the other, looming chaos. If this is the best of times, it is also the worst of times.

Just these circumstances, it seems to me, give Time, Space, and Knowledge ("TSK") its importance. There is no shortage of alternatives to the ruling ways of knowing, but TSK offers an approach so truly radical that it stands apart. At once precise and visionary, TSK takes the scientific spirit of inquiry into domains where science has refused to venture. Instead of tying knowledge to the substance of what is known, it offers knowledge as an intrinsic *capacity* of space and time. And that makes all the difference.

TSK stands out for its non-dogmatic openness. Instead of rejecting current forms of knowledge, it invites them to expand their scope. Interpreted through any set of concerns or any tradition of knowledge, it offers new inspiration. It shapes its own path, grounded in the insight that (as Tarthang Tulku writes in the foreword to this volume) knowledge is not what the knower knows. More complete than speculative philosophy, more immediate than theory, it is also more verifiable than religion and more fulfilling than academic discourse. It combines the indisputability of experience with the transformative power of visionary thinking. TSK offers more than new interpretations of how things have been or might be. You can *live* it, right now.

Publication of *Time, Space, and Knowledge* in 1977 generated considerable interest and appreciation. The book was quickly translated into four languages, and it has been studied and practiced across the country and around the world, in colleges and universities as well as countless informal study groups. Starting in 1987, Tarthang Tulku published four additional TSK-related works, each opening new aspects of the vision. Other students of TSK—philosophers, psychologists, meditators, systems theorists—have added to this body of inquiry, exploring in light of their own experience and concerns a way of thinking and knowing that ordinary knowledge finds quintessentially elusive.

Light of Knowledge, the fourth collection of essays by students of the TSK vision, seems to me an important step in bringing the potential of TSK closer to realization. This may reflect in part a more mature and considered response to the vision. But it also traces to the fact that society itself, in its concerns and its obsessions, is evolving toward the issues that TSK naturally brings to the fore. There is a growing sense that a great transition is underway; that something fundamental *must* change.

This is not the first time in recent decades that such a feeling has awakened, but this time it seems to be accompanied by a kind of blankness—a not-knowing what to do next. This very not-knowing is a hopeful sign, for it may encourage the kind of open hearing required for the radical vision of global knowledgeability that TSK offers—and this book explores.

The opening articles in *Light of Knowledge* present examples of a different knowledge in action. First comes an evocative essay by Tarthang Tulku that investigates the 'two-way pointing' of thoughts: outward toward what is happening, and inward toward the rhythms of mind in operation. As a way of giving balanced attention to both these aspects, the author suggests we can turn our conventional knowledge on edge. He gives to this metaphor an unexpected depth and aliveness.

The essay that follows, by Hal Gurish, presents the author's continuing experiments in making the 'data' and constructs of conventional knowledge transparent. Gurish writes in a style that is itself transparent, making the prospect for knowing differently seem natural, even self-evident. Don Beere's article adds strength to this conviction through its careful phenomenological analysis of nonordinary knowledge, intended to show that the nonordinary is in fact ordinary. It raises the question why this insight seems so difficult for us to comprehend and put into practice.

The next three essays stand together as critiques of standard knowledge, especially in the professional and academic domain. Ron Purser draws on his own experience of non-standard knowledge to suggest ways for implementing different ways of knowing, both personally and professionally. Steve Randall shows that each of us has the capacity to create and utilize his or her own vehicle for knowledge. He also presents his own model (for models too embody knowledge!) for classifying and relating alternative vehicles, analyzing the interrelated criteria of consistency, effectiveness, and comprehensiveness.

Alfonso Montuori (like Purser, a systems theorist) asks how knowledge can become more creative, and explores the ways in which conventional knowledge is opposed to creativity, even when it purports to foster it. He raises a theme explored in several essays (see especially the article by Osinovsky): the role of models and paradigms in our present ways of knowing, and the possibility of a knowledge that does not depend on either.

In an essay that stands at the midpoint of the book, Alan Malachowski points to the TSK vision as an alternative to epistemology. He makes the important point that TSK is presented not to criticize or even improve standard knowledge, but rather as a "benign gesture of communication" that draws attention to a wholly different alternative.

My own essay investigates the seeming impossibility in a fragmented society such as ours of going beyond private, selfish concerns. At the heart of this dilemma, I argue, lies the conviction that ignorance is not only inevitable, but actually constitutes a social good. My suggestion is to challenge this debilitating assumption by activating a knowledge that does not belong to the self.

In a somewhat similar vein, Lee Nichol takes on the claims of postmodernism to have decentered the self, as well as the claim that virtual reality has the power to free us from our identities. He shows that the advocates of both these views remain bound by forms of knowledge in which the self as knower remains as central as always. Concerned that we are at risk of sealing off from inquiry the way the self knows, he finds in TSK and the work of the physicist David Bohm an alternative: the embodied immediacy of experience.

Maxim Osinovsky, trained as a physicist, confronts the radical 'otherness' of TSK as a 'methodology' of knowing, exploring various ways in which it might interact with conventional knowledge (represented in his essay by the natural sciences). He raises the provocative question whether a science that radically transformed its methodology would still be science.

Finally, John Smyrl draws on the insights of the German thinker Jean Gebser to show how the categories and approaches of TSK could be used to open new avenues of exploration within conventional disciplines such as history and art. His observations on the ways that Gebser links shifts in perception to the structures of space can be fruitfully compared to the speculations on space geography with which Tarthang Tulku opens the volume.

Although there are themes that run through many of the essays in this volume, what truly unifies them is a certain tone: a realization that the alternative to our radically situated—and radically inadequate—contemporary knowledge is available here and now. This does not mean (as Malachowski notes) that we can readily give an instance of a special 'TSK bit of knowledge', for the knowledge that counts as such for TSK is phenomenological in its core, and cannot be packaged in words and concepts. Still, there shines through these essays an appreciation for what knowledge *could* be that many readers should find deeply encouraging.

TSK tells us that knowledge is inseparable from space and time. This means that cultivating a greater appreciation for what appears in time and space, or learning to embody time and space more fully, will lead directly to more knowledge. But it also means that anything written about TSK can only point *toward* a TSK knowing. For words and ideas do not transmit time and space directly; instead, they turn time into remembered or imagined experience, and make space into the perceived presence (or absence) of things.

This being so, we could never expect the essays collected here to add up to a 'how-to' manual for TSK. Rather, their success comes in making TSK accessible as the very potential for a new way of knowing, and in holding up a mirror to ordinary knowledge, revealing its limits and distortions.

In closing, let me say something about my own relation to TSK. For a dozen years now, I have been the principal editor for the books of the TSK series. Working closely and repeatedly with each text to refine the language and style, bring the syntax into compliance with standard English, and address issues of organization, my chief concern has been to preserve as accurately as possible the meaning of these visionary works, whose inner depths I do not pretend to understand. Throughout this time, I have been a deeply appreciative student of TSK, grateful that my editorial duties allowed me to work with it so intensively.

Through all these years, it has struck me as strange that not more people respond readily to the beauty and power that shine through TSK. That is one reason I am pleased with the form this volume has taken. For I sense that the collective intelligence and heartfelt enthusiasm of its contributors—the range of their concerns and experience, the playful dynamic of their inquiry, and the deep appreciation for knowledge that sparkles in their writing—may allow the spirit of TSK to manifest more fully in our time.

Light of Knowledge

GEOGRAPHIES OF KNOWLEDGE

Tarthang Tulku

Whenever we make assumptions and present viewpoints, take positions or interpret—whenever we create grounds for conflict—we base ourselves primarily on the content of our thoughts. But what are thoughts themselves based on? If we trace their arising in our own experience, we find that each thought is triggered by previous thoughts, or by perceptions that at once become the object of thought. Thoughts refer back to other thoughts, in proliferating patterns.

In shaping meaning, thoughts claim to give order and structure to phenomena that are known independent of thoughts. Yet this claim is difficult to justify. In pointing 'out' what is really happening, thoughts equally point 'in': back toward the rhythms of the mind in operation. Given this 'two-way pointing', what knowledge

3

do thoughts really 'contain' or rely on? Even when they are firmly grounded in sense perception, can thoughts ever go beyond sheer speculation?

Focused on the contents of thoughts, we largely ignore thoughts themselves, or else we settle for a superficial understanding of what they are. We accept thoughts for their instrumental value, and we continue to accept as authoritative their interplay with perception. Yet thought and mind as the subject or 'doer' of each perception or cognition remain mysterious. Knowledge of the mind in operation—its structure, patterns, and dynamics—remains largely undeveloped. Even the most basic question of all—the source of thought's ability to interpret and give meaning—is beyond our present capacity to analyze.

Despite the ever-increasing hoards of knowledge we are building up, the first steps toward an inner science of mind have yet to be taken. Nor do we have the tools available to do so. The 'here/there', 'at/from' patternings of analysis that thought applies to the physical realm seem inapplicable to mind and thoughts themselves. In any case, these fundamental patterns for cognition have been set in place by mind. How can we use them to make sense of mind?

Suppose that knowledge was not bound by thought's outward-directed lines of cognition, but was free to move in all directions. Suppose that beyond or within or at right angles to the body of knowledge that we currently investigate, another, invisible body of knowledge were available. Can we even imagine how to

4

explore this possibility? If not, can we say that we know how to know?

Space of Knowledge

Ordinary knowledge depends on the power of perception to focus the stream of experience, directing it toward specific objects that then become available for thought to identify and interpret. As thought 'reads out' the meaning of each appearance, it initiates a dynamic that is always moving forward. Our own position as the subject that knows is marked out by an 'x' that remains unknown. From a different angle, the 'x' is the cross of an x-y axis that defines the directions along which inquiry can proceed. In either view, mind cannot know its own knowing.

Within the dynamic of thought-perception, however, knowledge can be conducted differently. As perception points 'out', we can look differently, turning perception on edge. At first this may mean simply looking toward the borders or edges of what is perceived. More fundamentally, however, it means revealing the hidden dimensionality of perception itself.

Turned on edge, perception reveals a complex mental realm analogous to the world of subatomic particles discovered by the methods of modern physics. Here we can trace the power of thought to establish the content of appearance. It is not simply that we gain a new view on reality; rather, our sense of what is real and what is knowable shifts. We discover knowledge *within* thought's interpretations, *as* those interpretations. Old distinctions between known and unknown give way: The ordinary unknown melts into the knowledgeability of the edge like an ice floe melting into the sea. The *quality* of experience changes, so that defining limits and barriers to fulfillment vanish.

Turning perception on edge allows inner vision to develop. First, the distinction between what is outside the mind and inside the mind loses its usual significance. Second, the initial object-like structure of mental phenomena falls away; in a sense, there is nothing there. Third, it becomes possible to 'crack open' mental appearance to enter a new dimension.

In the dimension that inner vision makes available, the reality that previously appeared as the content of thoughts is reborn as an expression of knowledge. Appearance arises as the innovation of the knowledge that reveals, while thoughts become an instrumental transformation of this revealing knowledge. Within the limited space-body of thinking, a global knowledgeability allows the Body of Knowledge to transpire fully. Having discovered the space that conducts knowledge, we have discovered the source of being.

As an image for clarifying the different dimensionality of the knowledge-space, we might imagine that whatever appears has at its center an invisible hole, like the hole of a donut. Somehow, mysteriously, thought emerges from that hole to know the whole. Turning perception on edge, we bring the hole into view; entering the hole, we discover how appearance comes to be.

The hole at the center opens into the knowledge dimension. Light flows through this opening, revealing appearance as the expression of knowledge. We can still trace the standard lineage of each appearance: from the evolution of life on earth to the dynamic that turns happiness into sorrow and back again; from the complementary patterns of rationality and spirituality to the interplay of one sense faculty with all the others. Yet the substantiality of each appearance lightens, like the spray from an ocean wave. As thoughts are understood as expressions of knowledge, experience merges with the knowledge-space. Manifesting the open lightness of the hole, emotions, identifications, rigid causal chains, and self-confirming stories lose their heavy and compelling power. The vision of knowledge blossoms into the perfect beauty of freedom.

As the vision deepens, we find that we can turn the hole on edge as well, 'minding' the edge that separates hole and substance with the same freedom that we have discovered within thought and perception. Hole and substance merge, allowing the 'no-basis basis' of appearance to become the full expression of the vision of knowledge. We learn what it means to let go of each pattern, each new defining edge—even the edges that we use to mark out the boundaries of the self.

When 'minding' turns each edge on edge, revealing the edge itself as 'minding', distinctions disappear. A new understanding of space and knowledge and time allows the constructs of mind to merge into the intimacy of being. The hole becomes a non-excluding whole—a tunnel into a wholly different dimension of knowledgeability. 'Broader' and 'bigger' expand into brilliance, and segments and fragments give way to fullness.

Time of Wholeness

The merging of mind with space knowledge is also the emerging of time as the active domain for being. Before, thoughts moved out from mind with a steady momentum whose varying rhythms manifested the next point to be pointed out. Now, however, time's varying intensities exhibit a unitary presence, pristine, conclusive, and incisive. Inner vision opens actively to the presence of the whole.

To clarify the significance of this transformation, imagine a span of a hundred billion years, far exceeding the age of the universe. Now imagine a hundred such spans of time. Imagine that the whole of this complex is a tiny fragment of the whole of time; infinitely small in ratio to the whole. Finally, imagine that this entire range of time emerges and then vanishes, like a delicate flower. When the flower disappears, where has it gone? Does it have a root, or is the root born together with the blossom? When does the birth take place? The disappearing? Do such 'events' suggest a different way of conducting time?

In ordinary knowing, a back and forth rhythm of repetition and repudiation takes form as the varying content of thought and the stories that content supports. As soon as we let these structures fade out of focus, time becomes differently available. Each moment takes on its own significance. The rhythms of repetition shorten, until presence comes and goes in an instantaneous arising and passing away. In a single emerging instant, the patterns that shape our world—the whole range of human experience—are equally available, equally present.

In this immediate arising, all is in flux. The picture I piece together 'now' may differ as radically from the reality 'then' as two successive images in a kaleidoscope. Each specific happening is a mystery: We cannot express the place of its appearing, the how of its coming, or the when of its disappearing. Yet the mystery is no bar to knowledge, for each rhythmic transition that thought reveals is complete in itself—wholly open to knowledgeability.

In the time of the whole, the hole at the center of each appearance opens into nothing at all, like the tip of a rolled-up paper cone when the cone is unrolled. This 'nothing at all' is also 'nothing excluded': the whole of the hole. The absence of substance becomes the heart of the present: gateway to visions of knowledge.

In the presence of the whole, thought becomes the bridge uniting perception with vision. Tracing its own 'independent immanent', thought reveals the Body of Knowledge *within* the engagements we rely on to give meaning. Thinking its own presence, thought manifests the *quality* of knowledge.

At the beginning of the beginning, before anything at all has been 'pointed out', thought can introduce the presence of presence. Not bound to comparison or the ratios that establish rational order, it can move beyond speculation, neither 'taking hold' nor 'losing sight of'. Here there is no marking off as unknowable the regions of past and future; no restrictive 'source from'. Resting in the meaning of knowledge, thought is free to transmit the meanings of interpretation.

Relying on this intrinsic knowledgeability of thought, we draw close to our own being. We discover the extraordinary in ordinary knowing; the unrepeated in each repeating pattern. Departing from both subjective and objective perspectives, we gain immediate access to space, and also to the 'no-taking-place' of time. Fully engaged, we encompass experience without relying on positionings or 'wordings'. Multiple perspectives on previously closed dimensions open freely. The Body of Knowledge becomes the witness of its own arising. We too bear witness. We are 'inside' knowledge, and there is no outside.

Knowledge of Inspiration

Through all the centuries of civilization, knowledge has granted us incredible bounty. Yet we continue to filter the vision of knowledge through a subjective lens that cuts out its depth and cuts off our own capacities. Trusting in an artificial knowledge that adds and subtracts assumptions and distinctions, we cannot accurately map the shifting dynamics of being. All too easily, we fall out of balance. Our actions lead to suffering, our solutions create new problems, and the longings of our heart cannot be healed.

The Body of Knowledge offers an alternative: an appearance 'within' appearance that frees knowledge from the claims of substance. From within its within, there is no beyond the beyond—no witness proclaiming transcendence, no experience structured to conform to speculation, no truth limited by the way things 'really' are.

Focused differently, thought can inject the inspiration of the Body of Knowledge into present 'minding'. Instead of labeling content, thought can explore the space that exhibits content. Instead of tracing cause and effect, it can display the innovative time that presents appearance. Instead of proclaiming what is, it can investigate its own proclaiming. The rational and logical knowledge that define the who and where of what we are can be integrated with the intimacy of being. Contradiction can be transformed into the bonding of alternatives.

If we glimpse such new dimensions of knowledge in our own experience, we can honor their availability and cherish their power. Open to the knowledgeability of each presentation and alive to the wholeness of each arising moment, space and time become sacred. When the meaning of space unites the cosmos with our inner world of thought-perception, the meaning of time can inform our every thought and action. Resisting the call to label and to understand from a subjective point of view, we can embody knowledge as the heart of our own being.

Presented as a system of understanding, TSK relies on assigned meanings and puts forward speculations.

Yet even if the vision as expressed in words remains subject to the standard limitations on present knowledge, the presentation can resonate with our own inner knowledgeability, dancing a different way of wording. If we cannot say what we mean, we can invite every experience to speak. If we cannot leap into knowledge, we can let go of the secret pockets of identity and judgment. Entering the field of knowledgeability, we can face up to what we do not want to confront, accepting the authority of time and space and knowledge.

Knowledge is in the public domain, owned by no one. It is also a part of our thoughts and minds, enacted in each moment of being. TSK merges these two realities—the meanings of thought join forces with the meaningfulness of being. At both these levels, we *are* TSK, beyond any possibility of denial, affirmation, or attainment. When knowledge arises, we need not account for it; when experience opens, we need not specify the methodology at work. The closed circle that confines, the rhythms that shape and limit—these express the space-time presence of the knowledge that liberates. Today, when the rhythms of time seem hostile to innovative inner vision, TSK can heal our damaged way of being.

Within mind and thought, there is a body beyond the body we know. In any moment—at any 'within'—transforming richness is available. Toward the edge, at the edge, within the edge, thoughts melt into the vision of knowledge. Co-emerging, vision, thought, and presence reveal the unique trajectory of the present curve of time and space.

TRANSPARENCY

Hal Gurish

Transparency is an aspect of TSK that has enabled me to appreciate parts of my experience that might otherwise be lost. Within our experience are countless 'blank spaces' where nothing seems to be happening. These include such ordinary, unremarkable events as dreams which are not dreams in any visual or story form; moments charged with a vague feeling; jumbled aggregates that are not chaotic, yet have no organizing story or theme; smells that are faintly reminiscent but yield to the claim of no single memory; and inspiration that remains nascent rather than coming into idea or image. Such events or times usually pass without appreciation that they are knowledge. But TSK invites us to look differently. What of the possibilities that do not manifest, yet are imperceptibly present? Can we bear for once not to shrug them off?

Transparency is an excellent way to see more deeply into these events. Lucid and evocative, transparency shines through aspects of experience which might otherwise not be seen. To become aware of transparency is to acknowledge that knowing does not necessarily depend upon the object in the foreground to validate it.

Transparency evokes an openness of mind that values wonder and curiosity toward the odd experience alongside or within the ordinary. It alerts us to the faint, almost imperceptible feeling that pervades an otherwise blank space. This blankness is shaped by the conventional model of space. No thing is present, no boundaries or definitions are available. Yet the experience bears a curious feeling. If we looked with sensitivity to time rather than space, we could appreciate the moment's dynamic aspect: It is about to move us. Knowledge is imminent. It does not have to be lost.

I have often heard myself say with regard to a problem or situation: "Now I can see through it." In such a moment, I feel some pleasure and relaxation, the latter tipping me off to the underlying, preexisting tension. As the problem opens to a larger perspective there comes an increase of mental and physical energy. I feel as if I am in a larger space. A shift or jump to a qualitatively different knowing has occurred.

As I observe more closely this 'seeing through', I recognize that it follows from an intention to concentrate upon the problem or situation. The mental and physical energy tied up in it becomes more focused, more intensified. As this concentration builds to a critical intensity, the whole process breaks open. There is a release of physical tension and a feeling of energy moving in the body. This movement is often a rising sensation that turns into inspiration. Thoughts and memories become fluid and fluent; understanding comes easily as my perspective shifts. All this helps reveal that I am in another space.

In this new space, the problem is no longer so problematic. Yet it does not entirely disappear. An afterglow remains, filled with associated memories and feelings and an impression of the previous physical tension, still tending to emerge. Now, however, this residuum has been rendered transparent. It is infused by a larger perspective and understanding of the problem.

The ease I feel in my body at such times is more than a release of tension. It has a depth that often verges upon being immense, flowing out into vast regions. When this flow actually occurs, the quality of the tension changes markedly. Its borders are no longer hard-edged and confining. It no longer confines understanding either; instead, mental energy expands as well. Looking back, my sense is that the tension seems to have been intent upon maintaining its borders. At a different level, the tension seems to have aimed at avoiding the struggle involved in knowing the problem at greater depth. It is as if the incipient struggle had been checked and postponed indefinitely into tension.

There is another kind of experience where it is thoughts and thinking that become transparent. This usually does not involve the same kind of urgency as in the experience I have just described. I may be sitting quietly, fairly relaxed, observing thoughts in relation to space (and time). For example, I may be looking at the space between thoughts or even within thoughts. Ordinarily I do not regard thoughts as being solid, but when I practice such exercises I soon notice that thoughts are indeed impenetrable, completely obscuring my ability to observe the space between them, much less the space within. Thoughts 'take' me as the observer and carry me forward in a motion so strong it defies any reflection upon what is happening. The observer is completely enveloped, swallowed up and temporarily blinded by the power of the forward motion.

How does the observer extract himself from this encompassing environment? My first, rather imprecise answer is that I experience the shift as a sudden jump out of the motion of thinking, much like being startled: "What happened?" Perhaps it helps that I am already on guard at a deeper level, having had this happen so often before when doing such a practice.

I find this jump significant. It has a quantum characteristic that appears to operate at many levels of existence. Perhaps the accelerating speed and pressure of thoughts pile up, impinging more and more on the underlying intention to observe what is going on, until the breakout of the observer surfaces. At that moment perception is very sharp, even if only for a split second. I may see that I still have some tension in my body. Retrospectively, I may realize that this is not simply the tension of being startled, of jumping out. Instead, I discover a memory of its having been there for a while. When I look in terms of the momentary clarity I have experienced, I see that the release of thinking has a bodily counterpart—as if thought had been held firmly in the body to establish its ground, its substantiality. When I deliberately let the tension go, both body and mind are quiet for a while. Then thoughts come up and the cycle resumes.

If I have the presence of mind in such moments to look carefully at the relation between body and thought, I may observe that thoughts are usually preceded by movement in the body. Studying these movements over many episodes at different times in practice, I have found a relationship to gross or subtle movements in the breath. Gross sensations and breath correlate to thoughts that I consider heavy with emotion, which tend to move downward and establish themselves in tension and body postures. More subtle sensations and movements of the breath correlate with open and clear periods. More often than not, these open periods either move upward or expand. They are linked to inspiration, both in subtle breath and in mind.

As noted above, thoughts that are urgent tend to eclipse the observer. Emotion certainly makes thought more urgent, but often enough thoughts exhibit a momentum and urgency that have no obvious link to emotions. It takes long and repeated observations to finally see through the feelings at work here, which stubbornly resist revealing their purpose. But if I persist, I discover an underlying emotionality obscured by the thought's motion forward (as the word 'e-motion' already suggests). The specific quality of this emotion is apprehension or even anxiety: a literal 'holding on' through the body and holding on to the forward motion of thinking.

Again, transparency reveals this structure. As the holding tension is released, a brief moment of fear spikes, and there comes a relaxing 'whoosh' toward expansion. I see again that the apprehension served to maintain control of my established position; that the tension was the establishment of position, and that the position in turn supported my identity in that precarious moment when all orientation toward the self as observer is gone. Transparency comes when I am able to expand the experience deliberately. The openness that follows affords the opportunity to see through the anxiety driving the train of thoughts. With more practice, I grow familiar as well with the way the cycle tends to reassert itself.

As the practice of this process of observation and expanding is further cultivated, there may be a series of spontaneous jumps that transparentizes the whole process. With this greater transparency, openness prevails over the movements in the body and the forward motion of thoughts, and there is no need to cycle back down to ordinary thinking. All becomes quiet, for a brief period or perhaps longer. . . . During such moments, time seems to stop, even while there is a parallel sense 'outside' of this that can be aware of clock-time moving forward. This may account for the experiential impression of second-level time, described in the first TSK book as 'going without going'.

As thoughts become transparent, the space within them comes into view, and the quality of thinking becomes airy and light. At such times the observer is no longer eclipsed by the forward thrust of the thought. Time's more subtle, discriminating spirit can make distinctions in a new way, not having to exclude one object, idea, or feeling to establish another. My sense of self, the one asking questions, and the presentations of my mind can all be present together 'in' awareness, without obscuring one another or closing down awareness itself. Even different segments of ordinary time—past, present, and future—can display themselves simultaneously: a memory need not wipe out a present feeling. For example, if I feel hungry now, memories of other kinds of hunger may come up, all transparently super-posed, much like the sounds in a symphony. At such times I can view my life in various segments, ranging from the present to the recent and the distant past, attaining an overview without getting pulled in by the gravity of any one part. This can happen with a timing so infinitely precise that I may experience it as simultaneous, the whole coming together at once, accompanied by great clarity and understanding.

In TSK terms, I might consider this as an experience of second-level time. Alternately, I might regard it as a very rapid sequencing and alternating between observer and rememberer, closer to first level linearity. When I look more closely, I see that the line between these two levels of understanding or experience is arbitrary, or at best artificial. Seeing these two levels as both distinct *and* congruent may approach a third-level view. I consider it a transparent way of seeing, linked to the clarity and understanding available I find to be available within this kind of experience.

A closer look, retrospectively, at the clarity and understanding of this experience suggests that knowledge is not necessarily limited to what can be conceptualized as insight, nor does it have to be articulated to be valid. In that very brief moment of understanding there is certainty. I have to be quickened in awareness to see that and to accept it on its own terms.

The role of transparency in this process is to allow room for different layers of thinking. As it does so, it also fosters greater sharpness of mind. The dynamic aspect of thought comes to the fore, expanding geometrically, feeding time into time. With this dynamic activated, thought can go deeper, incisively plumbing emotions and exploring other levels of mind, such as dream-like visions rich with archetypal and mythical images. At the same time, the body's postural sculptures and muscle tensions are loosened, releasing energies that contribute to the quickening of mind. Livened with attentiveness and curiosity, body and mind give way to a kind of playful inquisitiveness.

Initially this process is quite unstable. A crescendo builds rapidly, and I lose my balance; in just a split second I drop into blank, dream-like confusion. When I wake up, I am back in ordinary, wandering thought. Yet some of the earlier curiosity may still be hovering, in the form of the simple question, "What happened?" Since the fall has been so sudden and deep, I have no direct recall. But as curiosity regains some of its earlier vitality, and the question sinks deeper, I am able to recall the dreamy miasma from which I have just emerged, with its drift into a waking-dreaming that is similar to the drift of ordinary thought. I experience this as restful, especially as compared to the high energy inquiry that preceded it, which now comes into view. Here is a clue to the reason for the fall: On the surface, at least, it is an escape from the intensity of what I had experienced.

"But why such a powerfully precipitous retreat?" Now inquiry is again stimulated, and with it comes a quickening of time. The earlier intensity reappears, and once more loss of balance looms. "What is this threat? Oh, it's the falling itself. . . . Does falling have to be threatening? Falling into space could be an expanding. . . . In fact, it feels cool and relaxing. . . . Ah, now it's more balanced. . . . That's it—that's how I lost my balance earlier! It was the intensity of inquiry and my response to it. I was tense in my body, my space constricted. The fall into dullness expanded my space, even while time congealed into a sloth-like darkness. Then the dream-like fantasies began to emerge."

After such a flood of knowing, I may fall silent. Often I overlook the silence, because it is featureless; nothing going on, and I have much to reflect on. Yet if I fail to appreciate the silence as another aspect of knowing, it is soon filled in with thought—the ordinary thought that is so familiar and unwittingly comforting.

Again, I look for transparency, finding my way in through curiosity. "Was that silence just now uncomfortable?" If I am quickened enough by curiosity, I may recall that the silence was perceptually very clear. Now I can appreciate it as another aspect of knowing. Brief as the moment of silence may have been in clock-time, it becomes infinite when time is allowed the infinity of space to expand the subtlety of knowing. Now, when I drop back once more into ordinary thought, it does not have the same power to obscure. It remains more transparent, perhaps more tentative—a derivative of awareness itself. As thinking occurs within awareness, its energy not captive to the story line, I find that thinking can enhance awareness. Curiosity has more space in which to play upon experience, recognizing it as ineffable. Knowledge deepens in its subtlety.

It is interesting to watch the ebb and flow of this process. It appears that every so often I have to withdraw from the intensity and the multi-dimensional aspects of thought and perception, returning to a single-layer linear process. But when I can more easily allow the ebb and flow, the speed and space for layering is also more available—between ordinary perceptions or, perhaps more accurately, within them. There is also more space for falling: The fall back into ordinary thought does not have to be so precipitous and obscuring. As the ebb and flow of it all relaxes, there is no need for me to hold on so anxiously to borders and definitions of myself. The process allows the transparency of multiple layers of experience to play.

Light and lightness are salient features of transparency. Light is immanent in awareness, and in the purest awareness light conveys its transparency. As awareness becomes more committed to form—perceiving a particular form, then naming it and creating it into object, imbuing it with meaning within a context of references, and finally adding to it values such as feeling—its transparency progressively diminishes, and light turns to opacity. The quick lightness of pure awareness progresses toward a slow heaviness, and there is a dimming of light as it becomes more committed to form.

This is reflected in a parallel trend toward heaviness and tension in the body. When a train of thought is more imbued with emotion, awareness tends to be obscured. The physical counterpart is that as thought becomes heavier with emotion, the body becomes more fixed in postures, which are held with strong tension. These postures are typically so opaque as not to be recognized as postures—the tension is below the threshold of awareness. Indeed, awareness appears to be swallowed up by this complex. On the other hand, when awareness is more transparent to form, the body is light, relaxed, and flowing in its energy. When awareness is most transparent, body flows can be so subtle as to be almost imperceptible, and the body can feel totally open and weightless.

To illustrate how mental attitudes ramify into bodily postures, consider the feeling or statement, "This practice is not going well for me." If I hear myself saying this, some awareness has emerged. I may understand that this comment is also a judgment, and I may be able to feel the heaviness of that judgment, linked to heaviness in my body. I may see or feel myself taking the position, "I am not doing well." This could manifest as excuses, a desire to stop practice, or starting to falling asleep. If I can see through this train of excuses and the tendency to give up, however, all of this becomes more transparent. I may see (feel) how the body has become fixed in a posture of holding back. Perhaps I ask, "What does 'doing well' mean in this context?" Is the judgment based on earlier, 'good' experiences? Can I see that the expectation of repeating former experience obscures what is actually going on at that moment in my body and my thought, damaging the quality of my awareness?

Once it is brought into play, the dynamic of such immediate inquiry heightens awareness. I literally wake 'up': my body lightens and lets go of its holding back, my spine straightens, and energies of which I was not previously aware begin to shudder and move. The TSK phrase 'seeing through my positioning' becomes an evocative metaphor. What was previously an unquestioned position and posture becomes movement. In fact, 'seeing through' is itself a moving through a fixed position. Here transparency is seen in its time aspect: not so much a state as an evocative transitioning through what appears as fixed.

The example of feeling pain illustrates the dynamic of fixed positions in a much more exaggerated way. Pain presents itself as being substantial, immovable, and inscrutable. When I go into pain with awareness, however, so that it ultimately becomes more transparent, I first discover an intense sensation. This seeing is already a change in definition and meaning, and thus a change in position. As sensation, the pain is not so tightly bound to its negative value. Its sharp, hard-edged substantiality loosens as well. Now the pain may reveal itself to be pulsating with movements. With increasingly lightened awareness, these movements may expand in quantum jumps (though the jumps may be separated by gaps in the ebb and flow of attention). Larger, slower movements emerge, lighter and thus less urgent. A pleasurable feeling manifests.

This whole picture depends on the pain being more transparent; still present, but not so dominant. Now the pain allows movement, accompanied by a release of energy and expanded feeling. The expansion of feelings may in turn reveal a play of conflicting emotions that had been locked up in the pain. As these emotions are given more scope, they manifest cascading impressions and memories that were previously hidden. They can also quicken impending insight, bringing the light of understanding to the dark inscrutability of the pain.

What is described here as a linear progression may unfold quite differently, with such a split-second timing that the layers are super-posed, each transparent to the others. Rapid flashes of time past, the now, and the future may also be super-posed, so that all of time seems available in this instant. Incipient impressions and would-be insights flood the horizon of awareness without obscuring it. There is no need to go off into a story line: All is in suspension. Though this blend may be inchoate at the outset, the transparency available in the moment of knowing may allow it to develop in the moments that follow, bringing articulated insight and physical ease.

A different way to investigate the relationship between transparency and awareness is to see awareness itself as being transparent. Thoughts, sounds, and body sensations can play in the presence of awareness without carrying it away. For example, as I walk, a carillon nearby may play a familiar melody, conveying a name, a verse, and memories, all of which appear without obscuring awareness. Even the lucency of the tones themselves can be appreciated without disturbing the presence of awareness. Indeed, it is as if all these aspects are *in* the transparent flow of awareness.

To take a different example, one where transparency is less evident, consider what happens when I seem to be lost dreamily in thought. There is dullness here, and yet awareness is standing by. Awareness is in suspension, possessing a kind of translucence that is mirrored by a subtle, viscous tension that seems also to be carrying thoughts and images in its thick flow. If the intention to be aware is strong, it seems to build up in the underflow and then surface from time to time. I suddenly wake up, and there is a very lucent moment before I sink back into the depths.

What I have just described is a linear development, as if taken from a tape that records a sequence of memories. But I wonder if it is the lucent moments that inform the whole sequence, rather than the memory-tape, which is faint and perhaps lost in the depths. And further: Is it necessary that these two views be mutually exclusive? It may be that in the instant of lucent awareness I see clearly whole aspects of the experience, though not as an image. It could be that the momentary lucency brightens the faint memories. Only retrospectively do I draw out the memories into a sequence in order to record them in memory.

These two aspects of time can apparently be transparent to one another, not in the ordinary visual sense, as the metaphor might suggest, but rather in the sense of an intense condensation. In the lucent moment all the memories are seen, though not imaged. In the drawn-out aspect, all the faint memories have to be re-membered, one at a time, as it were. Reflecting on this interconnection, my conclusion is that this re-mem-bering must be inspired by the moments of lucency.

I may find such condensation in more vivid form in a dream. For example, I dream of myself as an adult, but in a setting from my childhood. As the dream progresses, possibilities for a story-line develop. However, the scenes, situations, and actors are changing rapidly. Many of them are super-posed: for instance, my childhood home upon other households and settings I may or may not recognize. I might be trying to work out a problem, but the definition and circumstances of the "problem" keep changing, as do the actors. The dream may end in what seems to me a time in the future, perhaps beyond my lifetime. The landscape might be another planet. And though I navigate and negotiate in this landscape, it is not clear that I am of it.

As I awake and reflect on this dream, I gravitate toward a story I can relate to my life as I ordinarily know it. However, if I can appreciate the super-positioning of time, I may remain more open to the experience as a whole. Aware of this alternative, I may see that the overall difficulty here is my tendency to reject possibilities of being that do not fit with my identity as I have constructed it all these years. Now I may see in the problems that emerged in the dream new possibilities for change—for being quite different than I believe myself to be.

Usually I ignore a knowing imbued with such transparency, due to my conditioned tendency to look for identity, which in turn is more or less based on exclusion. Looking at the dream, I carefully determine that *this* aspect represents my childhood, *that* part is my imagination, and so forth. A condensed and transparent knowing, however, is lucent in a very different way. It reaches into many levels of my being which I would ordinarily ignore in order to maintain my official identity. Such lucency is not simply one more level added to the others; rather, it is a penetrating of the exclusionary boundaries. It reveals the boundless possibilities of being.

Another aspect of transparency is difficult for me to describe. I will point to it using the image of the aura. Some people actually see auras, and a few are skilled in making practical interpretations of them. But here I want to use the image in a more metaphoric way, letting it indicate a field around a person or object that heightens that person/object's presence.

This aura-like aspect of transparency may occur spontaneously. At times I am so tuned in to a person, thing, or situation that I pick up an ambience which heightens its presence. At those moments I feel a special alertness. I find myself looking with a sidelong glance instead of straight ahead, or listening as though I am eavesdropping on another conversation. When I want to stimulate this special sensitivity, I let go of the mindset that defines people and situations in terms of their specific characteristics—how I have known them before. I may allow my perception to become naive. Another way is to blur the distinction between foreground and background, letting go of the hard-edged exclusionary focus of linear identity.

This deliberate blurring offers a transition toward seeing through the conventionally established dominant or foreground meaning. During the transitional phase I may briefly lose sight of the conventional presentation, but not in a way that I become confused. Soon enough I find either that I can see through it without losing sight of it, or that I can alternate rapidly back and forth between the two perceptions.

To illustrate the spontaneous arising of such an aura-like transparency, I will describe a sight I came upon once during a long hike. In conventional terms, what I saw was a lone tree in a barren landscape. However, at the moment I came upon it I was out of my usual mindset, perhaps because I had been away from my conventional props for quite a while. Moreover, the sky was a deep blue and very wide, evoking a sense of space. In these circumstances I did not see the tree as a tree. What I remember now is a sense of wonder and admiration. I think it would be fair to say that the whole experience was radiant—and that the whole of my perception turned transparent. In fact, if I recall correctly, I had to look a little sideways, figuratively speaking, to avoiding clicking back into conventional perception. The whole situation had a high intensity, charged with meaning.

There is an outside-stander in me that tends to reduce the meaningfulness of this experience by claiming that I actually created the meaning. Perhaps I wanted to verify my interest in TSK and thus further assert my identity. However, this response misses a deeper aspect of what I am now appreciating from that experience. What I find meaningful is the interrelatedness of all aspects, including me. The fullness of meaning was revealed in the transparency of tree, landscape, and myself. Though all these aspects were still in sight as separate objects, as the defining boundaries became more permeable, the communication became communion. At a deeper level of knowing, this is really how it is.

The aura that I have learned to cultivate may not be dramatic in its onset and also may be slower to develop meaningfulness. Here is another example. I walk in on a gathering of people I know. I know why they have met, yet something I do not know flickers across my awareness. Like everyone else, I have been programmed to ignore this vague flicker and attend to the business at hand: greetings, finding out the agenda, and perhaps being filled in on what went on before I came. If instead I respect the flicker of awareness, I am already alert in a way that heightens my sensitivity. Now I look and listen 'sideways', even as I go about the usual routines. If I can tolerate the ambiguity between doing what is expected and not knowing fully what to do, a fuller knowing—one that I cannot explain or understand rationally—may come to inform my response.

Trusting this non-rational response may be even more difficult than accepting the initial ambiguity. Yet

I try to do so, for what I do not know in this situation may offer me a way to know it more fully. The very depth of my not knowing offers an expanded opportunity for a deeply full response, one in which transparency can emerge.

Of course, for this to happen I must deepen my trust in this way of looking and listening. Looking and listening transparently is like applying a code to a scrambled message. Though the message is not immediately made clear, I find that I have available a mode for negotiating the uncertainty.

Transparency is like a key to not knowing. For instance, it may happen that I lose my self-esteem in some encounter. The ongoing situation may demand a response, but the voices of self-blame within are dimming my view of it. Not knowing what to attend to, I experience a sinking feeling of something impending. Anxiety and despair are about to descend.

Right here in the sinking feeling can come a subtle shift in my breath, a possible signal to look transparently. Perhaps I see that my loss of self-esteem is uppermost, overshadowing the whole situation. But seen transparently, self-image shifts. It can be a little like the configuration of light in a kaleidoscope. With just a slight shift—being able to smile at my vanity, perhaps—the image changes ever so slightly. More light is passing through, and my response to the situation can also lighten.

Again my description of this situation is necessarily drawn out, making it seem that several seconds or more elapse, during which an awkward silence looms. But it does not have to be that way. The mind is very quick. With practice, self-blame, sinking, subtle breath, and seeing through self-image can all be transparently present in one moment. Transparency is as close as the next, subtle breath.

NONORDINARY
KNOWLEDGE

Donald Beere

Some of the experiences that serve as the backbone for this article I have never shared with anyone, let alone published. They represent "singularities" that violate everyday assumptions about how space, time, and knowledge "work." I describe them here as a way of getting greater clarity on the nature and possibilities for knowledge. In my view, these experiences also demonstrate that some of the assertions and conclusions reached by Tarthang Tulku in *Time, Space and Knowledge* (1977) and the other books of the TSK series are not abstractions distant from human experience. They are completely livable, and their availability suggests that we could have access to space, time, and knowledge in very different ways.

I have selected the following from among many personal experiences that (to use TSK terminology) go beyond 'first-level' experience to invoke 'second-level' knowledge. A frequent criterion for selection has been the consensual nature of the experience; that is, a reader could ask someone else to confirm as accurate what I have described. I chose this criterion because one of the methods the late twentieth-century culture of the United States uses to determine the truth (validity) of a knowledge event as experienced by an individual is whether other people can consensually report the same information. By conforming to this standard, I hope to convince the reader that the events described here did in fact occur. Otherwise the later analyses and conclusions cannot follow, or at least will be of less interest.

I understand the experiences collected here to be nonordinary in transcending everyday spatial and temporal limits. As I reflect on them, they represent brief openings in the fabric of my everyday world. In reporting them, I have tried to be honest and not distort. These kinds of experiences come and go: They are, as the reader will note, almost momentary. Speaking for myself, they do not happen frequently, but they occur with enough regularity that I no longer consider them low-probability events.

As will become apparent in the course of the article, one of my struggles has been satisfying myself that these experiences are not random occurrences; that they truly represent a "nonordinary knowledge" that transcends limits on knowing imposed by consensually defined space and time. For those cases where it seemed appropriate, I have attempted to do this by following the basic social science guideline that if an outcome occurs by chance less than five times in a hundred (a probability of .05 or less), then it is reasonable to look for some cause or explanation other than random chance. Thus, when a mental event coincides with a 'reality event' such that the mental event appears to represent nonordinary knowledge of that reality event, I attempt (1) to discount the likelihood of other possible sources for that knowledge; and (2) to estimate the probability that the mental event might match the reality event by pure chance. If I conclude that the probability of a match between the mental event and the reality event is less than .05, I assume that this significant improbability validates the mental event as nonordinary knowledge. In some cases, however, the mental event seems so unlikely by normal measures that it has not been possible to estimate probability in this way.

I caution and prepare the reader for a process of self-confrontation similar to the one I have gone through myself. When I experienced these incidents, I invariably questioned them and looked for alternative explanations. I anticipate that most readers will find they automatically and consistently do the same, picking out possible flaws in the arguments and explanations. Although I prize careful and considered argument and persuasion, my own experience suggests to me that this typical response reveals a tendency of everyday mind to establish certain conditions for what can be experienced and known, and to reject without real argument what does not meet those conditions. I invite the reader to investigate his or her response to the incidents described, to see whether such a response reveals his or her unique commitment to "the way things are." Such an inquiry while reading Part One of this article will prepare for the discussion of the beliefs and operation of the self in the later parts of the article.

The article is organized as follows. In Part One, I describe the experiences themselves. Each experience is followed by a discussion of its validity; that is, the reasons which lead me to consider it an instance of nonordinary knowledge. A brief phenomenological analysis of the experience follows, framing the incident in ways intended to educe commonalities and make it easier to assess implications. After describing several of my own experiences, I describe two instances of nonordinary knowing that come from a colleague. I have found these instances helpful in suggesting the generalizability of the results I arrive at, and also in raising additional issues that would not emerge from my own experience. In Part Two, I analyze the implications of these experiences for our understanding of knowledge and its relation to time and space. In Part Three, I make tentative links to the TSK vision and set forth some possible broader implications.

Before starting with this investigation, I would like to acknowledge that countless anecdotes about nonordinary knowledge circulate in our society, most of them more spectacular than the incidents described here. In addition, there is no shortage of systematic research that has attempted to establish the existence of nonordinary knowledge through thousands of carefully controlled trials. However, I have confined myself to situations that I knew of personally, or where I knew the person offering the experience. I did so for three reasons. First, these experiences are of interest just because they are (for the most part) quite ordinary. The transcendent and the everyday cannot be clearly distinguished. Second, because they happened to me personally, they gave me a chance to challenge my own understanding of time and space and to confront more directly the limitations I bring to knowledge. Third, because I have had to grapple with each experience myself, I can share with the reader a clearer exploration and elucidation of the experience and the layers of its meaning and significance. Perhaps the reader, reflecting on other similar experiences that he or she may have had, will be led to a similar kind of inquiry. When we choose not to discount our experiences of nonordinary knowledge, but instead, having satisfied ourselves of their validity, take them at face value, our ways of using the mind may open in healthy ways. The result could be to harmonize mind and body and bring the self more fully into balance with others and with the "objective" world.

PART ONE: THE EXPERIENCES

Experience One

I am driving our daughter to college. We (I, my wife, and my son, as well as my daughter) are in our new van, which features a computerized sensor for the fuel tank that continuously reads out the distance to empty ("DTE"). We have gotten on the freeway after lunch and decide to drive a while and then get fuel. Although the gas gauge indicates a quarter full, the DTE indicates around 140 miles. I decide that the first off-ramp after the DTE registers 90 that has three gas stations listed on the exit sign (the price should be cheaper due to competition) will mark our next stop. When the DTE is between 80 and 90, I get a little anxious. Will we really find a gas station?

I reassure myself that there are frequent exits and gas stations, and that eighty-five miles is a long way. I casually wonder what the DTE reading will be when the anticipated exit arrives. Relaxed, I shift my attention back to driving and then become aware of having a mental image of pulling onto the exit ramp as "74" registers on the DTE. I tell my family about my thinking and the mileage reading which came about with my image. The next exit with three gas stations finally appears and the DTE reading, as I pull onto the exit ramp, is "74."

Discussion of Validity   Was the '74' image a nonordinary presentation of knowledge, or was it a random mental event which I later indexed as knowledge because it coincidentally fit what happened? The image presented itself almost immediately after I had wondered about the distance to a gas station. It was a single image that came and went after I noted it. I did not have the sense, when the image came, that it was "my knowledge;" rather, it was a curiosity which I shared with my family. To phrase this differently, I did not have the subjective sense that "I know how far it will be to the next gas station."

To what extent might the number which appeared in the image be due to my unconscious access to other sources of information? I had never driven this particular freeway. I had not looked at a map; it is my wife's role to be the navigator on our trips. We had left Chicago earlier in the day and I had not read, looked at, or otherwise gotten information about the route, and there are no signs along the freeway alerting the driver to the next gas station. I am aware of no other sources of information from which I could have concluded the next exit with gas stations would be in approximately ten miles. I have also recently traveled this same route, so that I can verify the data presented here.

What is the likelihood of "74" being the correct mileage when we pulled off at the exit? On this particular stretch of road, a distance of 123 miles, there were 9 exits—one every 13.66 miles. The probability that an exit would be at any particular mile along this route is .073 (9 divided by 123). Over this distance, the number of gas stations per exit distributed almost evenly: one exit had three gas stations, and two each had zero, one, two and four gas stations. Therefore, the probability of finding at least three gas stations at an exit was three out of nine, or 33 out of a hundred. The likelihood of finding an exit at "mile 74" with at least three gas stations was .024 (.33 times .073).

Let us, however, analyze this differently. Having never driven this road previously, I could not anticipate the distance between exits. We had, for example, just left a tourist area with frequent exits and I did not know how far this pattern would extend. As well, I did not know we were entering a remote and rural area. In short, I did not know that exits distributed, on the average, every 13.66 miles. Nonetheless, using this figure, we can estimate the mileage each exit should appear from the beginning of this section of road: mileage 123 marks the start, then 109, 96, 82, and, finally, 68 indicate the "predicted" exits every 13.66 miles.

Notice that "74" is situated exactly between 82 and 68. Thus, even were I to know that exits occurred every 13.66 miles, I would have been unlikely to select "74" as mileage. That the exit was at "74" also points out the variability of the distances between exits and the difficulty of using 13.66 as an exact estimate of the distances. It appears that knowledge of "where" the exit was would be difficult to determine, especially for someone unacquainted with the road.

I conclude that for the "74" image to be randomly accurate is highly unlikely. That it was a single number, that it occurred immediately after I felt anxious, and that it followed my wondering about the next exit are all factors suggesting that the image was an accurate response, carrying real knowledge, to the inner question I had posed.

Phenomenological Analysis   S is engaged in an activity during which the happening or non-happening of a future event creates anxiety or worry. S wonders when and how the event might occur. S, in a relaxed state, attends to a current activity and an image comes spontaneously to mind that gives the answer to this question. Later, the image proves to be accurate.

Experience Two

This occurred while driving to our country cottage on July 22, 1994. My daughter has stomach problems and is sleeping. My wife is also sleeping. I have been sleepy and am worried about driving under those conditions. I also have a headache in the back of my head. I begin to feel a little better, though still sleepy.

I turn north after a small town to take the back way. A large "Road Closed" sign has been pushed off the pavement. I'm concerned about what this may mean. I can drive fast on this road and I speed up, eager to get there. About a half-mile away, I see a red dump truck. I assume that the truck is connected to the road construction and vaguely anticipate its stopping in front of me so its passengers can finish up parts of the road. I am also vaguely aware of a wish that it get off the road. For some reason I don't want to pass it; I'm anxious about the road conditions given the indications that road construction has been going on.

I drive into a dip at the bottom of a hill. My state of mind drifts a little, still somewhat sleepy. An image comes of the truck turning left onto a dirt road. The dirt is piled up a foot or so on each side and tall pines are set back about ten yards from either side of the road. On the right hand side of the road, the trees continue about fifteen yards, where an open but unfarmed field begins. I make nothing of the image and no other images arise. Coming up out of the dip, the road flattens out. I look for the truck and am surprised not to see it. I wonder, "Was it further in front than I thought?" I notice a dirt road coming up on the left and I look down it. There is the dump truck, driving away. What I see is identical to the image I had seen a minute or so previously: the position of the truck on the road, the road itself and the terrain surrounding the road is identical to what appeared in the image.

Discussion of Validity   Did the image embody knowledge? As in the preceding case, I did not "know" until later that the image presented a "reality event." Nonetheless, the image did accurately portray what I later saw.

A reader might question this last sentence. First, I may have distorted my perception of the scene to accord with my image, or else distorted my memory of the image to accord with the scene. I cannot dismiss this possibility. What I recall is my surprise: first, my surprise that the truck was not on the road and, second, my surprise that the image was "identical" to the scene I saw as I glanced down the road. The surprise suggests to me that I did not anticipate either.

Is there a way to estimate the probability that a random image would be accurate? Since I had a wish for the truck to leave the road, the image might have been a fantasy of wish fulfillment that randomly matched what followed. But why would my wish have manifested as a single, detailed image? Is it not more reasonable to anticipate that the wish would have unfolded as a series of possibilities, each granting the wish?

In addition, I had driven this road often enough to know unconsciously where various crossroads would be. But this counter-argument ignores the specificity of the image. I had not driven this road for several months and thus had not seen the surface of the dirt road, the mounds of graded dirt along the side of the road, and the height and color of the field. These details would be difficult to anticipate. How difficult—what probabilities to assign—I cannot say.

Phenomenological Analysis   S is engaged in an activity about whose future unfolding he is worried, anxious, or concerned. He is aware of a wish for events to change. While his mind is "sleepy," a spontaneous, detailed image of a change in events that fulfills this wish occurs. A short while later the image proves to represent accurately his lived experience.

Experience Three

During the summer of 1974 we were trying to sell our house. I am waiting in the house for a potential buyer, whose precise arrival time I do not know. The house is totally empty. I decide to do a meditation practice (counting my breath) as I wait. I alternate between focusing on my breath and frustrated anticipation of the buyer's arrival. I pace. I look out the window. Cars drive by, each of which I scan. None of them brings our potential buyers.

Eventually I give up. I stop tracking cars, looking out the window, or carrying out any of the other future-focused activities I have been doing. I simply count my breath while I stand there. At one point a voice in my "mind" says, "They come now." I open my eyes, and at the same time I hear the noise of a car accelerating a block or so away. It sounds no different from any other car I have heard earlier in my wait. The noise of the engine slows, a car parks at the front walkway, and two people get out to look at our house. They do not, to finish the story, buy the house.

Discussion of Validity   What is unusual in this example is the inner cue, "They come now," ostensibly in response to no external stimulus. The sound of the car occurred after the inner words. A critic might point out that I might well have heard the engine, yet simply been consciously unaware of it. Still , I had no way to differentiate our potential buyer's car from any prior car: I did not know the buyer's car and had never heard its engine. Even if I had heard the engine, it would not have meant anything to me.

Could the driver have been driving hesitantly, looking for the correct address? Possibly. My recollection, however, is as follows. The buyers were longtime residents of our small city. I believe they had been to the house previously, but I can not be certain. More to the point, when I heard the engine, after the inner words, the car had still not turned down our block, which is when the buyer would begin to look for numbers. Would the driver have been cautious prior to turning down our block? I cannot say. My impression is that when I heard the engine it sounded like any other car's in the neighborhood.

Could the words I heard have been randomly accurate? If we conservatively assume that during the forty-five minutes I was waiting a car might have driven up during any thirty second period, there were 90 occasions when the inner words, having arisen, might have been right by chance. They arose only once. The probability of .011 makes this a highly unlikely event.

Phenomenological Analysis The mind is focused on a particular event in the future, with some anxiety or anticipation. The mind becomes quiet, with no particular focus on outside events. At a certain point, when there would be no overt perception of the desired event, words spontaneously surface in the mind to indicate its imminent occurrence. A short while later the event happens.

Experience Four

The following experience is similar to many I have had; in this case there is the possibility of consensual validation. A job candidate for my department at the university and I were getting out of the car to go into a local restaurant around 6:30 in the evening. She was Native American, which may have helped me feel comfortable in saying what I said. The sky was overcast but not darkly-clouded, as might be the case before rain.

"Should we take an umbrella?" she asked.

I have difficulty describing what happened next. I "sent" my "awareness" out to the west, (from where the weather generally comes in Michigan) to "feel" the clouds/sky. There then came a "knowing" that it would rain later, quite heavily.

"It'll be raining when we come out of the restaurant," I answered. I hesitated to take an umbrella and then decided against it based on the inconvenience. I remember feeling foolish at having made the prediction and wondered about how my job candidate/colleague reacted. This contributed to my deciding not to take the umbrella. When we left the restaurant an hour and a half later, I needed to run through a drenching downpour to get the car. The rain had just started, and it had not rained while we were eating.

Discussion of Validity I often anticipate the day's weather. In this situation, we had driven through rain once on the ninety-mile drive to Mt. Pleasant, and the prospect of rain should not have been surprising. On the other hand, the rain had been inconsistent. It had not rained for hours, and the clouds at the time we got out of the car did not seem threatening. While partly a general prediction that it would rain later in the day, my statement reflected a more precise 'sense' that it would be raining when we left the restaurant. It did not rain during our dinner, and the downpour began about five minutes before we left. The meal had come to a natural conclusion and we had begun preparing to leave prior to the rain's beginning. The position of the table, the blinds on the window and the depth of the overhang of the roof blocked a view of the outside.

In other words, the facts do not support a claim that I had us wait to leave until it was about to rain. In fact, I had forgotten what I said on getting out of the car until, just after I signed the check, I heard thunder and the shushing of rain on the street. Only then did I look out the window and see rain cascading down.

Phenomenological Analysis S is in a situation in which an unknown future possibility becomes the focus of attention. S focuses awareness on that future possibility, opening the mind to it, and an accurate foretelling spontaneously arises.

Experience Five

My daughter has lost a toy. I have never seen it so I don't know what it looks like. My wife asks if I would help look for it. I look around, rather cursorily. The search continues with no success, and my daughter gets more frustrated. Once again my wife asks me to help. My subjective sense is not knowing where or how to look. The rest of the family has looked all over. Spontaneously I close my eyes and relax. A single image of the living room couch, focusing on the left cushion, appears. Something is under the cushion. I suggest looking there. My son finds the lost toy right where the image suggests.

Discussion of Validity What is the likelihood that a single, spontaneous image would pinpoint the location of an object no one else could find? I had not been with my daughter while she was playing with the toy, so I would not have known where she had it, let alone where she had it last. In addition, family members had been looking all over the house. From my point of view, there is no reason to consider the living room or the couch a more likely location than any other room or piece of furniture in the house. The living room holds four additional cushions, and there are various other possible locations for the toy in that room. There are eleven "room-like" locations in the house, all of which have their nooks and crannies, pieces of furniture and so on. If I estimate eight hiding places per location, then there are eighty-eight possible spots for the toy, giving a probability by chance for this event of .011. On the other hand, I might have had some unconscious awareness of where my daughter had been playing and where my family had already looked.

Phenomenological Analysis   S feels a subtle demand to know ("find") something hidden, along with a subjective sense of an inability/incapacity to do so. S focuses the mind inward and then consciously relaxes. A visual image of the location of the hidden unknown arises in the mind and proves accurate.

Experience Six

For years my family and I took vacations in our motor home. On these trips I would always try to practice TaiJi in the early morning before everyone else woke up. On this occasion, we are driving across the country and have stopped at a rural campground in Oklahoma, pulling in well after dark. In the morning, tired from the long drive the previous day, I keep dozing off. I know we have another long drive in front of us, yet struggle mentally with getting up to do TaiJi.

As I am again considering slipping out of bed, I imagine stepping out the door and wonder what it is like outside. I settle back again into a drifting state. A beautiful image comes to mind—one which is still vivid. The horizon is pink and orange, slightly streaked, with one cloud to the right, a little above the horizon. The earth stretches away from me flat and plain-like. To the left, a single tree is silhouetted by the dawn. The image is so striking that I roll over and peek around the shade—which happens to be on the same side of the motor home. The scene which has come to mind is identical to the one I now see. As I reflect on this, I realize I had no prior information about the terrain, since we had been traveling at night and I had never been there before.

Discussion of Validity To start with the counter-argument, I might have noticed subliminally various aspects of the terrain as we drove to the campsite. After all, I did go outside to hook the motor home up to electricity and used the restroom facilities of the campground. What is worthy of remark, however, are the details of the image which matched the real scene. Even having a clear knowledge of the terrain, the possible variety of scenes is huge and changes moment to moment as the day progresses. Ten minutes earlier or later, the scene would have been significantly different. The likelihood of the mental image matching so precisely the real scene outside is small.

Phenomenological Analysis S directs the mind toward an upcoming event and wonders about present conditions, unavailable to sight. A visual image comes

49

to mind. When S looks at the actual visual details of the scene, they precisely match the image.

Experience Seven

I am in a rush, driving to get something from the store. I am concerned about getting a good parking place when I reach the store, because in my state of mind, seconds count. I am considering how to pull into the parking lot so I don't circle needlessly. A short while later, while I am still a block away and before the parking lot can be seen, an image springs to mind of a white car leaving the third space in front of the entrance to the store. As I turn off the street into the lot, I look to the front of the store and a white car is beginning to pull out of the third space in front of the entrance.

Discussion of Validity Can the image of the car pulling out be construed as a random mental event that intersects with a likely occurrence in the world? Since I could not see the parking lot at the moment the image came, there were no unconscious cues available to process. The parking lot was arranged so that cars could park at an angle in long rows, facing other cars parked the opposite direction. There were about fifteen spaces per side in three rows, or approximately ninety spaces in all. The lot was full when I got there, and I would have anticipated that, given that it was a busy time on a Saturday.

However, assume that spaces closer to store entrance are preferable and therefore more likely to be filled; given that, we can arbitrarily halve the number of spaces to consider. Most of the close spaces would be filled and have cars leaving, so the likelihood of having an image of just the right space would be one in 45, or approximately .02. Assume six different car colors that I might differentiate; including this one in six probability in the prior calculation yields a probability of .004. I ignore the time element, because on a busy shopping day it would be a safe assumption that a car would almost always be pulling out at any given moment.

Phenomenological Analysis   S is concerned about a future situation. As he anticipates the future, an image comes to mind of what will happen, one that fulfills his wished-for outcome. The image proves to represent the actual event.

Conclusion: A Preliminary Phenomenological Reduction of the Situated Structure of Nonordinary Knowing

The above experiences as a whole provide a context for educing the essence of the experience of nonordinary knowing. The process, as described in Giorgi (1985), involves seeking the commonalities among the descriptions. In other words, the final phenomenological reduction must fit each of the individual descriptions. The assumption made is that what is in common between the descriptions captures the essential qualities of this particular experience. I offer the following as a synthesis. The reader can evaluate whether the synthesis fits the previous seven descriptions.

51

The experience of nonordinary knowing occurs after the individual has focused awareness in a questioning or inquiring way on some aspect of experience ordinarily construed as unknowable. The individual then lets go of the focusing and the questioning. Next, typical everyday mental activity stops or slows. A short while later, the individual notices that a single mental event has spontaneously taken form and later coincides with what was "unknowable."

Experience Seven seems partly discrepant from the reduction, since in that case there was no overt letting go of the concern about parking followed by stopping or slowing mental activity. However, I bring the reader's attention to the phrase "a short while later" which precedes the emergence of the image of the white car pulling out. For me, driving tends to be an automatic and focused activity which is relaxing and does not activate my day to day goal-oriented thinking. Note that three of the examples occur while driving. I think of driving as a kind of mindless doing. Thus, in Experience Seven, after my concerns focused my mind, I returned to the passive and automatic activity of driving—in effect, letting go of the focus and concern. As I shifted into my "driving mode," my usual mental activity slowed. It was then that the image popped into awareness. I conclude that the reduction as given does capture what occurred, though less explicitly, in Experience Seven.

Various implications of this reduction will be considered more extensively in the next part of this article, but several observations should be made before proceeding. First, though most descriptions involve mild distress, concern or worry, the rainfall incident does not, so I have eliminated this as a factor. What seems critical is a focusing of the mind accompanied by a sense of questioning. Second, all examples share an absence of intense emotion. Third, identifying the knowing as knowing at the time does not seem critical. In most of the examples, it is only after the event has occurred that I realize I might have accurately "known" something.

The Experiences of a Colleague

I turn now to two examples related to me by a colleague, who has reviewed the accounts given here for accuracy. The first is quite similar to the prior seven examples; the second is quite different.

Experience Eight

S's husband cannot find his pipecutter, a tool S has never seen. Very frustrated, he asks her if she had seen it. She asks him what it looks like, and he replies that it was orange when new but is now old and rusty, and that it is about the size of a large baseball.

"Where did you have it last," she asks. He doesn't know. She becomes frustrated with his inability to find it since he is interfering with what she is doing. She says to herself, " Oh, I can find this if I put my mind to it. I can do this right now." She takes a deep breath, closes her eyes, relaxes, and lets her mind go blank. A grey space arises within which she allows an image of the object to appear.

"It's downstairs in the basement, underneath a pile of junk on the left side of your workbench."

"I've looked there. It isn't there," he said.

"It's there. Go look again."

When he picks up all the junk, the pipecutter is exactly where she has said. She asks to see it, and it looks just like the image which had come to mind.

Discussion of Validity   Perhaps S had previously seen the pipecutter on or near the workbench and simply forgotten. Even if she had not seen it, a likely location for the pipecutter would be on the workbench. The specific details—its precise location and the match of the image with the pipecutter's appearance—are more difficult to explain. What is striking about this description is its similarity in form to the preliminary phenomenological reduction, given above.

Phenomenological Analysis   S focuses on discovering what is objectively unknowable. She relaxes her mind, allowing it to become inactive, and a picture forms in mind which accurately depicts what had previously been unknowable.

Experience Nine

While S was an undergraduate student in college, her grandmother, with whom she felt very close, had been hospitalized for a broken hip. S had visited her grand-mother a few days previously in a nursing home and it seemed she was getting well and would return home soon. S is taking a four-hour evening art class. Well before it is due to end, she gets an internal sense that she needs to go to her grandmother. She continues to sit, working on her project, for ten to fifteen minutes more, until the inner sense "says" she must go. She is sure her grandmother is much worse. She packs up her materials and leaves. On her way out, the instructor asks why she is leaving, and she replies, "My grand-mother's dying and I've got to go."

After hurriedly packing a few things, S starts to drive to Detroit. When she gets close to the city, it crosses her mind to go to her parent's house, but that does not feel right. Without "conscious" intervention, the car "drives itself" to a hospital she has never been to before. It is around 10:45 at night. She enters through the emergency room, goes up to intensive care, and asks for her grandmother, who is in fact located in that unit of the hospital. No one has questioned or stopped her, and she has not questioned her own actions: She "knew" the whole time that what she was doing was right. Later she learns the background: Her grandmother's condition had worsened earlier that day, and she had contracted pneumonia and was not expect-ed to survive. In the hope of treating her, she had been transferred to the hospital to which S has driven. Soon afterwards, her grandmother dies.

Discussion of Validity   Although there was no overt information motivating S to leave her class, she did have a sense of her grandmother's ill health. It might be possible to rationalize her abrupt departure as motivated by anxiety tied to an accurate intuitive understanding of her grandmother's health. But this leaves numerous aspects unexplained. The day S drove to Detroit was the same day her grandmother was transferred to the new hospital. The reason for the transfer was that her condition had quickly deteriorated following the onset of pneumonia after hip surgery. S drove there without, to the best of her knowledge, having been told about that move. In fact, she expected her grandmother to be getting better so that she would be discharged. She did not know where the hospital was, yet she drove directly to it. Having arrived, she went directly to the right location.

Phenomenological Analysis   In the midst of everyday activity, S discovers herself to know that an event of grave emotional significance has occurred to someone about whom she cares deeply. Feeling confident of this nonordinary knowing, she makes choices about how to act that are not guided by ordinary knowledge, but which turn out to be accurate, as was her knowing about the event.

Application of the Preliminary Phenomenological Reduction to these Events

The pipecutter incident displays almost the same phenomenological structure as my own experiences, and thus provides some limited generalizability to the conclusions I have reached. The incident with S's grand-mother shows that there are other kinds of nonordinary knowing which do not seem to arise from a direct focusing of the mind. We can not generalize from this single experience, but we can compare it to the tentative phenomenological reduction developed earlier. One distinction between this incident and most (but not all) of the others is the absence of a conscious state of concern, interest, or worry to focus the mind or to conduct this particular nonordinary knowing. Clearly, the health of S's grandmother was of significance and concern to her, but not that particular evening. In fact, she had thought her grandmother was getting well. She responds to an event of concern or interest which is not currently a focus of her mind.

PART TWO: DISCUSSION

The mundane content of the experiences described above (apart from the final example) may seem at first disappointing. In my own experiences, everyday concerns and trivia generally come to the surface. In contrast, the frequent reports by many people of claims to nonordinary knowledge are often quite spectacular; for example, stories of psychics who help police track down killers or finding missing persons. However, evaluating the truth of these stories is difficult given the usual lack of information available to someone like myself who hears of them only through the media. This is the significance of Part I to my own understanding of space and time and their relation to knowledge. The examples given seem to me to establish firmly the possibility of nonordinary knowing—a possibility available in the everyday world.

Once nonordinary knowing is established, numerous questions arise. How does it arise? When it arises, how does it show itself? Can we determine the source of this knowledge? What does nonordinary knowledge imply about everyday knowledge? What does it reveal about space and time? These questions and others will be considered in the following parts of this article.

What Allows Nonordinary Knowledge to Arise?

Although the experiences I have reported are insignificant in themselves, they beckon toward possibilities and actualities for knowledge that are usually excluded even from fantasy. The processes they hint at are far from trivial, for they point to how mind operates, point to knowledge, and point especially to space and time. The experiences transcend themselves.

The following sections present my own speculations as to how these experiences occurred. I look at the following factors: mental preparation, focusing on a place or time, mental inactivity, and mental receptivity.

Mental Preparation

I have been meditating for over thirty years, learning and practicing TaiJi for over twenty years, and working with *Time, Space and Knowledge* and the subsequent books in the same series for over seventeen years. During this time, there has been a gradual but notable increase in the frequency of nonordinary knowing events. Thirty years ago, nonordinary experiences never happened. A few occurred over the next ten years. The following ten years, during which I began learning TaiJi and TSK, showed a marked increase in such experiences. The past ten years has yielded the greatest number. (Note that my colleague has also had mental training, though not formal, and reports that she has learned how to quiet the mind and to shift mental states readily.)

This progression suggests to me that the mental inactivity and receptivity which (as discussed below) seem to be necessary for the emergence of nonordinary knowing become more likely through training the mind. Tarthang Tulku repeatedly suggests something similar in the TSK books when he remarks that opening experience and activating inquiry make non-standard (second-level or third-level) experiences more frequent.

True, there are anecdotal accounts of instances of nonordinary knowing in times of intense stress or emotional upheaval that appear to emerge with no preparation. But the pervasive consistency in the structure of my own experiences makes me think this a less likely alternative. I believe that what I describe here captures one set of significant conditions for nonordinary knowing, even though it clearly does not capture the full range of circumstances under which such knowing may in fact occur.

The nature of this preparation goes beyond relaxing and quieting the mind. TSK and Tai Ji both force the involved individual to confront assumptions about self, world, and beliefs. As I note in more detail below, such assumptions are among the mental structures and typical patterns of mental activity that I consider key factors in hindering or making possible nonordinary knowing, so training that encourages this kind of confrontation seems to me important.

In addition, my almost daily practice of TaiJi for twenty years and my frequent and intense practice of TSK "exercises" seem to have trained my mind/ awareness to stop or to arrive at a "neutral state" conducive to nonordinary knowing. This state might be relaxed or quiet, or simply open and receptive. It is, as it were, non-active or "passive," but not in the sense of being lethargic and dull. Instead, it is a state that is responsive without being directed toward particulars either "inside" or "outside" the mind. My assumption is that my mind has learned to settle into this inactive state with some regularity. Just standing, getting sleepy, or quietly focusing inwardly all allow this particular state of mind to manifest quite naturally.

The term "inactive" or "neutral" might seem inconsistent with the mild anxiety that was often an aspect of the situations I have described. I will clarify this point further below, but to anticipate, the anxiety seems to function as a stimulus for focusing the mind; afterwards, I let go. It seems to me that the ability, in such situations, to quiet the mind and to let go of mild anxiety is the result of mental training.

Focusing on a Time or Place

My experiences of nonordinary knowing involve the nitty gritty aspects of everyday concerns. They are neither transcendent nor spiritually uplifting. But each seems to involve a focus of the mind toward a space or time which is of interest or concern, followed by a letting go so that the ordinary mind becomes inactive, at which point knowing arises on its own.

The example of my colleague's grandmother might seem to contradict this, since in that case there was no deliberate focusing at all. However, a similar focusing element was provided there by a mental state receptive to an event of unusual significance. Consider the everyday situation in which someone calls out your name. Because your name is significant to you, this event breaks through whatever else you are doing into your awareness, and you respond. In the same way, if you are attuned to other significant events, they also tend to break into awareness. This seems to me to capture my colleague's situation with her grandmother. It allows for the kind of receptivity that I discuss below.

Receptivity

Nonordinary knowledge could be thought of as arising in response to what is asked, whether the question is actually put in words or not. However, the recipient must be open to the answer. "Open" means that the answer must be acceptable given the belief structures of the individual. One might describe this process as the "mind receiving or accepting knowledge." For instance, a question of interest or importance comes to me; I hold it in mind, then quiet the mind and wait; a response comes. If mind will not receive or acknowledge the response of knowledge, it can never accept the gifts knowledge could bring.

The subjective sense or belief that certain experiences are possible or not possible seems to establish what can, what cannot, and what might happen. Further, one's conscious willingness to engage an experience makes it possible. As an example, I will describe an experience I vowed never to do again, because it scared me. I had been practicing connecting to the feelings in my heart center. As I walked by a window, I saw a robin sitting on the branch of a tree about fifteen feet from the window. I spontaneously decided to connect my heart to the robin. As I did so, it felt as if a cone opened outward, with its apex at my heart. Immediately the robin flew straight at the tip of the cone, headed straight for the window. I was so startled I immediately broke the connection. I remember saying to myself, "I'm not going to do that again."

True to my word, I have never experienced this again. I even now experience a kind of fear of what would happen were I to "connect" with another robin. On the other hand, I have "tried" unsuccessfully to do so a number of times since that event. My working assumption at this point is that "I" have simply shut off the possibility of this kind of experience.

The phenomenon of potential knowledge helps clarify some of these issues. Consider the following situation: I approach an airline departure gate in a rush, wondering when my flight is leaving. In front of me is the sign indicating when the plane leaves, but I am not aware of seeing it. I ask a fellow passenger who tells me that the plane does not leave for twenty minutes. I relax and suddenly see, in front of me, the sign which clearly indicates the plane's departure time. The sign was perceivable, potential knowledge from the first moment I arrived, but it became knowledge only when I allowed it to come to me, or when I made myself available to it. In this regard, knowledge cannot arise without receptivity.

We can conclude that time and space—and the events and objects that arise 'within' and 'as' them—are open to us and available as potential knowledge. We must, however, be receptive to this knowledge. This simple proviso encompasses a great deal, for the knowledge must accord with my beliefs and assumptions, I must be willing to acknowledge it as knowledge, and it must fit with my purposes—with what is significant for me at this moment.

Mental Inactivity

Almost all of the experiences I have described emerge spontaneously, when the ego or self is not too active, and present themselves as not-mine. That is, they come to the self (come to mind) but are not from the self directly (not *from* me), except that they arise as "my image" or "my sense." This leads me to suspect that the sense of self as presently constituted simply does not allow for nonordinary knowledge. Were the self to be reconstituted so as to include the possibility of such nonordinary knowing, this knowing would probably not be sequential temporally, or separated into "knower-known" spatially. In that case, would the self be the self? In other words, when there is no distinction between knower and known, does the term "self" continue to apply? Or would this mark such a radical transformation that everyday concepts cannot capture the experience?

A further observation seems relevant. To try to achieve experiences of nonordinary knowledge—to work for these kinds of results—will most likely fail. Nonordinary knowing, though natural, would seem to be an artifact of receptivity. The effort or intention to evoke it deliberately would interfere with the mental inactivity necessary for its spontaneous emergence. Knowledge simply pops up, as if the mind allows or opens to it. Effort interferes.

To go into this point further, I have attempted to duplicate some of the experiences described above at other times. I have tried to "see" which parking place is available and never been successful. Likewise, I have (I admit with some embarrassment) attempted to "see" the winning lottery number. Once again I have not been successful. The latter example helps clarify the issue. In trying to see the lottery number, I am filled with so many conflicting feelings that I am not in a consciously receptive state. My conclusion is that effort and strong emotion interfere both with the initial clear focusing of the mind and with the open receptivity or spontaneity which seem to be a part of the phenomenological structure of nonordinary knowing.

This might illuminate why mild concern or worry is associated with many of the incidents I have described. Such concern helps focus attention, but it is also easy to let go. More intense emotion might focus the mind on many different times and places, and would certainly be more difficult to let go.

To make this point from a different angle, I will point out that some nonordinary knowings happen quite regularly in my life. Sensing the weather—rain in particular—is one example. Finding lost objects also occurs regularly. However, nowadays my wife will tell people that I have a special ability to locate lost objects: I just get an image and find what is missing. I experience this as pressure, take it on as something "I" can do, and find that images do not come so readily. The effort and self-consciousness impede the activity.

Summary

Based on the consistent elements in my own experience of nonordinary knowledge, I conclude that at least one such form of knowing requires a focusing of the mind on a place or time, a settling of the mind into inactivity, and a receptivity of the mind to what forms spontaneously. These three mental processes (focusing, settling into inactivity and receptivity) are developed in training of the mind.

In addition, various other mental states can hinder the arising of nonordinary knowing. Strong emotion, for example, would scatter the initial focus, hinder the settling into inactivity, and lead to an investment in the "outcome"—what might be known. Effort, intention, and beliefs also can interfere, since they structure consciousness in restrictive ways.

This set of conditions illuminates why nonordinary knowledge can more readily arise in dreams, during reverie, or, possibly, at times of emotional upheaval (provided that at those times the individual is allowing emotions and thoughts to bubble up and the self-constitution has shifted so as to accept different experience). These are the situations in which the sense of self loosens or broadens, so that it does not restrict the potential emergence of such knowledge. I relinquish the tight structuring of experience, and become more available to different experience, and thus to nonordinary knowledge.

What Lets Me Identify Nonordinary Knowledge as Knowledge?

When a mental event occurs, how do I know it is knowledge? It is beyond the scope of this article to offer a summary or critique of the basic structures of Western epistemology, the branch of philosophy that addresses that question. The examples given in Part One, however, establish a foundation for investigating several basic issues related to the nature of knowledge.

The experiences I have described, and the discussions of validation that followed each of them, suggest that confirmation of the accuracy of nonordinary knowledge comes about in the future. If I experience an item of possible knowledge, it either is or is not knowledge. Let us say I "know" that "something is over there." This is knowledge of the existence of something, and it appears to be quite immediate and direct. Suppose, however, that as I step to one side, the "thing" changes appearance, and I realize that what I thought was solid is actually shadow. What I knew—or, rather, what I thought I knew—was wrong.

This description confirms that knowledge is proved true or false in the future. Even the most elemental knowledge—the knowledge that something exists—is validated when the experienced "something" persists over time. In some sense, then, all knowledge of the world (which all of the described experiences entail) is tentative, depending on future validation. Yet on a day to day level, we simply trust or believe that "experience" is "accurate" without question. What seems in the first instance to be objectively so proves to depend more on our subjective sense of certainty. (Compare the discussion in LOK, 143.)

With ordinary perception, the subjective component of certainty does not usually come to the fore. *Seeing* a truck turn left a quarter of a mile in front of me is an event I would consider that I *knew* as soon as I saw it. There would be neither doubt nor question concerning what I experienced. The mental *image* of the truck turning, however, would be a curiosity . . . a curiosity which only later might prove correct. Most of my own nonordinary experiences had this quality: They were of sufficient note to engage my interest at the time and again later when events proved them correct. But they were not accompanied by any sense of subjective certainty.

The two examples drawn from my colleague, on the other hand, *were* accompanied by the subjective certainty of their accuracy. I must note that demonstrating them to be correct depended on later verification, so my earlier conclusion still holds: All sense-based knowledge is tentative and depends on the future for validation. These events were accompanied by a sense of certainty that my experiences did not have. Yet the presence or absence of this subjective sense does not seem to affect whether the knowledge was "true."

Still, there is an interesting distinction to be made. My colleague seems much more comfortable with and able to feel certain of nonordinary knowing. I tend to be more skeptical, putting to question what arises in experience. It is possible, therefore, that my colleague and I structure consciousness differently. In other words, subjective certainty—or rather, comfort with being certain—may be associated with a particular kind of constituted self or state of mind. As will be discussed later, such a self might have more frequent experiences of nonordinary knowing, which would be more consistent with the self as it is constituted.

To explore the issue of subjective certainty associated with a mental event further, let us consider the difference between nonordinary knowledge and a wish. Among the distinguishing characteristics of the nonordinary-knowing events I have described are that they are spontaneous (non-willed), and that each is a single mental event, as opposed to a stream of possibilities. In contrast, a wish or want on my part usually tends to elicit a stream of varied images, all of which are possible ways the wish or want might be satisfied. Interestingly, if I relax into a particular mental state, an almost constant stream of images come to mind, sometimes repeating, sometimes changing. I discover this same response when the stream of mental events is guided by my needs and wishes: spontaneous mental images flow with variety. That is, for me the anticipated result of a wish is almost never a single image, with regard to which I could be certain. But this is exactly what nonordinary knowledge does offer.

True, sometimes I do actively construct as a fantasy a particular wished-for outcome. When I do this, I live out the fantasy one way, and frequently a short while later do it slightly differently, sometimes even altering parts along the way. What is more, these fantasies are an active response to a wish (even when I do not deliberately initiate them); in this sense, they are not spontaneous. Experiences of nonordinary knowledge share neither of these characteristics. They are spontaneous, and they appear as a single mental event (whether image or sound or sense).

It might seem to the reader that dismissing or ignoring the issue of certainty misses what knowledge is. How can there be knowledge when we do not know it is knowledge? In this context, I would simply point out that the situation is not so simple. I can be certain of something and then, on discovering new information, decide that what I had been certain was knowledge is actually an error. This is clear in interpersonal conflict when one party is convinced of the ill will of the other, only to discover that the other was simply acting on misinformation. At the other extreme, we often know something but do not acknowledge that knowledge. After the fact, we may say, "Yes, I knew it all along but I sort of ignored it." Again this is clear in interpersonal relationships. For instance, after a divorce someone might say that the signs of marital trouble were evident, but the parties did not admit what was obvious. These examples verify what was said earlier: that everyday knowledge is identified as knowledge later on, in the future, and that present subjective certainty need not be related to accurate everyday knowledge.

Although subjective certainty is not crucial for valid knowledge, this does not leave us with no standards at all. In fact, some standards have already been articulated. Nonordinary knowing is totally spontaneous. It seems to form in consciousness on its own, in the absence of volition or effort on the part of the knower, and it arises as a single mental event.

Taken together, these criteria offer an alternative to looking at "outcome" as the test for whether the knowing is accurate or not. They consider the experience of the knowing-in-itself, the sense of subjective knowing. This is a departure from the "future verification" model we have been following until now.

The absence of effort or volition as a criterion needs clarification. My colleague clearly intended to find the tool for her husband. Likewise, I intended to find my daughter's lost toy and anticipate whether it might rain. In each case a volition was at work. However, this volition only structured the initial focusing of the mind. Immediately afterwards, the focus was let go and the mind opened. At that point nonordinary knowledge arose spontaneously.

Would a reliance on the sense of knowing-in-itself yield different conclusions from the prior analyses? The following example addresses this issue.

Experience Ten

I am participating in a small, work-related meeting of six people. I suddenly have an impulse to go check something in my office and, even though it is inappropriate and disruptive, I immediately leave with no explanation. As I begin down the hallway to my office, my son is hurriedly turning the corner at the other end. I call out to him and we talk. He had run into the building to seek my help since he had locked the keys in the car and hoped I could drive him across town. My wife, who would be there momentarily, had a meeting she would have to miss in order to drive him back.

In this example, there is a subjective sense of knowing what to do. Following an impulse, I chose a course of action which turned out to coincide with what one of my family members wished. The experience is "uncanny," since I appeared when and where I would not be expected either by me or by the other person.

If the last example is considered a response to my son's wishes, then I was responding to something distant in space. The impulse entered awareness or came to mind and I chose to act on it. What was atypical was my acting in ways which "violated" expectations: I walked out of a small work meeting with no adequate reason. This shows a different kind of certainty—a certainty that does not know something to be so, but knows what to do. It also reveals a different facet of nonordinary knowledge, a facet which coincides with my colleague's grandmother incident. Unfortunately, I have too few examples to make generalizations or do a phenomenological reduction. Perhaps readers would like to share some of their own examples.

What are the Characteristics of Nonordinary Knowing?

Almost all of the experiences I have described emerge spontaneously, when the ego or self is not too active, and present themselves as "not directly mine," rather than arising as "my image" or "my sense". In other words, self gets out of the way, and mind opens and allows the nonordinary knowing to take form. The knowledge that results seems not to belong to the self.

This leads to a puzzling question: If the knowledge is not mine, if it is not "in here" with me, then where is the knowledge? My answer: Knowledge is located *between* the subject and the object. Knowledge is neither in the world (the known) nor in the subject (the knower), but, as it were, in their meeting in a certain way. Let me try to flesh this out.

An everyday understanding of visual knowledge is that what I know—let us say, the color of the rose—comes to me because the light reflected off the petals stimulates the cones in my eye and, thence, neurons in my occipital lobe. The rose does not *do* anything: It simply reflects light. I am the one that "knows" its color when I interpret that light in a certain way. At that point the light becomes knowledge-for-me. Without the appropriate cones in my eyes, without the necessary connections between my eyes and my occipital lobe, and without a functional cortex, I would not see or know the color of the rose.

The description just given translates a scientific and neurological understanding of perception into everyday terms, but I do not think the translation undermines the conclusion that knowledge arises from a coming together of the known and the knower consistent with the purposes and capacities of the knower. Most striking to me is the spatial distance separating the knower and known. Given this distance, there must also be a process that links the knower and known across space and through time. In that linking or coming together, knowledge arises.

"Knowledge," from this view, is not an absolute given, a fundamental truth, which, as it were, one can ultimately know. Rather, knowledge is a potential- and meaning-filled coming together of subject and object or knower and known, which represents them both. My knowledge cannot be independent of my purposes. It embodies the meanings I bring to it, and it represents the possibility or potentiality of the known. As for the standard philosophical view that knowledge must be somehow objectively true, this is just another approach to knowledge, which brings its own view and purposes and, as a result, demonstrates those aspects of the experience which coincide with that philosophical view and purpose.

Returning again to the most elemental of knowings, my knowing the rose is red or knowing the mountain exists depends on *their* potential for being known as red or as existent. In other words, that I can know them as "this" requires that they have this particular potentiality for being. If the flower were not "red" or the mountain were "non-existent," I could not know them as "red" or "existent." Most likely the mountain would not ascribe the word "existent" to itself, nor would the flower call itself "red." But this simply points out that "how and what I know" is filtered through my "view." As Tarthang Tulku writes in TSK, it is "a function of focus or perspective."

One more facet of "potential knowledge" and "potentiality for being" must be clarified. The red flower could "be" a boutonniere. When I regard it in this way, I "know" it would be an attractive addition to my outfit. Thus, the flower's potentiality for being is also potential knowledge for me vis-à-vis my purposes and point of view. However, that possibility might conflict with the flower's potentiality. To use it as a boutonniere requires cutting the flower from its stem: killing the flower for my own purpose.

Let us return to the emergence of nonordinary knowledge. In DTS, Tarthang Tulku uses the puzzling phrase, "mind conducting knowledge." It was only as I was writing the prior sections of this article that what this might refer to occurred to me. Mind, in its focus or intention, conducts—leads or directs—the knowledge that is relevant to its current purposes. In the context of the prior analysis, the way mind would conduct nonordinary knowledge is to invite such knowledge to show itself. In response, mind must allow or open to that knowledge. That is, it must become inactive—receptive, non-interfering — following a prior intention to know. At that point the nonordinary knowledge emerges spontaneously and can assume various forms. That is, the knowing need not be visual but can be auditory, a "sense of something," or "just knowing."

In this model, nonordinary knowledge comes in response to a focus of the mind, an intention, need, or question, followed by openness or inactivity. It arises in response to a question, as long as the recipient is open to the answer. "Open" here means that the answer must be acceptable given the beliefs of the individual, which structure what can be known. This might be the process described as "mind conducting knowledge." My specific methods and channels for knowing are utilized by knowledge to communicate.

PART THREE
BROADER IMPLICATIONS

The previous discussion has proceeded in terms I would characterize, from a TSK perspective, as belonging to first-level knowledge. Nonordinary knowledge experiences point toward the availability of second-level experience, and I have tried to describe some of the circumstances or conditions for this to arise. From there, it is possible to draw broader implications, speculations, and conclusions that may move toward the third-level of the TSK vision.

What is intriguing about the nonordinary knowledge experiences and their analyses presented above is that other facets of knowledge, space, and time "shine through." Thus, even though the structure of most of these events show themselves in terms of the here/there, knower/known or subject/object polarity, their unity or connection within space and through time "speaks" of something different. This aspect is what I want to explore now.

Nonordinary Knowing Does Not Depend on the Senses But on Mind

How can we understand knowing "objective, real world situations" in the absence of overt sensory stimulation? How can one know—"see in one's mind"—that which is so but which one cannot see with the eyes? How can one know—"see in one's mind"—a scene which will occur in the future? These are the ways of knowing found in all of the examples described. And all of them involve the mind.

Everyday mind is curtailed or limited by beliefs. One typical belief is that mind is located in the head;

is, in fact, the brain. To live out this latter view means that the mind follows the limitations established by everyday beliefs about how reality functions. Examples of nonordinary knowing, however, indicate that these assumptions are not always operative. Since they do not consistently operate, the claim that their view is "the way things are" must be in error.

In this regard, it is critical to note that actual experiences of nonordinary knowing arose when the everyday structuring activity or everyday operating processes of the mind stopped. The everyday beliefs which limit what can be known were temporarily set aside and, in those moments, a "response arose" after a prior focusing of the mind. If we can say that nonordinary knowing occurs "in" the mind, we can conclude that mind or awareness has access to spaces and times that would be closed off to it under everyday understanding.

From a TSK perspective, one hypothesis to account for this would be that when everyday beliefs and limitations cease to operate, we discover the oneness of mind/awareness with space and time. In brief openings, knowing appears able to access any point in space or time. Such knowledge "knows" that "this" space is not separated from all other space; that this point has access to all other points. Likewise, this time is connected and not separate from all other times.

If nonordinary knowing suggests that the beliefs that limit mind can be temporarily set aside, do other beliefs take their place? This seems to be one possibility. It is conceivable that someone could hold beliefs that include the possibility of certain non-standard kinds of experience or knowledge, and that these experiences might then arise for this individual. However, that is not what I am pointing toward, for it seems to me that any set of beliefs is limiting and conducts only the knowledge consistent with its structures. What I am suggesting is the possibility of a temporary suspension of all beliefs. In that case, nonordinary knowledge can spontaneously present itself, but that is only a first step. The next step would be to discover that mind/awareness are one with space and time.

Distinguishing and "Connecting" Mind and Awareness

It seems useful to distinguish mind from awareness in the following way. The mind is where I experience intentions, thoughts, and my sense of identity, while awareness—for example, awareness of sounds, sights, or sensations in the body—is not shaped by these structures. I can, of course, also be aware of the activity of the mind, and mind in turn seems to guide or focus (given the earlier discussion, could we say "conduct?") awareness. I am able, for example, to ignore the music in the background or to pay close attention to it. Awareness seems more fundamental. I can only know something when it is in awareness, which is broader or more encompassing than mind or than any sensory activity. Spatially speaking, we could say that mind and the senses are "within" awareness. More broadly, we could say that awareness is my experience of connection with the known.

This distinction between mind and senses helps us clarify what happens with nonordinary knowing. For mind and the senses, locked into the body and how it is embodied in the physical world, inherently limit what is knowable by "defining" as knowable only what can come from the senses. The kinds of "singularities" described above—events which seem not to follow ordinary "natural laws"—are simply not available. But awareness is not bound in the same way. Awareness can bring all kinds of knowledge to the mind, even if mind does not necessarily take as potential knowledge that which arises in awareness. In turn, it is the capacity of mind to open, that is, make itself available to what arises in awareness, that connects it to knowing beyond the limits of the everyday.

I have already suggested, based on my own experience, that nonordinary knowing can arise when the mind becomes inactive. I do not yet know how to bring this about as a part of the way that I structure my everyday experience. What is apparent to me, however, is that the usual assumptions and beliefs that guide how most people construe "everyday reality" are not so rigid or clear.

As Humans We Are
Connected to Space and Time

I return to the question of how it is possible that nonordinary knowing occurs. The answer plumbed exhaustively by the TSK books is that we, as human beings, are not separated from space and time. Nonordinary knowledge reveals this facet of being and potentiality as it slips into the everyday. And the emphasis on time, space, and knowledge in turn clarifies or illuminates why effort, belief, and other processes associated with self seem to get in the way of nonordinary knowing. Such knowing is not brought about or created by the self, but is an ongoing response by space and time.

My TaiJi teacher, H.H. Lui, told the following story. A master had a student who wanted to learn from other great masters. His master supported him not only emotionally but also financially. He traveled for many years, finally finding another teacher. After fifteen years, he excitedly returned home to show his teacher what he had learned. He happened to find his master about to cross a river on a ferry boat. Proud of his accomplishments, he refused to join his master in the boat and instead crossed the river by walking alongside the boat on the water. When they got to the other side, his master said, "Poor boy. Twenty years of practice and all this money, only to save a quarter's toll."

There are many ways to understand this story. The one I want to note is that effort and work to develop the nonordinary for its own sake miss the deepest profundities and the inherent wondrousness and "magic" that underlies them. The self structures mind and ways of knowing, and the self could also be structured differently, allowing different possibilities. Can we consider the possibility of going beyond the self, and beyond the linear time and separated spatiality that it structures?

From a first-level point of view, the answer to this question will turn on the intriguing facets of knowledge, space, and time that we glimpse "through" the ordinary and everyday. This is what happened in most of the nonordinary examples described in Part One, where the unity of consciousness with space and time revealed itself, even though consciousness continued to structure experience into subject/object polarities. Although self continued to structure the way things are known—the point of view taken in that knowing—a "different" space and time did shine through, revealing through nonordinary knowledge that one point is linked to all points.

Yet this whole process can be understood in ways that go beyond the first level. Knowledge reveals itself, but it does so from the point of view of the knower. In an almost magical way, it uses the individual's methods of knowing to communicate nonordinary knowledge. This is both a great gift of knowledge and a reflection of the limitations of the self.

The way that knowledge manifests shows that the self uses both mind and awareness from a particular point of view. It reveals a polarizing tendency within mind/awareness to "split" into subject-object. This polarization is mirrored in other distinctions such as mind/awareness, mind/body, mind/world, and now/then.

In the cases of nonordinary knowledge described, these structures are maintained: a thought or image presents itself via awareness to the mind of the self. Yet if we assume that the open availability of space and time to knowledge is correct, an inexhaustible number of views, not linked to the self, are available. The reason they do not manifest is that knowledge reveals only in response to a request by mind, and thus remains bound by the everyday point of view of the "knower."

Recall the precise pictures that came to my mind of the truck turning, the morning sunrise at the campground, and the car leaving the parking place. Each image presented exactly what I later experienced in ordinary terms. From this I conclude that while the self (its beliefs, needs, emotions, purposes, and attitudes) structures (that is, invites and limits) what can be known and how it can be known, space and time can present themselves fluidly. Put more broadly, space and time are openly available to and as knowledge.

If we go a step further, the distinctions we have been making between self, mind, and awareness begin to break down. Let us consider again the presentation of nonordinary knowledge:

a) "I" am in an inactive state of mind and a picture "enters my mental awareness."

b) Sometimes "I" notice images and sometimes "I" do not. On this occasion, "I" notice the image.

c) Later, "I" discover that the image coincides with a "reality event."

In this sequence, what is the role of the self or "I?" In the books of the TSK series, Tarthang Tulku suggests that the self manifests as a structuring or polarizing of mind/awareness such that there is a subject and an object. The self, that is, is simply one of many potentialities of mind/awareness—and should probably be written as "self/mind/awareness" to capture that inseparability. And indeed, we can see why this is so. Since the "self" is constituted by and in "mind/awareness," how can it be different from mind/awareness? Nonordinary knowledge reveals this alternative understanding in our own experience.

The next analytical step now presents itself. Almost all of the prior discussion seems to describe self/mind/awareness as distinct from space and time. To distill this, we can use the phrasing, "I come to know about space and time." Yet mind also manifests as space and unfolds in and as time. Considering the spatial aspect, space differentiates itself into self, mind, body, and world, distinctions established and maintained through time. Again, this spatial element is obvious if we focus there. Awareness pervades my experience of my body and my world. It opens them to me, making them available.

Recall, however, that awareness cannot so readily be separated from self or mind. We could, as a result, rewrite the previous sentence as follows: "Self/mind/awareness pervades the experience of my body and my world, of space and of time." And further, despite the experience of articulated distinctions, self/mind/awareness pervades space and time. Space and time are fluid (not limited, partitioned or constricting) and available to knowledge.

Nonordinary experiences of knowing reveal knowledge which is not bound by the usual, everyday constraints apparently established by ordinary space and time. They show that we are all linked within space and time. Space is open and available. Time is open and available. Self/mind/awareness is connected to space and time by being space and time. As Tarthang Tulku has written, "One point is all points."

REFERENCES

Giorgi, A., ed. 1985. *Phenomenology and Psychological Research*. Pittsburgh, PA: Duquesne Univ. Press.

EXPLORING TIME, SPACE AND KNOWLEDGE IN THE CONDUCTING OF PROFESSIONAL LIFE

Ronald E. Purser

PART ONE

One

On one cool and pleasant summer evening in the town of Kenosha where I live, I elected to go for a bike ride. After riding on a path alongside Lake Michigan, I stopped at one of my favorite parks and sat on a bench overlooking the lake. As I gazed out onto the lake, I decided to allow a TSK exercise to unfold. The sky and the water were a rich blue color, so I felt that a Space practice would be both nice and appropriate. The one that came to mind was Exercise 9 in *Dynamics of Time and Space*, "Generating Space."

As I looked out onto the lake I saw several sail boats slowly making their way across the water. I noticed how things like the horizon, the boats, the water, the sounds felt to be "out there" and away from me "here." As I gazed at the object I called "boat," I began to see or know, perhaps simultaneously, that the "boat" was made of wood, the sail was made of fiber, and the figures of people on the boat were human bodies composed of organs, cells, molecules, and so on. I began to question the perception that space was simply the absence of these things that "I" was perceiving, or that space was simply a container for things. A bird flew overhead, and the whole picture of me sitting there looking out at objects seemed to shift to a sense that a tremendous, uninhibited openness was allowing all these myriad forms to appear.

Suddenly, all that was appearing, including my own presence, was sensed as space doing space, time doing time, and knowledge appreciating that this was so. Things appeared as space, and space appeared as things, but not in the sense that space was behind these things, or that these things were at some level space. No. . . . The perception and the event itself were somehow space, not dependent on any prior cause or substance.

As I contemplated and allowed the space presentation to unfold, a notion of space-depth became more apparent. This space-depth, or depth of space, gave a blissful feeling of unified, non-dimensionalized extension. It offered a knowing that while things appear to be separate and distant, the truth of space reveals that they are in reality no-where and no-things—"there" in the sense that they are perceivable, yet not fixed in any substantial position or location.

As I reflected later, it seemed that this space-depth dimension can apply to whole events and to mental states as well as physical objects. In other words, space is a realm without borders and without distinctions, so open and accommodating of possibilities that the lack of limits allows appearance to burst forth. Anything can happen, or nothing—the property of space continues to manifest, undisturbed by such referents.

Two

The Christian tradition in which I was raised tends to place a partition between intellectual and philosophical inquiry and the inner, experiential, and mystical dimensions. In Catholicism, for example, those educated in scholastic theology and the liberal arts, such as the Jesuits, are trained to enter the "active life." Monks, on the other hand, are sequestered to lead the isolated "contemplative life." TSK is quite different, and that is one of the reasons I was so drawn to it from the beginning. It offers a unique opportunity for melding intense intellectual and philosophical analysis of the nature of reality with an experiential and imaginative expansion of consciousness.

In 1995, soon after a TSK e-mail group had been established, Tarthang Tulku contributed several e-mail messages to the group. In one message he commented that TSK practice in and of itself may not lead to fruitful results with the vision. On an intuitive level, I already knew this was the case, given the TSK emphasis on combining rational inquiry with experiential exercises. Recently, however, I have come to appreciate this comment in a deeper way. Certainly experiential practice should not be put aside, but the danger of practicing with the hopes of having "good and unusual experiences" struck a chord for me.

For many years I fell prey to this "experience seeking" approach. It was not that I avoided or gave short shrift to textual and analytical study of the TSK books. Far from it: I probably read and reflected on each one to a far greater degree than practicing the exercises. Rather, I think the trap of experiential practice was in making stories about the experiences I did have. Each new and unusual experience became another story for the self to tell, an account of its wonderful progress and discoveries along the TSK path. I relished the TSK exercises for the liberating and expansive feeling they would evoke. In many cases, I would actually sit down to practice with the expectation of "having" these expansive and unusual experiences. I am sure that many others too have been prone to think that such experiences were signs of "progress," or indicators that the vision was "working."

Such unusual experiences were not limited to sessions when I was formally practicing TSK exercises. I will recount a few incidents: stories about the stories I so much liked to tell myself and others.

In 1983, when I was a student in a nine-month TSK program at the Nyingma Institute in Berkeley, spontaneous paranormal experiences began manifesting in my daily life. Events such as precognition and clairvoyance had begun to happen several years earlier, but now they came with much greater frequency. For instance, I remember a conversation I was having with my sister in Chicago as I talked with her from a phone at the Nyingma Institute. It was around Christmas time, and I suddenly had a visual impression of the presents that were sitting under my family's Christmas tree. I described these presents with great accuracy.

On other occasions I would meet people for the first time and find that an inner voice seemed to give me instantaneous knowledge of their physical problems or ailments. I remember meeting one woman at a friend's party and knowing immediately she had an ulcer, a fact she confirmed. Another time I met someone and instantly had a visual impression of seeing this person falling off a horse and being seriously injured when she was a child; again, my impression was confirmed. In another strange instance, I visited someone's apartment and found I could hear conversations that had actually transpired days earlier. I had never been to this apartment before, and I had just met the person who had invited me there. This person had a roomate, whom I never had met either and who was not physically present at the apartment. I heard her name "in the air." "Your roomate's name is Susan," I said, "and she had a big argument with her boyfriend a few days ago." Of course, we were both amazed at the words uttered out of my mouth.

During this period, it was as if I was able to see and hear with different eyes and ears—as though a different space for knowledge had suddenly become available. Tarthang Tulku notes such possibilities (TSK, 207):

> By opening ourselves up to 'time', it can act and speak more freely through us. Our speech and gestures become totally irrepressible and spontaneous, welling up from 'time', the dynamic center of our being. . . . Initially, this may result in a surfacing of unpremeditated action perfectly suited to the situation at hand. It may also give rise to a keen predictive ability (precognition). Although making predictions may seem to require seeing the 'future' and then reporting back to the present, predictive knowing actually does not go forward or elsewhere and return. Precognition is possible, because it—and we— are not 'pre', not 'before'. For just this reason, such knowing and speaking are due to a deep abiding in a more inclusive form of 'the present'.

Looking back on these early and impressive experiences with TSK, I realize that the way I fit them into my understanding of the vision was much too compartmentalized and immature. I was infatuated with these "extra-ordinary" experiences, and I actually began to seek them out. This applied as well to the more expansive and blissful meditative states that can often arise while doing TSK practice. Anticipating such tendencies and traps, Tarthang Tulku warns (TSK, 149):

> It is important not to congratulate ourselves when discontinuities and miraculous events occur.

They are not to be taken as achievements or as something to consolidate 'ourselves' against, thus shutting them out. Either of these approaches, which involve trying to maintain a 'self' on very shaky ground, is likely to lead to psychological disorientation—since 'time' would, as always, work against such consolidation.

And (204):

On the second level, where the visions gain their meaning, they can become a subtle trap; they may cause stagnation or infatuation. Such visions have a tendency to prevent full resolution and at-one-ment because of this difficulty in going beyond them.

Perhaps it is normal to go through a phase of being enticed by and attached to such unusual experiences. At least it provides a sense of faith that TSK can indeed facilitate a miraculous yet natural opening into the potentialities of space and time. Nevertheless, I eventually realized that I had constructed a boundary between my ordinary life experiences and these more extraordinary perceptions and 'mystical' states. In these early years of working with TSK, I did not heed Tarthang Tulku's warnings.

The results were ultimately disappointing. The new possibilities I tasted were brief and fleeting. Insights gained during practice would soon fade. Times when everything in my life seemed to go smoothly eventually ran their course. Times when I felt I had tremendous physical and mental energy would soon give way to lethargy and mental laziness. Periods of inspiration and creativity and intense concentration would last for awhile, only to be followed by more routine rhythms and habitual patterns. Since I first started studying and practicing TSK, I have noticed how these fluctuating rhythms and cyclic trends alternate "from and to," from being closed to open, from being lazy and frustrated to being energetic and creative, from being confused and distracted to being clear, focused, and sharply aware, and then back again.

Even now, I suspect that such subtle tendencies continue. I can still get into an orientation of seeking "special experiences," not so much paranormal events, but simply states that I judge or classify as higher versus lower, mundane versus creative. And then there are periods of stagnation—TSK downtime, so to speak—in which dull and habitual routines seem to take over. Still, something has shifted. What is different now is that all the while there is a continuity of awareness of light, knowledge, and the confidence that "things" can be different.

My approach and understanding began to shift after Tarthang Tulku published *Visions of Knowledge* in 1993. At that time I began to focus more on the arising of "ordinary experience" as a TSK practice. Both *Visions of Knowledge* and *Dynamics of Time and Space* (1994) placed more of an emphasis on the dynamic of tracing how our experience arises in space and time. These presentations of the TSK vision seemed to integrate cognitive with experiential inquiry in ways that were not as accessible in prior TSK books.

Lately, guided by this insight, I have allowed cognitive inquiry to work more in parallel with experiential practice. I have found that a deeper understanding of the TSK vision can guide everyday thinking, knowing, and doing. I think that the core of this understanding has to do with seeing and questioning how our everyday experience 'with' and 'in' space and time and knowledge is constructed. How are the mechanisms put into motion? How are they ignored and maintained in our daily experience?

I am perhaps most intrigued with the notion of "embodying knowledge," rather than simply "possessing knowledge." This approach seems central to TSK, for Tarthang Tulku has often emphasized the importance of "living the vision." In this sense, TSK is not a tool or technique to be used in an instrumental way.

Another personal vignette might help illustrate this point. In late May of 1992 I returned to Chicago from a Kum Nye retreat at the Nyingma Institute in Berkeley. During the retreat, I practiced many of the TSK exercises while doing the Kum Nye practices (which focus on meditative movement and awareness). The months that followed were one of those magical and creative times of my life.

My main focus at that time was preparing to teach a summer course in ethics at Loyola University. My habit was to over-prepare for my classes, loading each session with information and specifics that I wanted students to learn: I *possessed* a lot of knowledge, and it was my job to disseminate that knowledge to students (whether they liked it or not). Now, however, my deep sense and feeling was that this sort of activity was unproductive and ineffective. Instead, I confidently went into the first class session and allowed my active presence and words to flow from a deeper knowledge-ability. My memory and recall of material was much improved, which added to my newfound confidence in speaking extemporaneously. Of course, I had a basic idea of the issues and topics I wanted to share with students, but I felt no need to drag out my "to-do list." I even started the class by inviting students to do a short Kum Nye exercise! A few days later a colleague received a call from one of my students, who remarked on the change, saying, "What's happened to Ron Purser? He's a different person!" That was more or less my sense as well. Previous limits on knowledge had definitely been transcended.

TSK tells us that time and space are not merely background factors for the experience of a self-in-a-world. This idea is deeply inspiring for me, and I have learned to use the sense of "space and time as background" (versus "direct participation in and as space and time") as an early warning system to help me see when knowledge of time and space is being ignored. Through this and other means, I have found that my familiarity or knowledge of space has shifted or changed. Conceptually I have always acknowledged that embodiment of the Great Space aspect of the TSK vision is fundamental to a change in focal setting, but it is only recently, after working with TSK on and off for fourteen years, that I really feel that I am beginning to open in a limited way to the boundaryless depths of Space. I have found the sections on Space in DTS to be particularly helpful in using cognition and reason as tools for inquiry. Using such tools, I can deconstruct—analytically and experientially—what we normally take to be the substance of things as they appear to exist.

Beneath this way of inquiry lies the realization that the great and liberating power of the TSK vision must be measured by the quality of our lives. Our own experience is the only place we can authentically begin. Far from being an abstract philosophical system, TSK confronts our experience head-on. How are we living in space and time? Do we act wisely and for the long-term benefit of others? Do we respond creatively to events in our lives? Still better, do we allow Time, Space, and Knowledge to create the events in our lives?

Three

For several months last year I felt I was squandering precious time and energy in procrastination and avoidance of my next big writing project—a new book. I had become withdrawn, frustrated, and lazy, often letting days go by without sitting down to write or even plan what I needed to do. I made up tons of excuses: "There's plenty of time;" "I deserve a rest;" "I'll do some other little things;" "I'll start when I feel inspired;" "I need to read more to prepare." . . . I am sure I could fill several pages with other justifications for inaction that I tried out and sometimes adopted.

Although I went along with these mutterings, trying to make myself feel comfortable with a lackadaisical, drift-along lifestyle, the TSK books glared at me from my bookshelf—those imposing fractal colors beckoning me to drop the game-playing and charades. It was hard to keep up the pretense, knowing very well that I was wasting valuable time.

Still, I believe there was some valuable knowledge concealed within this mind-muck. I knew that I wanted to conduct the task of writing in a different way than I had on a previous book project. I could tell that if I simply forced myself to write, the form would be wrong and my performance erratic—a constant struggle. Although my hesitation and reluctance to start writing was perhaps ninety percent avoidance-driven, my sense that space seemed constricted also pointed to something else. The frustration and feeling of avoidance seemed to be related to a cramped mental attitude that accompanied my physical sluggishness.

At some point a new thought emerged. Could I apply a TSK approach to the writing process and the project? Of course I could! Even to think that this was a possibility brought a sigh of relief and ray of hope. I decided that this would be an implicit personal theme for me to contemplate at a week-long TSK retreat that I was planning to attend in Colorado.

The same theme is at work as I write now. My usual procedure at this point would be to start a new sub-heading, "TSK-Retreat, Stillpoint, July, 1996," in which I described how the retreat was beneficial to my stated needs. Actually, I did start to do this, but at once I felt stuck. Instead, I decided to aim for a more TSK-like approach. I asked, "Do I really have to proceed this way? Is this 'stuckness' the final say on the matter?"

Instead of playing out the stuckness, I playfully challenged the notion of linear sequencing. Did I need to write this essay in the usual chronological order? Once the question was there, Exercise 3 in DTS spontaneously wriggled in between the lines, clearing a space for more knowledge to shine through. While what I have just written is hardly earth-shattering or profound in content, I certainly feel more confident in the creative force that will let me continue writing.

Someone might say, "Ah, that is a well-known creative technique; some people call it 'free-writing.' It's no big deal." Well, maybe so, but I certainly didn't intend to try "free-writing" as a technique to go beyond the "constriction of the subhead." Instead, I engaged my experience through inquiry: Is this "stuckness" the final limit? How have I constructed the stuckness? Could it be constructed differently?

Four

Perhaps the example I just gave is enough to make the point: TSK can be applied to the writing process. But I want to share another, related discovery: The Time aspect of the TSK vision can be brought into play to inform the activity of writing—or any other project.

For the 1996–97 academic year, I had been awarded a sabbatical leave. I planned to use this time to read widely and start work on a book that would examine new ways of bringing about change in social systems, using TSK-related ideas. However, to take a whole year off meant taking a fifty percent reduction in salary. To make up for the lost income, I submitted a proposal for another, more conventional book-project in my field to three well-known trade publishers. To my surprise, they all made offers on the book, complete with a healthy advance that would solve my financial needs.

Now I had a new problem. The demands of this new project threatened to occupy all of my time and attention, overriding the very purpose of my sabbatical. Not to mention the fact that I felt little intrinsic motivation for the project I had proposed. I was faced with a mixed blessing: I had solved the financial problem, but I had just signed away the next year of my life to a project that seemed likely to overshadow everything that I hoped to do during my sabbatical. And so the story went. Indeed, I was constantly caught up in stories concerning this dilemma.

One morning during the TSK retreat at Stillpoint, I brought this dilemma up with the group. Bob Pasternak asked me, "If you were to do a TSK exercise right now to help you tap your creative resources, which one would you do?" Without hesitation, and seemingly without much conscious thought, I responded, "Reversing Temporal Structure (Exercise 22 in the first TSK book)." And so we all did it on the spot.

I imagined myself in the future, after the book had been written and was circulating in the hands of readers. Imagining the book as a finished product, with cover and all, I felt a sense of ease and joy. As I continued, an expanded vision of the future unfolded. I now saw managers and business leaders reading the book and discussing it with employees in their organizations. I saw numerous executives being influenced by what I had written and making significant organizational changes as a result. These changes affected the lives of employees in a beneficial way. That benefit in turn affected the lives of the employees' families. The ripple effects of the book continued to be revealed. I thought, "If these changes occur in an organization, a worker may not go home and physically abuse his children." The energy of the future was alive with potential, and this aliveness fed back into 'the present'.

The exercise left with me a vision for the book. The energy and creativity of the future had infused my task with a larger vision, purpose, and meaning. This book could significantly improve the quality of work lives of thousands of people for the better. Instead of sitting down each day at my desk and cajoling myself to write, struggling as a isolated bystander—the subject as writer opposite the computer screen as object—I could now relax. Writing could 'do' me, instead of me doing the writing. I could conduct differently, using time as an ally. The task of writing would no longer need to be confined to a tight, constricting space in the corner of my mind, in the corner of my room.

As I reflected on what had changed, I saw that my old way of looking at the book project was based on the model of the maestro who conducts time, as described in Chapter 15 of DTS. The maestro identifies himself as the active agent of his own experience, conducting in the present, which is always slipping away. To affirm his own existence, the maestro tells stories that confirm his continuous identity, ignoring the larger and more energetic conducting of time that makes the storytelling possible.

The world that unfolds in this way, linear in its temporal structure, is stripped of its energy and meaning. For the maestro to make sense of his own self-understanding, he must reject the creativity of time and the freedom of space, conducting instead a continuous sameness.

As long as I followed this model, I would write in a flat and uninspired way. But I sensed the possibility of a different way of writing, based on improvisation instead of linear structure. As improvisation, the words of the book could be "danced into being" (DTS, 145).

Five

With no previous design in mind, the retreat at Stillpoint focused on chapter fifteen in DTS, "Dancing a Challenge to the Whole," a chapter that discusses the cultivation of improvisational skills. I have always been drawn to jazz because of its spirit of improvisation, and some of my academic articles have used jazz improvisation as a metaphor for how companies and groups of people could be organized for creative business performances. So I was delighted to have this opportunity to explore improvisation as a TSK practice.

Chapter fifteen of DTS suggests conducting experience less as a maestro conducts a symphony orchestra and more as an electrical wire conducts electricity. Taken as a practice, this seems similar to the idea of putting Time at the center of experience. Instead of thinking that you are the one who is thinking and making things happen, or else that things are happening to you, you can open to the wider view of all activity as Time manifesting.

Conducting like a wire means that I do not always have to locate myself in time by getting caught in the constant chatter of the narrative mind. The solidity of the storyteller can relax and become more spacious, allowing more time to enter the picture. As knowing rides the wave of time along the fluctuating wire, it transmits past, present, and future as a unified presence. While the field communiqué (DTS, 27) and conventional thinking still generate references to things that appear to be in the remote past or distant future, or otherwise separate from me, a higher knowing knows that this view is one of many messages of time, not the way things really are. The result is more flexibility, more intuition regarding the future, more creativity, and a sense of being able to take advantage of possibilities at the right time. There is also a stronger sense of knowing when one has slipped back into the rigid structures of identity and lower time. There is less tolerance for wasting time or for accepting one's stories as excuses for being lazy.

Chapter fifteen of DTS invites the reader to cultivate such possibilities through imaginative perception. Instead of allowing our knowing capacity to become entranced by the appearance of substance, we can develop a sort of bio-feedback capability (DTS, 150–51):

A special kind of 'bio-feedback' is called for: a self-projecting of what has been perceived, without identification. . . . Clear awareness can improvise differently. Instead of insisting on pronouncements, mental projection can practice the instant reflection of images, arising within memory or awareness like an image in a mirror, but never entering the mirror itself.

Instead of identifying with the substantive content associated with the stories and images active in the order that operates in the mirror-like world, we can remember that our own appearance and perceptions are also images of space and time. An awareness that can begin to glimpse and see images as images, rather than as substantial things that exist independent of space and time, can feed this way of seeing back into itself. This in turn allows for a new way of knowing to loosen the hold of what appear to be fixed patterns or patternings, while experimenting with knowing capacities not confined to the standard linear order of time.

PART TWO

One

Over the last five or six years, TSK has increasingly influenced my professional and intellectual life. My orientation has changed significantly as I have ventured farther away from the mainstream thinking in the field of organizational theory and development.

Mainstream organization theories and managerial practices tend to be highly rational and instrumental in nature. They are preoccupied with problem-solving techniques and tools for accomplishing existing ends. Conversely, many of the deep-seated issues of organizational life are conveniently ignored.

For example, organization theories and managerial practices do not address or acknowledge the problems of human emotionality in the workplace: emotions such as pride, arrogance, jealousy, envy, and greed. These emotions are tied to such problems as inequality, conflict, domination, subordination, and manipulation, which do register as issues for organizational theorists. However, mainstream theories and practices limit their attention and discourse in regard to these matters to such issues as "motivation," "social skills," "group process," and "efficiency."

Through learning to focus their inquiry in these ways, managers learn to privilege technological knowing and instrumental discourse. They learn that their job is not to ask critical questions, but to use whatever means are available to get their jobs done in the most effective and efficient manner possible, even if this is often times accomplished at the expense of human beings and the natural environment.

My connection to TSK has given me the confidence to trust my own independent judgment in rejecting such approaches as the only ones available. It has also encouraged me to be open to complex questions. In this sense, the knowing evoked by TSK study and practice infiltrates everything that I do. For this I can only be grateful, for I would have found it extremely unsettling to follow the herd, learning to be a "true professional" while remaining silent about the issues that are of deepest concern to me.

One of the major problems in almost any field is that there is little inquiry into how our embodied assumptions of space and time influence the type of knowledge we have access to, leaving us with characteristic problems that result from a "lower-knowledge" perspective. The field of organizational theory and development is no exception. It offers a lot of ideas and techniques intended to help people and organizations change and adapt, but these theories and practices assume that space and time are invariable dimensions.

If that assumption could be challenged, many fruitful avenues of inquiry could be opened up, possibly leading to personal and professional change of the deepest sort. In the next several parts of this essay, I make some preliminary moves in this direction, reflecting on various developments in my field through TSK eyes. These ideas are thumbnail sketches of an inquiry that I hope to pursue further in the near future.

A good way to begin is to examine how modern industrial societies became standardized and routinized to conform to the rhythms of the machine, thus transforming our relationship to time. The starting point was the rise of the factory system, which marked an abrupt break with the craft tradition and the temporal rhythms it sustained. And here the first step was the division of labor, popularized toward the end of the eighteenth century in Adam Smith's famous description of a pin-making factory.

The idea that tasks could be divided and subdivided, parceled out to different specialists, allowed capitalists to assemble many workers under one roof, giving them control over the total process of manufacture. However, the wheel of mechanization would not go into full gear until the discovery that work could be broken down into even more detail by timing the motions of workers measured against the stopwatch.

As has often been noted (Rice, 1989) the early factory system required a regimented and standardized relationship to time. It is not coincidental that the invention of the clock was modeled after the waterwheel—one of the classic mechanical devices.

Mechanized time (as opposed to the digitized time we have today) conjures up the image of gears turning round and round—a wheel that churns away, repeating the same movements over and over. As cultural artifacts, both machines and mechanical clocks are bound up in a rhythm of temporal sameness. This sameness in turn manifests not only in the techniques of production, but also in the products themselves. The mass production of consumer goods both requires and reflects standardization, synchronized methods, and a submission to the dictates of technique, and the goods that result bear the hallmarks of the methods that have been used to create them.

With the introduction of Taylorist scientific management techniques early in this century, workers who had already lost control over the final product of their efforts also lost control over the pace of their work. In the age of the artisan and the craftsman, work was both an activity valuable in itself and one resulting in things that were of value for others. Now, however, such "real work" disappeared, transformed into "labor:" activity with no intrinsic value for the laborer. Thus, the trend toward the fractionalization of work also resulted also in the degradation of work.

This process of fractionalization and degradation was paralleled by a shift in in our attitude toward time. As human activity came to be valued only as a set of standardized motions that efficiently produced desired results, time was valued only as a device for standardized measurement. In both cases, it was less the rule of reason than the rule of measure that came to dominate. Just as the laborer's product is a commodity that can be bought for a fixed price, his labor became a commodity that can be exchanged for a fixed wage. This labor is measured out in fixed, standardized units of time: the sixty-minute hour, the eight-hour day, and so on. In this way time itself becomes a commodity. Laborers are alienated from the time in which they work, unable to engage it in a playful and creative way.

Much has certainly been written on the problem of alienated work. However, from a TSK perspective, the phenomenology of alienated work-experience can best be understood in terms of time. Compared to the measured-out activity of the laborer, the "real" work of the artisan contains within it a fuller and more open relationship to time. In such work, labor and leisure are integrated, both intrinsically valuable. Work can be playful because it is not cut off from the creativity of time. For the laborer, this is no longer the case.

Today the mechanization of time has spread into the realm of leisure as well. The dynamic of conducting temporal sameness constructs and maintains an economic order where mass production requires mass consumption as its analog. While the consumer has available an infinite variety of goods and services to choose from, "real leisure" and "real recreation" give way to the temporal dynamic of "free time" (meaning time "away" from work). The resulting "leisure-time" activities generate the same feelings of dissatisfaction, anxiety, and lack of fulfillment that we find in our jobs. A blank numbness takes over, making us ideal candidates for the diversions and distractions of consumption. The mass media condition us to a special kind of "efficiency" in our pursuit of enjoyment that parallels the routines of the Taylorist workplace. Habitual television watching and channel flipping, shopping binges, and the like are all part of the same dynamic. The words of Tarthang Tulku describing temporal sameness apply fully (DTS, 121):

> In each case, the mechanism works in the same way. We find ourselves isolated within the borders of the established model. We cannot know and do not have the answer; cannot think what is new. We move in a narrow circle: the pattern of sameness on the surface, the blank numbness of repetition on the interior.

Two

The cultural dynamic of temporal sameness came to the fore and intensified in the mechanical age. Now we have entered a different time, sometimes called the post-industrial or the information age. Does the dynamic of temporal sameness operate in this new era?

In *Understanding Media*, Marshall McLuhan (1964) described the social transformations that might come about through new communication technologies. He prophesied a new era—the age of electromagnetism—in which a global information network would emerge that would model or mirror the complexity of our central nervous system. Today that prophecy is becoming a reality. The information superhighway, with its capacity for instantaneous communication and multimedia transmission, is spreading so fast that within ten years or so it will likely approach the level of a single unified field-state (which McLuhan likened to the type of organic unity that exists in the human brain). Anticipating this development, McLuhan foresaw a complete discontinuity in cultural patterns, requiring a whole different mindset from machine-age thinking.

For McLuhan, the age of electromagnetism represented a break with the principles of mechanization. The speed of electromagnetic transmission not only *parallels* the speed of neural firings that occur within our central nervous system; it actually becomes an *extension* of our nervous system. Electromagnetic transmission does not recognize the conventional boundaries that delineated territories in the mechanical age, nor does it obey the requirements for linear movement of physical entities, as in the production-flow of materials on an assembly-line. McLuhan pointed to some of the consequences (1973, 104):

. . . [T]he tendency is to speak of electricity as painters speak of space; namely, that it is a variable condition that involves the special position of two or more bodies. There is no longer any tendency to speak of electricity as 'contained' in anything. Painters have long known that objects are not contained in space, but that they generate their own spaces. It was the dawning awareness of this in the mathematical world a century ago that enabled Lewis Carroll, the Oxford mathematician, to contrive *Alice in Wonderland*, in which times and spaces are neither uniform nor continuous, as they had seemed to be since the arrival of Renaissance perspective.

McLuhan associated the electronic age with light and illumination, suggesting a potential transformation of the temporal sameness of industrial modernism. And there is no doubt that momentous changes are in the air. Human society is learning how to control the forces of electromagnetism to ever greater degrees, and the effects are breaking down space-time boundaries as we know them. Already we can communicate instantaneously with people in distant parts of the world. We can send images and distribute gigabytes of information through the vast interconnected networks of cyberspace. Surely these changes point toward important new possibilities.

Yet I question whether these possibilities in turn point to anything new. In terms of content, child pornography, recipes for making pipe bombs, and racist propaganda are now accessible to the average cyber-junkie over the Internet. Can we call this progress? Has the capacity for emitting electromagnetism through conventional space and time really led to any significant or fundamental transformations in human consciousness—*in the human relationship to time*?

Let us attempt a small thought experiment. Imagine that the electromagnetism coursing through cyberspace is indeed an extension of the electromagnetism arcing across our brain synapses. Better, imagine that our own identity is like a sophisticated website. In my case, the address for my home page would be "www.identity.net/ ron_purser.htm."

If we opened up our home page, we would see all sorts of files associated in hierarchical order under our main identity file. Inside those would be numerous hyperlinks to other files, and so on. We would have a multitude of files to call upon for different self-images and varying moods, as well as a data bank of memories we could click on as needed. Each memory file would, of course, be hyperlinked to virtually every other file that had some sort of association with it. And image and audio files would allow us to experience a multimedia world.

Here is the rub. If I did a search within this site for the real "ron purser," my "real identity," all I would find is one file pointing to another file, pointing to another, and so on. We can go even further. The identity website will include the image of a viewer who appears to be standing back viewing the site, having thoughts and memories and spinning narratives about its own identity. This is the conventional bystander (TSK, 72), the strong sense that "I am the one sitting at my desk looking at the images on the video screen." Once we understand how the programming for the website works, we see that the sense of the "I who am the one doing the viewing" is itself part of the program. There is no one standing outside of the website, which is complete and also completely self-contained.

We might put the same point in this way: If we picture an image of the person watching the website display, that image is not different from the image that appears on the screen. There is nothing behind or inside the 'watcher image' that is substantially there or existent, causing that image to appear.

Let us return to McLuhan's original description. If we look at the image being projected on a video screen, "magnifying" what we see, we find only electromagnetic waves. If we magnify the workings of the human body until we reach the atomic level, we likewise find only electromagnetic waves. And if we explode this view in turn, we encounter the vast void of space. (TSK, 42) Space appears to be the foundation for cyberspace, ordinary space, the human body, the central nervous system, the mind, identity, and everything else.

From a time perspective, the same point applies:

The flow of time can be understood in much the same way: waves of energy whose rhythms carry information, without anything subtantial moving from space to space. In terms of the analogy, first-level objects are these rhythms. (KTS, 70)

Still, to recognize the constructed nature of virtual reality in terms of space, time, or knowledge does not have the liberating effect that McLuhan seems to have anticipated. The simulacra worlds of cyberspace, with their virtual images, are easy to intellectualize about and imagine in the abstract. The extension from the atomic to the electromagnetic world, or the journey through temporal rhythms, is likewise an abstraction. But it is much more difficult to actually inhabit such a world (LOK). We seem unable to allow our everyday thinking, knowing, and acting to embody the knowledge that reality itself is a construct, virtual and phantasmagorical—a magical display.

Even though virtual technologies can construct powerful simulations of the physical world through electronic means, the construct that a physical world "out there" exists cannot be so readily challenged. As long as that construct operates, the creation of alternative, virtual realities will merely simulate—and thus confirm—our taken-for-granted notions of time, space, and knowledge. While these mechanical notions are in place, the electromagnetic age will not bring about any significant change after all. Instead, it will only speed up the same limitations and mistakes we have encountered and produced in the age of mechanization.

Three

Perhaps we can draw on McLuhan in another way. McLuhan suggested that thinking and perception of reality is influenced by the medium or vehicle through which messages are received. Our thinking and perception are so closely tied to the mode in which such activity occurs that McLuhan coined the famous aphorism, "the medium is the message."

McLuhan was of course writing primarily about the influence of television on culture and society, so let us start there. We can see how television as a medium has transformed the messages of politics and "the news." It has also shaped our cultural identity, sending a barrage of messages about (for example) sexuality. Today, when talk shows often exploit people's suffering, TV has also redrawn the border between public and private experience. Perhaps most importantly, it has shaped our preferences for receiving information. Knowledge now has to be condensed into "sound bites;" ideas have to be "packaged," and any presentation must contain "visuals" or "graphics" if it is to "grab people's attention."

There is no denying the fact that communication media like television, and now the Internet, can profoundly alter the form and content of cultural messages. But what if we looked at both the medium and its message as being given together as a presentation of time? What if we viewed the medium and its message as part of a meta-message, transmitted by what Tarthang Tulku in DTS refers to as the "field communiqué"? This perspective reverses McLuhan, reminding us that "the message is the medium." In other words, the message transmitted presupposes a medium in which space and time can operate in a particular way.

We usually do not look at messages in this manner; instead we attend to the content of the transmission. By doing so, we "look past the field communiqué to accept the truth of the story being communicated" (DTS, 23). Once the process is in motion, the momentum of the transmission keeps our consciousness and central nervous system faithfully committed to playing within the rules and confines of the medium. We are largely unaware that the messages we are engaged with are bound to a particular order. Commenting on this point, Tarthang Tulku states (DTS, 17–20):

> The individual appearances that make up the content of experience manifest *in terms of* the field communiqué, which unites them in somewhat the way that stock ownership unites the shareholders of a corporation. Emerging from the field, entities appear hand in hand. . . . In this communication forward, we ourselves emerge in the role of manifestor, the one who knows. But though our role is central to the enactment of the whole, it is also restricted. Our knowing conforms to the logic of naming; our minds reacts to what has been identified. We have no choice but to engage and participate, for the mind has no other way of working.

The field communiqué is a heuristic for contemplating the arising of messages within a space-time medium. Let us note some of its implications, as presented in the works of the TSK series.

Ordinarily the messages that our senses convey and transmit about "self and world" are not seen as being shaped by the operation of a spatial and temporal order that gives meaning to all sense data. This order is taken for granted, and our attention and awareness are completely given over to responding and reacting to the messages that transpire within the limits of the medium. For ordinary sense perception, the temporal order gives us objects that are substantial, with space as their container. Conventional logic operates, and things exist as "substance" or as substantial entities, so that space is already "pre-occupied" by an object orientation (DTS, 7).

Similarly, our awareness is too busy responding and reacting to a constant flow of messages to be aware of the temporal order that gives these messages. Moving rapidly from one message to the next, we lose sight of the fact that everything that happens, all the messages that transpire, have to fit into the structure and narrow channel-capacity of the medium.

As messages fill up and speed up through linear time, fueling reactions and counterreactions to the point of mental overload and emotional exhaustion, the medium itself is subject to "space-time compression" (a term I will return to shortly below). Knowledge cannot gain access to wider vision, and instead must stay within the boundaries defined by the rules and logic of a container-medium.

TSK opens up possibilities for transforming the space-time nature of the medium. The notion of the field communiqué challenges conventional understanding on just this point (DTS, 26–27):

> If substance is itself insubstantial, then inquiry knows no limits. . . . Once we see that the ongoing communiqué invariably presents the whole

of time and space as the 'character' of reality, we can play with this reality however we wish. . . . 'Before' the present manifestation, 'before' the 'before' that manifestation presupposes, appearance without substance offers the other side of birth and the beneath of zero. . . .

A knowledge based on substance accepts that objects appear *to* the mind through sense perception, thoughts, and so on. It proclaims the substance *of* appearance by insisting on the dance of subject and object as the interior truth of what presents itself. But the forward communication of the field communiqué presents a very different picture. Here substance arises *through* the mind, taking form in the act of naming.

To name is to enact knowledge. If substance arises through naming, the knowledge that makes naming possible must be directly available 'within' each appearance. We arrive at this intrinsic knowledgeability by tuning in to the field communiqué. Without withdrawing into blankness, we can let go of our reliance on words and language, name and form. We can touch the nameless and formless within appearance that make naming and giving form possible.

All of the above statements call into question the claims of substance. They invite us to look with "space eyes" and "knowledge eyes."

In my own experience, one way to glimpse this possibility is to investigate the nature of messages as they appear in the medium of dreams. Here are two dreams I have had recently which I think point to how it is possible to see through the act of naming.

The Dream Elevator

In this dream, I find myself in an elevator, but I do not know exactly where I am. I realize that I am concerned about the fact that I do not know this. Another person boards the elevator. I push the button to go down to the first floor, but the person in the elevator reminds me the first level no longer exists, and that I will have to get off at level three. As I look at the numbers on the panel, I suddenly can see that I am really "no-where," that I am in a dream, and all of these referents are constructs of my own knowledge. It seems that my concerns for locatedness actually began to set the dream in motion, together with its story and objects and my actions and responses. Even though I continue dreaming, I now no longer see or hear any story unfolding. I am still in the elevator, and the numbers on the panel are there, but now I know these apperances are just that—appearances, echo-like in nature—including my own image as the one who is dreaming!

The Dream House

I am in a house looking out a window and I see what appears to be a Tibetan monk with a long pole and bucket at the end. I seem to think that the monk wants to enter the house so he can fill his bucket with water, so I let him in. As the monk comes inside, I realize that

I have my eyes closed. The monk holds my hand and says, "I'll show you the way," and leads me up a flight of stairs. As this happens, my awareness becomes very expansive, clear and light, even though I still have my eyes closed. Upstairs is a group of Americans who are being very disruptive, noisy, running around, restless. I say, "Oh, don't mind them." Suddenly, I open my eyes and look at the room. What I see is a dazzling display of images. The normal items and objects in the room are there, but they have no solidity. There is a feeling of wonderment and sense of vast openness within and as each object appears.

It appears easier to tune in to the field communiqué within the dream medium because the rhythm of objects as they appear are not based on the rhythm of the physical senses. The mental acts of naming that we utilize in the waking medium are still carried over into the dream state. However, if lucid dreaming occurs, we can literally see that the objects being pointed out in dreams are insubstantial. Then, as Tarthang Tulku points out, "We can tell a story that in its telling evokes a 'no stories' knowing: a story about time that does not link it so irreducibly to the ways of knowing of the witness." (DTS, 116).

Perhaps such a dream awareness points to how messages might appear within a third-level space, time, and knowledge medium. Could we perhaps look at dream objects (and physical objects) as expressions of different rhythms of space, time, and knowledge (which in turn express the field communiqué)? When we see more lucidly the nature of dream reality, we see with "knowledge eyes." TSK makes us lucid while we are awake as well. This is the power of the TSK vision.

Waking dreams and "moments" of pristine lucidity have often arisen as a shared group experience during TSK retreats. I can recall two events in particular that stand out.

The first occurred at a TSK retreat held in Boulder in July of 1995. The retreat had been in session for several days, but a new person who had not been part of the retreat joined us to participate in the evening sessions. That evening, we practiced Exercise 22 from TSK, "Diving into Time." Normally after we had finished a formal practice, there would be an informal sharing of our phenomenological experience with the exercise. In this case, as we all opened our eyes there seemed to be a dynamic elasticity to appearances in the room. I described that I felt like a "time puppet," and that we were all like dangling puppets dancing on a stage, with time pulling the strings. There was a fluid feeling of smoothness to all the interactions between us, and a sense that our presence to each other was not caught in a "sequence of unfoldings." As "time dolls," we seemed to have a peerless ability to enter a different realm of time, one that was not subject to the point-by-point, moment-by-moment movement of linear time. The whole group found itself swimming in this slippery dimension, at one point triggering a period of uncontrollable laughter among us.

The second event had a similar dynamic, coupled with the emergence of a more "inward-outward knowing" (DTS, 159) at the group level. At the Stillpoint retreat in July of 1996, we had spent a good part of one afternoon doing one of the time exercises from DTS. During TSK retreats a qualitative shift often occurs, in which my presence (and everyone else's) becomes intensified. There is a deep sense of relaxation, settledness, and calm abiding, a "not-doing" or "not-going" that I liken to what is often described in the TSK books as a sense of "active presence."

In this instance, with this experiential sense of active presence pervasive among us, Tom Morse was sharing his post-exercise experience with the group. I had the urge to ask him, "Can you feel how we all seem to be non-located right now?" Something seemed to shift among us. Tom replied, "Your question just seemed to put me in a trance."

I think we all recognized that Time was working one of its miracles. We sat in the silence of this pristine-like presence in the room, and Tom humbly commented on how auspicious and unique was the play of events in which we were all participating. We seemed to have collectively entered an inward medium that allowed us to interact with "reality" with the knowledge that the appearances in the room—including our own bodies and minds—were just that: object-facets of appearances, appearing as substance.

In each of the descriptions I have just given, the perception of objects shifted to seeing objects as appearances without substance. I believe that this shift is linked to a number of key changes in the way we know and embody time. Tarthang Tulku elaborates (TSK, 143–45):

'We' can learn to allow brief 'knowings' which track more of 'time' and which are broad and impartial enough to take into account our self, observed objects, and other background items as all being given with 'time'. It therefore becomes possible for such a 'knowing' to 'tap' the dynamism of 'time.'

As our perspective becomes less rigid and more open, we can develop an appreciation of 'things' as inspiring symbols. The ordinary view of time has the effect of embedding all situations in a linear series so that they gain their significance from their environment or location between the orienting past and the confining future. . . . First, all drab items, facts, and trends can become alive, inspiring symbols. . . . They are no longer seen as produced by—and tied to—a 'horizontal' temporal series. So they, in their giveness with us, can point in what seems at first like a different, more vertical and liberating direction. They do not then have a specific content or referent (referring along or within the ordinary series). Rather, they signal the beginning of an unfolding path of discovery, *off the beaten track*. The second phase of this path consist in the concrete presentations or manifestations indicating what is even less prosaic and more dynamic, namely *manifesting* or *presenting* [emphasis in original].

Let us return to the idea that objects do not appear to the mind, but *through* the mind. Certainly it is easy to see how this can be the case in lucid dreaming.

Usually we take the separation between subject and object as a given, rather than the output of a view taken on mind. However, if we take the view that objects appear through the mind, then the "subject-knowing-object" type of knowing is not the only way to know. If this three-part structure has developed, there will also be a knowing before that development, a knowing more inherent in the medium itself.

This knowing does not have to rely on the messages of conceptual thought or the rhythms of the senses. We could think of it as a kind of "centerless" knowing, since it operates within the act of naming, and before name and form take place. Centerless knowing knows no limits within our ordinary medium, since the referents to location, boundaries, and points in time that are required to establish limits are themselves messages produced by subject-object knowing.

Centerless knowing is not bound by the messages of the field communiqué (DTS, 159). Knowing *through* the mind, we need not be bound by what is seen, said, or thought. By tuning in to the field communiqué, we can allow our mind to relax into the space of knowledge that is not partitioned into subject and object. Simultaneously, we can enter the silence present in the act of naming, in the act of seeing and hearing, allowing such relaxation to loosen the hold of our usual tracing of messages within the medium. We can embody knowledge in a new way.

This new approach entails paying more attention to the medium through which appearance appears. In DTS, Tarthang Tulku describes this in terms of "light transmission." He asks us to look at the light of mind as a sort of medium through which objects appear. Instead of attending only to messages of the medium, we can tune our attention more directly to light. Instead of reducing appearance to a world of fixed and substantial objects, with time and space in the background, we can conduct a different knowledge. Instead of listening to the content of our messages and limiting our perception to seeing objects, we can allow knowledge to be shaped more by the power of the medium: Great Space, Great Time and Great Knowledge. In Tarthang Tulku's eloquent words (DTS, 212–13):

> [We can] invite light as source by sinking beneath the contents of mind, turning to inward illumination. Soon we learn that we can contact our thoughts and feelings more directly and deeply than we had imagined.
>
> Once we engage the position we have presently adopted, we find ourselves amidst the prevailing patterns of the mind, observing with new clarity. As more patterns emerge, we react as we have been conditioned to react, only to discover that this reaction is its own position. For a moment we gaze at this position and at the thoughts and other patterns that accompany it; then we enter it, fearlessly conducting forward.
>
> Exploring in this way, we activate a stream of thoughts. We circle through rings of thought, expanding standards ways of knowing. Neither accepting thoughts as guides nor rejecting them

as enemies, we grow intimate with the byways of the ordinary.

Through this emergent intimacy, our journey changes character. Starting from the ordinary light of day, we find that we have entered the light-filled womb of experience. Here we can abide, embracing the truly unknown, allowing the presence of a lucent awareness.

Yet this is only a preliminary stage. For what happens next, I refer the reader to the original.

Four

One factor that distinguishes the modern age is what David Harvey (1989, 240) describes as "time-space compression:"

> I mean to signal by [the term 'time-space compression'] processes that so revolutionize the objective qualities of space and time that we are forced to alter, sometimes in quite radical ways, how we represent the world to ourselves. I use the word 'compression' because a strong case can be made that the history of capitalism has been characterized by speed-up in the pace of life, while so overcoming spatial barriers that the world sometimes seems to collapse inward upon us. The time taken to traverse space and the way we commonly represent that fact to ourselves are useful indicators of the kind of phenomena I have in mind. As space appears to shrink to a 'global village' of telecommunica-

tions and a 'spaceship earth' of economic and ecological interdependencies—to use just two familiar and everyday images—and as time horizons shorten to the point where the present is all there is (the world of the schizophrenic), so we have to learn how to cope with an overwhelming sense of *compression* of our spatial and temporal worlds.

Time-space compression as it is evolving today has much to do with electronic technologies, with their increased capacity to digitize information and connect disparate entities in space and time. Not only is more information being generated, but the rate at which information is being generated is itself increasing. As the temporal and spatial constraints on the flow of information and knowledge are obliterated, the dynamic presenting of linear time intensifies, invading spaces that were previously more stable. Changes in one part of the economy or world now reverberate rapidly across space-time, increasing the level of turbulence and relevant uncertainty in the social environment (Emery and Trist, 1965). People increasingly feel they are on shaky ground, anxious about the future, unsure of what to do.

An intriguing way to trace this speed up is in terms of the new language that is constructing social reality. We can start with the relation between language, sound, and time. Sound has a sense of immediacy, linked to its being transitory (cf. TSK, 188). Beyond that, K.S. Lashley, the famous American physiological psychologist, has pointed out that syntax in speech and language is organized temporally, through rhythm,

while Edward Hall, in his classic anthropological studies, illustrates that different cultures display different
linguistic rhythms.

Whitrow (1988) helps spell out the significance of
such observation. The rhythms of a language can be
linked to the specifics that language describes. For
instance, the vocabularies of so-called primitive peoples are more extensive and refined than our own when
it comes to concrete descriptions of the natural world.
By the same token, their syntax is more linked to the
present. Scholars have determined that verb tenses in
most early languages are more descriptive of duration
than of actual distinctions between past, present and
future. Even Old English, a language of the early Middle
Ages, has no distinct verb forms for the future tense.

These differences in turn reflect and influence
shifts in cultural values and concerns. For example,
Fleischmann (1982) has linked Christianity's new
emphasis on moral obligation in the fifth century AD to
a change in Latin sentence structure from SOV (sub-
ject-object-verb) to SVO (subject-verb-object). Again,
Steiner (1975) notes with regard to Sanskrit that "the
development of a grammatical system of futurity may
have coincided with an interest in recursive series of
very large numbers."

In *Time in History* (1988, 14), G.J. Whitrow discusses the relation of language and time:

[T]he origin of the concept of number, like the
origin of language, is closely connected with the
way in which our minds work in time, that is,

by our being able to attend, strictly speaking, to only one thing at a time and our inability to do this for long without our minds wandering. Our idea of time is thus closely linked with the fact that our process of thinking consists of a linear sequence of discrete acts of attention. As a result, time is naturally associated by us with counting, which is the simplest of all rhythms. It is surely no accident that the words 'arithmetic' and 'rhythm' come from two Greek terms which are derived from a common root meaning 'to flow.'

Bearing the connections between time, language, and counting in mind, consider that our contemporary world is increasingly governed by the new language of binary code: the building blocks of all computer languages and all software. Binary code, based on endless on/off messages, is what allows microprocessors to do their counting in nanoseconds. It has the capacity to compress itself into ever smaller discrete units of information, which has the effect of producing more information in less time (speed). The growing ability of technology to miniaturize computer chips and circuits (thus shrinking space) contributes to this change. In effect, it is the ability to speed up the process of counting that is speeding up our society's way of life.

Still—and this is the point—the changes brought about by binary language have until now only served to perpetuate and intensify the cultural structures of the mechanical age. Although the events that matter to us are speeding up, *the process of our thinking remains fundamentally the same.* On the first, or conventional level of time and space, Whitrow's description continues to apply: We think primarily through a linear sequence of discrete acts of attention. But now this sequencing is being driven to an extreme.

As long as it functions as a container for storing bits of information, the human mind cannot cope with our ability to count at faster and faster speeds. In the face of so much information, it experiences a sense of overload, disequilibrium, and helplessness. Always on the edge of disorder, we feel that we have to play catch up, rushing here and there, going from and to, scurrying around in a space-time compression chamber. Entranced by and entrained to (dazed and confused?) the compression of a linear sequencing of events, we are literally unable to take account of what is happening. We are "caught up" in the flow of linear time to a degree never seen before in human history.

Five

Today we are witnessing a fundamental reordering of how social systems are constructed and deconstructed in space and time. Anthony Giddens, a sociologist at Stanford, attributes the specific dynamism characteristic of modernity to the *separation of space and time—*what he refers to as *time-space distanciation* (1990, 14). His inquiry leads him to pose the question of how social systems in general "bind" space and time.

Giddens starts from the observation that in more traditional agrarian cultures, time's movement was expressed through reference to natural occurrences, such as the position of the sun in the sky or the shadow-lines on a sun-clock. Even abstracted from the agrarian cycles of growth and decay, time was always closely linked with space ("Meet me at mid-day in the town square.")

The universal acceptance of mechanical clock-time in the late eighteenth century broke this linkage. Time became an abstract dimension that could easily be quantified into hours and minutes. Social organizations were able to standardize and synchronize their operations (as symbolized by the adoption a century ago of standard time zones), and space itself could be controlled in new ways.

Giddens points out that the transformation in the technology of time was accompanied by a separate transformation in the technology of space. The charting and mapping of the globe led to a perspective in which space could be seen as independent of any particular place or region. In turn, this innovation traced to the rise of linear perspective in painting during the Renaissance. When painters began to depict landscapes from an elevated, fixed, and distant vantage point, they fostered a geometric and systematic view of space and place that provided the foundation for the revolution in map-making (Edgerton 1976). Space now began to be represented as an objective ordering of geographic coordinates. Not surprisingly, access to maps and geographical knowledge of the world was a highly valued commodity, for it offered a command over space that in turn promised command over wealth and capital.

According to Giddens, the resulting standardization of both space and time has in effect made them into "empty" dimensions, increasingly abstract and removed from our daily awareness. In agrarian societies, space and the sense of place were one and the same: To be somewhere, one had to have a physical presence. But modernity ripped space away from place, making absent communications possible.

Contemporary information technology, as epitomized by the birth of virtual reality, has heightened this sense of communication without presence. To be somewhere in modern society does not require a presence at all. Mark Poster (1985, 85) explains:

> [When language is made electronic,] words cannot any longer be located in space and time, whether it be the 'real time' of spoken utterance in a spatial context of presence or the abstract time of documents in a bureaucrat's file cabinet. . . . Speech is framed by space/time coordinates of dramatic action. Writing is framed by space/time coordinates of books and sheets of paper. . . . Electronic language, on the contrary, does not lend itself to being so framed. It is everywhere and nowhere, always and never. It is truly material/immaterial.

Six

I think it should be apparent by now just how relevant our modes of spatial and temporal experiencing are to the reproduction and conducting of social and technological structures. Because technology affects our relation to space and time, it has the power of reconfiguring social space and social interactions in time. New telecommunication technologies have increased time-space distanciation and are speeding up the compression of space and time. Such changes have brought both benefits and added complexity. But do they bring any qualitative shift in our sense of intrinsic freedom? In the quality of our life? Or do they intensify and make it more unmanageable?

Today we have access to more conveniences, more labor-saving devices, and a wider ability to communicate across vast distances in myriad ways. Yet my sense is that many of these innovations have hidden costs and externalities of which we are dimly (but perhaps increasingly) aware. In the industrial age, the major quality of working life issue had to do with workers being treated as if they were merely "cogs"—extensions of a machine, dispensable parts. Now, in the post-industrial age, white-collar professionals are chained electronically to their information-technology devices.

Our symbiotic relationship to technology is restructuring the way we think and how we make sense of reality, but it does so in ways that only embed us more completely within the strictures of technological knowing. As conventional space and time are compressed, we find it more difficult to reflect on the consequences of our actions. In the midst of an electronic speed-up, we are always running out of time. Off-balance and anxious, we do not know how we could possibly change this dynamic.

The TSK vision suggests that the turbulence of modernity needs to be seen through the lens of space and time. Space and time are the "stuff" of our lives, dimensions that are inseparable from how we live. As we tear apart the fabric of space and time (Giddens), we experience the consequences in the turbulence of the field we inhabit. Yet we have no recourse: Rather than taking stock of our situation, we seem to tug away even harder at the fabric of existence.

Today the invisible hand doles out a pervasive malaise. Constantly busy, for what higher purpose we do not know, we may not even know that we do not know. In the midst of this not-knowing we rush to catch up. If we stumble and fall, we dust ourselves off and get back on the treadmill. And those entrusted with authority are infected with this same space-time disease. Zengotita's comments on this change express most eloquently my own concerns (1996, 18):

> One of the Lincoln-Douglas debates took seven hours, with one break. In 1960, uninterrupted segments of speech by a presidential candidate on nightly news coverage averaged forty seconds; in 1992, 9.5 seconds. Explaining why he was resigning, Senator David Boren described "fourteen-hour days" in which there "was no time for reflection, no time to exchange ideas with fellow senators," as when "the President. . . asked four senators from each party . . . to work on a civil rights compromise" and, even then, the "eight entered and left the meeting at different times" so that "no more than four were ever

together for more than fifteen minutes." Sound familiar?

This particular quality of rushed busy-ness expresses in action the absence of vision under which issues become iconic rather than grounded. Busy-ness is a way of hiding from a truth that must be faced if our politics is to be renewed in the postmodern age. The phenomenon has been glimpsed as the "end of ideology," but that locution eludes what most needs to be faced—namely, that *no one really has any idea what's going on anymore, let alone what to do about it.* [emphasis in original].

When I listen to managers and employees lament the problems of organizational life, the single dominant complaint is not having enough time. But enough time for what? For more of the same? For more routine tasks and thoughts that only repeat variations on the theme of temporal sameness?

In the modern realm, not only space and time are compressed, but knowledge as well. Carried along on the jagged waves of turbulence, we cannot see where we are headed. Strung out along the surface of linear time, our attention is too scattered to take in the whole. We might say that the truly scarce resource in modernity is attention, and that "we experience that scarcity most directly as time pressure" (Zengotita 1996, 18). When we fail to pay adequate attention to space and time, these ever-shifting "fundamental facets of being" (TSK, 303), should this be surprising?

PART THREE

One

In today's post-industrial society, many critical decisions that will affect the quality of our lives are in the hands of professionals. We may therefore well wish to ask: What does it really mean to be a professional? Do professionals have the knowledge we need? For instance, do they know how to pay attention? Or do they contribute to the "attention deficit disorder" that plagues our time? What is the role of knowledge and inquiry in professional practice?

These questions have concerned me for years. Since I teach graduate courses in a "professional program" and consult as a professional to business organizations, I have long tried to come to grips with the meaning of professionalism in the context of a rapidly changing world. My comments on these concerns in the sections that follow are specifically directed to professionals in the world of business and management consulting, since this is the area that I most familiar with.

Whenever the word "professional" is pronounced to invoke the authority of expertise, I feel uneasy. Maybe this has something to do with why I dislike wearing a suit and tie. For a long time I thought these feelings were purely a private matter, linked to my blue-collar upbringing. But today I realize my discomfort stems in part from a more fundamental set of issues related to professional practice. Looking with TSK eyes, I see

134

around me strong evidence for what I call "the pathologies of professional practice."

By professional practice, I mean the ways professionals think, perceive, and act in the settings where they are employed. Professionals are involved in solving problems, providing expert advice and counsel, and making decisions. A long and arduous education is required for them to master the canons of a given discipline and to hone the skills for rational, critical, and methodical thinking. Practitioners are socialized to behave in accordance with the ethical standards of their professional. Often, continuing education is required in order to maintain competence.

Then why, with all this focus on training and intellectual skills, is genuine inquiry among professionals more the exception than the rule? Why do professionals so often avoid engaging fundamental questions concerning human well-being and fulfillment, or close off such questioning prematurely? Why do they not pay attention to what is really happening? This is where the pathology comes in—a dark side to professionalism that suppresses the practice of free and open inquiry.

Two

Knowledge in the usual perspective is the accumulation of facts, data, and information that can be manipulated at will. It is lifeless and neutral, something to be collected as we might collect specimens. Yet this view is hopelessly naive. The historian knows that knowledge takes shape and direction through the impetus of powerful emotive forces. Palmer (1990) suggests that knowledge has typically arisen out of human passions and needs. Driven by a desire to control our environment, we create weapons of mass destruction, conduct experiments in recombinant DNA, and produce a steady stream of labor-saving devices.

Tarthang Tulku refers to the knowledge that originates in desire as "technological knowledge," thus highlighting its link to a technique-driven way of knowing. Technological knowledge is essentially a means toward a goal. It moves forward in time along a linear trajectory, toward the achievement of ends that are given in advance (DTS, 80). The triumph of technological knowledge in modern times is what gives technological development its seemingly autonomous character—a forward, onrushing momentum that appears unstoppable, inevitable—what we customarily label as the march of progress.

Technological knowledge sets its own limits. As "technology makes knowledge itself into a tool" (VOK, 96), it ceases to serve as a support for independent inquiry. The resulting narrowness makes it difficult to trace the patterns of technological development to their originating source in the desires of the self (LOK, 34).

Because technological knowledge turns knowledge itself into something inherently limited, it reinforces the professional's reliance on techniques (VOK, 167):

[K]nowledge [is seen] as something dull and routine, something to possess and make use of like a sophisticated tool. We apply knowledge to our situation as we might try to fix a machine by following an instruction manual. But this way of knowing puts us at a distance from what we are trying to know. There is the thing and there is our knowledge of it, and the two are separate. To apply our knowledge, we must turn away from what we seek to know, like turning from a new machine to read its assembly instructions.

Bound by this model, whenever problems arise, we reach for the tool at hand. Thank God for tools and techniques, we tell ourselves, for we simply lack the time to think more deeply about our problems and how our life is actually unfolding in the midst of them. But are we really cognizant of the effects that the application of our techniques is having or will have on others? As Tarthang Tulku warns (DTS, xxxviii):

On the surface our experience may seem interesting enough, but when we conduct knowledge inward, we soon see that the patterns that space and time at present allow only confirm our limits. Dedicated to conventional ways of knowing, we may perfect a specific livelihood. We may follow the model flawlessly—true professionals. Yet invariably we conduct problems and shortages forward into being as well. Insisting on the right and true, we establish the wrong and false. Even if our own lives unfold in ways we find satisfying, we are sowing the seeds for competition and conflict on a broader scale. Simply in supporting one model over another, we foster a system in which some individuals are inevitably more successful in communicating the prevailing knowledge forward than others."

In psychological terms, living in this way constitutes denial. Though our quality of life and well-being may be deteriorating, we never question the "how" and "why" of our situation. We are like a besieged firefighter who puts out each new blaze, never finding the time to track down the arsonist. Our techniques help us to look away from a deeper knowledge that might truly provide healing and illumination.

We can also trace this fragmentation of knowing to the emergence of modern scholarly praxis, which began to appear in twelfth century Europe. It is at this point in time that scholasticism attempted to dissociate itself from the inner, experiential dimensions of monastic education. A new school of philosophical and theological thought emerged which focused on the abstract idea of information, factual knowledge, which was gradually separated from the knowledge of the individual. As Brain Stock (1983, 328) points out, twelfth-century scholasticism began to recognize a difference

> between the knower as inquiring subject and the knowledge which was the object of his investigations. Unlike the Eastern 'wise man' and the early medieval sage, the twelfth-century intellectual did not *embody* a subject personally, he taught it. Being an intellectual was a profession, even a social role [emphasis added].

Following this lead, we can see that over time there has been an increasing depersonalization of scholarly inquiry and philosophical discourse. The experiential and inner life of the knower is progressively removed from scholarly praxis, to the point that the figure of the modern intellectual emerges in the pursuit of disembodied knowledge for its own sake. Possession (not embodiment) of knowledge arises as the central task.

The limits of this way of knowing are concealed by our unquestioning acceptance of the myth of objectivity. According to this myth, a knower takes a position that gives the appearance of standing apart from that which is known. This stance is necessary, as Barrett points out (1979, 26), because the whole premise of a technique depends upon a "distinct separation of the objective and subjective components of a situation in order for us to take rational hold of a problem." Once an objective problem is isolated, the technicians can rush in and apply their logical, step-wise procedures.

The myth of objectivity is intimately bound up with knowledge as method. The link comes through the Cartesian notion that thinking can establish itself as separate from the objects it attempts to know. The Latin root of "objective" means "to put against," "what lies over against," "what stands in opposition;" similarly, the German "Gegenstand" can be translated as "standing-over-againstness." For objective knowing, the world is outside us, and we are the bystanders and spectators of that world. The corollary is that knowing is an activity that exists inside one's head. The insentient world is simply its distanced raw material.

Professionals trained in technological knowledge—knowledge as a tool—and the myth of objectivity are encouraged to discipline their stand against the world. On the one hand they are engaged in an attempt to acquire facts or apprehend phenomena, but on the other their aim is to gain possession, ownership, and control over an insentient environment. Their position as professional "bias-standers" (DTS, 174) is ultimately egocentric, in the quite literal sense that it is centered on the ego.

Committed to being objective, professionals have learned to reject the interiority of human experience, while their fixation on tools and techniques has led them to focus on only those external representations of problems that lend themselves to technological observation and measurement. Professionals assume that in manipulating the data they generate, they are in fact dealing with the problems and their solutions that exist "out there," in the "objective" world, when in fact they are engaged in manipulating their own data.

The result is to contribute to a profound confusion. Human intelligence is equated with IQ scores; personality with one's Myers Briggs (MBTI) type; management potential with competency-based assessments; academic performance with the letter grade. Guided by this vision of knowledge, professionals naturally aim to change behavior, skills, and external structures, since it is precisely those aspects of human experience that can be objectified, molded, and manipulated through application of the proper techniques.

Given these assumptions, it is little wonder that the machine becomes the root metaphor for thinking (Postman 1993). For example, computing metaphors have infiltrated our way of thinking of intelligence. Today the brain is often viewed as a sophisticated "information processor" that is "hard-wired" to interact with the outside world in specific ways. The inner life of human beings is largely ignored—a black box, off-limits to disciplined inquiry—and social problems are conceptualized in mechanistic terms.

The real victims of this mindset are in some ways the professionals themselves, who must learn to ignore their own values and moral sensibilties in the quest for the purity of objective knowing. Although professionals often do enjoy considerable prestige and status, this only supports the one-sidedness of their training and encourages them to cut off their own experience. Many professionals live one-sided lives, addicted to their work to such an extent that they have merged their whole identity into their role. Empty on the inside, they have nothing but their successful professional persona. Ambition drives them to seek more power, more fame, more money, more achievement. They are largely unaware why they are so restless, agitated, and driven. Their inner life is but a dark shadow, both to themselves and to the outer world.

Take the scientists working at Los Alamos during the making of the atomic bomb: Their accounts indicate that they were beset by inner struggles, cognitive dissonance, and psychological conflicts (Segre, 1993). However, only on the day after testing the explosion did they begin to listen to their conscience. Recently I read an article in the *New York Times* that conveyed the same flavor in quoting a high-level executive from

141

Philip Morris dying from lung cancer: "I knew all along it was wrong, but the culture of the company acted as a potent tranquilizer which numbed me from the painful realization that we were producing products that were deadly." The pain, trouble, and hurt associated with professional knowledge are derived from the psychic pain of suppression. In a sense, the dominant attitude of objectivism has led to a form of psychic tyranny, elevating mind over body, intellect over feeling, and practice over ethics.

Three

Over the last several years, our TSK e-mail group has had numerous discussions as to whether it would be appropriate to "apply" TSK in a more explicit way to professional practice.There has been talk about developing workshops, writing papers or books, and similar sorts of projects, all with the intention of making TSK both more accessible and more immediately practical in solving social or personal problems or addressing issues within different disciplines. Some have proposed or considered applications such as "TSK and Business," "TSK and Psychotherapy," "TSK and Time Management," "TSK and Creativity."

Consider in this context Parker Palmer's eloquent description (1990, 44) of the "true professional:"

> [The true professional is one who] makes *a profession of faith*—faith in something larger and wiser than his or her own powers. The true professional is the opposite of someone who makes

objects of other people by creating dependencies. Instead, the true professional is a person whose action points beyond his or her self to that underlying reality, that hidden wholeness, on which we can all rely. [emphasis in original]

Palmer here implies as the source of "vocation" (literally, a calling) a transcendent dimension that is rarely talked about in professional education or even among professionals. Looking to this dimension, could we say that the true professional is open to a deeper Space and a more creative Time, able to command insight through Great Knowledge?

My own view is that all great minds have intuitively been in touch with such higher dimensions of Space, Time, and Knowledge. Such rare individuals have developed a truly scientific attitude that frees them from the pathologies of professionalism. Albert Einstein is an icon exemplifying what it means to be a professional in this sense.

A scientific attitude in this sense, one informed by higher dimensions, is linked to TSK by a "spirit of inquiry" that relentlessly questions the appearance of reality and the reality of appearance. TSK and science share a commitment to an experimental approach to testing reality. Whereas TSK questions the nature of appearance and how things have come to be the way they are, science takes a hypothetical and tentative stance, rigorously submitting all truth claims to empirical tests. Both depend on an experimental or practice component to save them from becoming scholastic language games, and both depend on imagination to take practice and experimentation to new levels, beyond the excitement of unusual experiences on the one hand and a dust-bowl empiricism on the other.

As habits of mind, experimentalism combined with a hypothetical, imaginative stance underlie both the methodological rules of science and the vigorous appreciation for intelligence in TSK. Together, they sustain the spirit of inquiry—the love of knowledge—that all great minds, all true professionals have pursued.

I make these comparisons with one important qualification: TSK is not science. As Tarthang Tulku points out, "TSK does not pursue knowledge through beliefs founded on reasons. Instead, it proceeds through active inquiry, which is seen as embodying knowledge directly" (DTS, xvii). But TSK shares with a true scientific attitude a commitment to active inquiry. Such inquiry may or may not be present in the practice of normal science, based on an objectivist stance. But it can certainly guide scientists, just as it can guide monks, managers, students, and professionals of all stripes. To the extent that it does so, the professional may return once again to the sense of calling, with significant consequences for our whole society.

In my view, a true professional is someone who eschews any form of dogmatism, totalitarianism, domination, elitism, mechanization, conformism, or blind obedience to customs or fashions. Simply put, true professionals seek the truth. Love of knowledge guides their conduct: a spirit of inquiry that borders the religious in its call to go beyond conventional truths. Yet this approach is not encouraged by professional education or by contemporary standards of professional practice. Perhaps this explains why many great scientists were also humanists, and why many breakthrough ideas in different professional disciplines have been made by individuals working outside the confines of traditional organizations.

The spirit of inquiry is rarely found in our social institutions. Jacob Bronowski (1959) has pointed out this out in stirring words:

> I have said that the invention of organization was Man's first most important achievement; I now add that the development of inquiry will be his second. Both of these inventions change the species and are necessary for its survival. But both must become a part of the nature of Man himself, not just given house room in certain groups. Organization is by now a part of every man, but inquiry is not. The significant product of science and education will be the incorporation within the human animal of the capability and habit of inquiry. . . . What science has to teach us here is not its techniques but its spirit; the irresistible need to explore.

The "inquiry deficiency" in professional practice has today spread to every sector of society: to the workplace, to schools, government, the media, and religious institutions. Homogenization of thinking is a disease more deadly than cancer, for it attacks and destroys without our even knowing that we are at risk. The thought virus that saps the spirit of inquiry looks innocuous and normal. As socially responsible professionals, we must track its appearance and provide the antidote that will reverse its spread.

As the author of the TSK books, Tarthang Tulku has issued an invitation (DTS, xxvii):

> Knowledge is usually understood as something to possess and accumulate. . . . Suppose that instead of possessing knowledge, we could successfully embody it.

What if professionals did learn to embody knowledge directly? What if they learned to expand their focal setting on time, space, and knowledge? Based on my own tentative steps in this direction, I believe a change of this order of significance would entail a shift from a reliance on models and techniques to a reliance on creativity and wisdom. Professionals guided in this way—true professionals—would not only be technically proficient in what they do, but would embody the knowledge to act wisely for the benefit of the whole.

Yet this does not mean the professional as philosopher-king. If everyone has the innate capacity to embody knowledge, the professional leads not through his or her special expertise, but through commitment to active inquiry, dialogue, and ongoing civic discourse. This amounts to a revival of what once was known as the public intellectual.

The TSK vision teaches that we need not rely upon a higher authority—whether a professional or a guru. In a society shaped by this realization, how the professional puts his or her expertise to use, justifying the use of power and privilege, will be a matter open to intense and continuing scrutiny.

Perhaps we could take as a model the stance adopted by Tarthang Tulku, who makes clear that he is not the sole authority or "high priest" of TSK, but simply a facilitator and student (surely an advanced student!) of the TSK vision (DTS, xv):

> Instead of claiming to possess knowledge that I could pass on to others, I have tried to encourage an ongoing dialogue between and among space, time and knowledge.

To encourage such dialogue seems a worthy vision for professional practice. Whatever the profession, active inquiry centered on time, space and knowledge can inspire creativity. It can offer insights in various disciplines that lead to greater balance and harmony in our world.

Four

One evening at the Stillpoint retreat we all sat without any specific exercise to do. I do not wish to refer to what happened as "my experience," or even to say that it "happeneded" (DTS, 85); instead, I offer a simple description.

Sitting in the stillness of time and space, all thirty-five of the exercises from the first TSK book started to unfold. First, I found myself practicing each exercise sequentially, spending a few minutes on each one before moving on to the next. I continued this round of mini-practices, going from Exercise 1 through Exercise 35 several times. Then a shift came. Instead of going through each exercise sequentially, I found my awareness had expanded, allowing all the exercises to take place simultaneously. A sense of awe and feeling of acceleration manifested. As this mega-practice deepened, I had a series of insights, ideas that might have come from a TSK book, but which came from a more direct perception. Here is what I wrote down later:

Improvisational Being has never been born into time. It does not exist in time nor does it not not exist, and it will never pass away. Not being located in time, yet still exhibiting an active presence, it does not need to resort to telling stories to make sense of reality.

Not subject to the strictures of substantial identity, Improvisational Being is deeply playful. It sees through the presentations of the senses, since objects, the light reflected off objects, and the senses themselves are also seen as Time projections, conducted in the arena of Space. There is the presence of presentations appearing, but such light awareness (or knowledge eyes) can see that appearances do not block the dynamic energy of Time, nor do they occupy the non-dimensionalized, non-located openness of Space.

In this light awareness, the stories of identity lose their grip and substance. The present moment is seen as a construct, an overlay on a dynamic that is not limited to a measuring out into sequential moments. The presenting of future time is like a chaotic wave of energy that presents infinite possibilities for manifesting. Like a wire, I can allow this dynamic conducting to flow through and infuse my Being. The present moment is but one infinitesimal flash of this infinite, light-presenting presence.

The threefold notion of birth, existence, and death appears as a celebration of finity in a cosmic dance of Time. There is an intimate sensing of the universal unique, the cosmic passion play conducting without inhibition, without freezing what is presented into some fixed order.

Now, seeing can play in Time, knowing more of Time, looking at right angles to what appears to be a linear unfolding. Past can mingle with future and future can energize Being's presencing. Now, imagination can be illuminated with a different light. Ideas, perceptions, insights seem readily available. Anything not known, any border, or any limit is welcomed as an invitation into light. Any situation, any sensation, any pattern, can be touched by this infinite opening capacity that allows for new possibilities to be danced into being.

Now, there is truly nowhere to go and nothing to do that requires striving or effort. Instead there is a gracious appreciation and deepening of feeling that expands and keeps feeding the opening, the dance, and the play. There is receptivity to light, allowing the light to rain into the senses and flood the imagination with its healing and creative powers.

Later that evening I left the cabin where our group had been sitting and went outside to gaze at the starry Colorado sky. Because there were no lights for miles, and the sky that night was crystal clear, the expanse of stars was truly breathtaking. The incredible beauty of Being simply kept unfolding, in the wonderment of the vastness of cosmic Space.

REFERENCES

Barrett, W. 1979. *The Illusion of Technique*. New York: Anchor Books.

Bowers, C. 1993. *Education, Cultural Myths, and the Ecological Crisis: Toward Deep Changes*. Albany, NY: State University of New York Press.

Bronowski, J. 1959. *Science and Human Values*. New York: Harper & Row.

Deetz, S. 1992. *Democracy in an Age of Corporate Colonization*. Albany, New York: State University of New York Press.

Edgerton, S. 1976. *The Renaissance Re-discovery of Linear Perspective*. New York.

Fleischman, S. 1982. *The Future in Thought and Language*. Cambridge: Cambridge University Press.

Giddens, A. 1990. *The Consequences of Modernity*. Stanford, CA: Stanford University Press.

Harvey, D. 1989. *The Condition of Postmodernity: An Enquiry into the Origins of Cultural Change*. Oxford: Basil Blackwell.

Lasch, C. 1995. *Revolt of the Elites and the Betrayal of Democracy*. New York: W.W. Norton.

McLuhan, M. 1964. *Understanding Media: The Extensions of Man*. New York: McGraw-Hill.

McLuhan, M. 1973. "Learning a Living." In *The Future of Work*. ed. F. Best. Englewood Cliffs, N.J.: Prentice Hall.

Palmer, P. 1990. *The Active Life: Wisdom for Work, Creativity andCaring*. New York: Harper Collins.

Postman, N. 1993. *Technopoly: The Surrender of Culture to Technology*. New York: Vintage.

Purser, R.E. 1993. "'Opening up' Open Systems Theory." In *Mastery of Mind*. Berkeley: Dharma Publishing.

Rice, P. 1989. *Timesource: A Handy Compendium of Facts and Uses*. Berkeley: Ten Speed Press.

Scott, W., and Hart. 1979. *Organizational America*. Boston: Houghton-Mifflin.

Segri, A. 1993. *A Mind Always in Motion*. Berkeley: University of California Press.

Steiner, G. 1975. *After Babel: Aspects of Language and Translation*. Oxford: Oxford University Press.

Stock, B. 1983. *The Implication of Literacy: Written Language and Models of Interpretation in the Eleventh and Twelfth Centuries.* Princeton, NJ: Princeton University Press.

Weisbord, M. 1987. *Productive Workplaces.* San Francisco: Jossey-Bass.

Whitrow, G.D. 1988. *Time in History.* Oxford: Oxford University Press.

Zengotita, 1996. "Celebrity, Irony, and You: How Political Attitudes Are Shaped by our Spectator Syndrome." *The Nation,* (December 2), Vol. 263, No. 18, 15–17.

TSK: VEHICLE, COMMON GROUND, AND VISION

Steve Randall

In the books in the Time, Space, and Knowledge series, TSK is often referred to as a vision. But what is a vision? The American Heritage dictionary gives two meanings (among others): "unusual competence in discernment or perception;" and "the mystical experience of seeing."

With this focus on a way of seeing, consider the following statements in the first TSK book:

> It would seem that now is the time for a new venturing out, for a vision which would integrate and unite all aspects of being . . . . Space and Time themselves have now presented such a vision, and I hope that it will be helpful to the contemporary world. (xxxiv)

We can develop a mode of 'seeing' which is not limited to a particular position or 'point of view' at all. (27)

There is no longer a 'looker', but instead, only a 'knowingness' which can see more broadly, from all sides and points of view at once. More precisely, the 'knowing' clarity does not radiate from a center, but is rather in everything, and everything is in it. There is neither an 'outside' nor an 'inside' in the ordinary sense, but rather a pervasive and intimate 'in' or 'within' as an open-ended knowingness. (282)

Drawing on this, I propose that vision be considered "a mode of 'seeing' which is not limited to any particular position or 'point of view', and which integrates and unites all aspects of being." To my understanding the TSK vision is what the Time-Space-Knowledge books point at in descriptions of "the third level."

A Vehicle Is Different from a Vision

Of course, the descriptions of the vision in the books, as precise they are, can only point to the vision. They cannot constitute the vision, just as numerous descriptions and analyses of a symphony do not add up to the sounds of the music. Tarthang Tulku has made this same distinction (DOT, xlix):

The vision is the essence of unity and simplicity. But the system of ordinary knowledge, which the [TSK] book attempts to communicate with and open up, is very complicated and given to such a diversity of positions that, in order to speak to it and challenge it successfully, you have to try many different approaches and analyses.

For me, this distinction is related to a distinction between the TSK vision and the TSK books. The "different approaches and analyses" are what I would consider the "vehicle" for the unified simplicity of the vision. Here the dictionary defines the word "vehicle" in part as "a medium through which something is transmitted, expressed, or accomplished." For TSK purposes, we can define "vehicle" broadly as a system of writings, principles, actual use of techniques, actual practice of exercises, art, movements, presentations, workshops, environments, social groups, etc.—structures, spaces, activities, content, and pointings used to facilitate some kind of beneficial change in relation to an implicitly or explicitly identified guiding vision.

I want to call the text of the books written by Tarthang Tulku, plus the actual practice of exercises in the books, the "initial TSK vehicle." This initial TSK vehicle is not the same as the TSK vision. As defined, the initial vehicle is a combination of ordinary objects and events, while the TSK vision is a profound 'seeing'.

Now, suppose that all human 'experiences' (using the word very broadly) or all possible 'focal settings' (to use a term frequently seen in the TSK books) on time, space, and knowledge can be represented by points within a circle, and that the distance of any one of these points from the center of the circle is a measure of the depth of the experience or breadth of the focal setting, with the deepest, highest, or most nearly enlight-ened focal settings nearest the center. This set of points will be called the "circle of settings." In TSK terms, first-level experiences will be at the periphery, second-level settings will be midway between periphery and center, and third-level will be at or near the center.[1] A given *vehicle*, in facilitating "beneficial change," will operate on a subset of the "circle of settings." In doing so, it will lead to a range of other settings that, in general, are closer to the center of the circle.

Now, by focusing on the possibility of such "vehi-cles," I hope to help open up the tendency to treat the original TSK books as 'sacred', infallible, or the final word. Seeing them as part of one vehicle, of and for the vision, may make it more likely that other, possibly more effective vehicles will be developed for different audiences, fields, disciplines, and purposes. Tarthang Tulku himself expresses considerable openness about different ways that TSK might be presented (LOK, xvi):

> My hope is that in the future students of TSK will make use of the insights they gain to pre-sent the vision in new and more fruitful ways. In considering this prospect, I sense that others have much more to contribute to the TSK vision than I do. A dynamic of great potential is wait-ing to be activated.

The Vehicle Reflects the Vision

Although a vehicle is not identical to a guiding vision, it will ideally be closely or precisely related to the vision, in somewhat the way that objects closely resemble their reflections in a mirror. Tarthang Tulku wanted *Time, Space, and Knowledge* to reflect the TSK vision in a way that typical theories or paradigms, with their insistence on 'objective representation' of 'reality', could not. After the first book was published, he put the issue this way in an interview conducted by Steven Tainer (Tarthang Tulku 1977, 5):

> Tainer: [TSK] should say something definite that can be tested out as true or false.

> Tarthang Tulku: That's a sound propositional view of the matter, but I'm thinking more in terms of a kind of poetry of reality, which can keep up with reality in all its presentations. I don't think reality is just "this way" or "that way," and I want something that can reflect that.

This distinction is important. Rather than pointing to some 'objective reality', the pointings of the TSK vehicle show the openness of the vision (TSK, 206):

> Even the pointings utilized in presenting this new vision are really not pointing out anything at all. They do not 'mean' anything, in the way that theories and systems usually do. A great deal is being said, but only to find it possible to say 'nothing'. For this presentation actually undermines all 'saying', including even itself. These ideas and pointings say 'nothing' because they lead us from a lower condition (the first level) to a higher one (the third level) that, in a

certain respect, turns out to be 'the same' as our beginning.

Reflections of Vision in Our Lives

Most of us are implicitly or explicitly using some kind of vehicle consisting of a set of beliefs, affirmations, principles, practices, and techniques. Through this vehicle, we have embodied or are living our guiding vision to some extent. Most of us would like to embody certain aspects of the vision more fully.

Usually, some of our beliefs, affirmations, principles, practices, and techniques help improve things, while others contradict each other, have unwanted side-effects, or are destructive, even though they may have been beneficial at one time. Often it is unclear for what circumstances, or for what domain of time, space, and knowledge a given belief, affirmation, principle, practice, or technique best applies. And often a vehicle would be improved by principles that are missing, implicit, or only suggested.

In investigating the effectiveness of vehicles, I have identified three distinct and particularly important properties that vehicles may possess: comprehensiveness, consistency, and effectiveness. These properties are closely interrelated.

Comprehensiveness

One property of vehicles is comprehensiveness: the percentage of the circle of settings upon which a vehicle operates. A completely comprehensive vehicle will operate on all significant aspects of the entire domain of human experience—the whole circle of settings.

Note that comprehensiveness is not defined in terms of the circumstances or environments that a vehicle addresses, but in terms of focal settings. Many, if not most, vehicles severely limit their comprehensiveness by specifying particular physical or psychological circumstances or processes. Consider this principle: "In communicating with people, honesty is the best policy." This would not be useful when one is not thinking about or actually communicating with people.

Vehicles Less Comprehensive than TSK

Even when vehicles do not limit their applicability to particular circumstances or environments, they still usually address only a subset of the domain of human experience (a part of the circle of settings). Consider, for example, the system of "positive thinking," which was quite popular some years ago. In this system, whenever a negative thought arises, you try to negate the negative by thinking something positive, using what is sometimes called an affirmation. Though useful and somewhat effective within a certain domain of one's experience, this vehicle eventually proves ineffective in bringing about substantial change.

At what point does such ineffectiveness come about? LOK (xli) suggests that higher-level knowledge "does not depend on taking one position or rejecting another." Using this as our guideline, we can conclude that when higher-level knowledge starts to become dominant, decision-making or action based on 'positive' and 'negative' no longer works. Therefore, positive thinking, to the degree it works, will apply only towards the periphery of the circle of settings.

As another example, consider the vehicles commonly used in Western psychological systems. These vehicles address a domain of focal settings that all involve the self as the perceiver, actor, and holder of psyche, personality, and experience. This domain does not include what are often referred to as spiritual or transpersonal perspectives. Thus, when a higher-level knowledge replaces the self as causal principle in one's life (cf. TSK, 33–34), psychological methods no longer lead to progress. Using a vehicle designed for land in order to cross a body of water won't get you very far.

A vehicle that is comprehensive will address all 'experience', encompassing the fields of psychology, philosophy, religion, spiritual disciplines, science, and education. It will offer a common ground—the circle of settings—within which the principles, ideas, and practices of these fields can be compared.

Comprehensiveness of the Initial TSK Vehicle

I have found that the initial TSK vehicle seems to be comprehensive, encompassing the entire domain of human experience. In TSK terms, the vastness of this domain is sometimes described in terms of development from "first level" to "second level" and "third level" (cf. TSK, 111-14, 136-62). Being comprehensive does not mean that every possible guiding principle or proposition is contained within the vision, but that all essential aspects of human experience and transformation are addressed, even if only succinctly, implicitly, or suggestively. Nothing is left out.

The following quotes point to the comprehensiveness of the initial TSK vehicle:

"Space, "time," and "knowledge" have resonances that offer a comprehensive perspective on what we ordinarily call "reality," but can also facilitate infinite personal growth, which includes going beyond particular theories, views, or experiences—you never get bogged down or tied to some view of how or what things are. (Tarthang Tulku 1977, 5)

. . . a vision which would integrate and unite all aspects of being . . . . Space and Time themselves have now presented such a vision . . . . (TSK, xxxiv)

All scientific, religious, and psychological disciplines are confronting space and time, too—what else, at bottom, is there for them to explore? (DOT, xxvi)

You have everything you need in this 'step', Time, Space, and Knowledge. There is no truth or realization that's in principle beyond your reach. (DOT, xxiv)

It puts you in touch with facets of reality that are truly *central* and wholesome . . . . Space, time and knowledge can ground you wherever

you may find yourself, and can always point the
way to new insight . . . . (Tarthang Tulku 1977, 9)

The Initial TSK Vehicle as Common Ground

If TSK is truly this encompassing, it offers a forum or
common ground for the comparison of various principles. Since any two principles would apply to subsets of
the domain, these principles should be relatable by
means of TSK propositions and descriptions.

How useful such descriptions would be as a common ground will depend a great deal on the vehicle's
inner consistency and effectiveness, to be discussed
shortly. Yet in principle such comparisons and relationships could be very helpful. Arguments between
and within different fields of knowledge often portray
various principles as being simply right or wrong, but
the availability of common ground suggests that this is
an oversimplification. Principles have a certain range
of application, a certain sphere of usefulness beyond
which they are ineffective, or possibly even produce
harmful side-effects. In other words, principles should
be regarded as appropriate for a certain domain of time,
space, and knowledge.

Here is an example of how principles can be compared within TSK. Consider the statement, "While working, the faster you produce things, the better." This
principle is somewhat effective for improving productivity within lower space and time (near the periphery
of the circle of settings; cf. TSK, 111–12; 136–41). From
a TSK perspective, it is formulated in terms of lower-

level existents (TSK, 7): "Our ordinary world view has an implicit preference for tangible 'things'—existence, existents, interactions, causes and effects, and events." Use of this principle to the exclusion of others would thus restrict potential improvements in productivity to the domain of first-level settings.

Compare the following principle: "The more involved we are in our work, and the less distinction there is between ourselves, our work process, and time, the greater the productivity." This principle not only applies to first-level experience, but opens toward second-level possibilities by not focusing on things and events. It should be usable over a greater domain of experience.

Inspired use of the initial TSK vehicle as a forum for comparing principles would accord with Tarthang Tulku's early suggestion (TSK, xxxi) that TSK could be "a visionary medium through which a common ground could be found in the pursuits of knowledge carried out by the various sciences and religions."

Consistency

A second property of vehicles is consistency. A vehicle is totally consistent when it has no inner contradictions. In general, inconsistency corresponds to less than optimal effectiveness of the principles, propositions, practices, etc., within a vehicle.

Various thinkers have noted repeatedly that inconsistency of one's vehicle is the rule rather than the exception. For instance, Charles Hobbs writes: "We have all spent thousands of hours of our lives struggling with the disunification of principles inappropriately espoused" (1987, 30).

Testing Consistency

Inquiry into the consistency of various principles that make up part of a vehicle can be a means of evoking knowledge. Such inquiry may show either (1) the vehicle is imprecise, faulty, or confusing (perhaps it can be improved), or (2) the apparent contradiction was based only on an initial perspective on the principles, and now a different and clearer way of relating them has emerged. This testing of, or inquiring into, apparent inconsistency is probably one of the most important and productive ways of exploring a vehicle.

Here, for example, are three statements from the initial TSK vehicle that could be tested for contradiction:

(1) "We take time merely as a structure for indexing states of objects, which involves the picture of objects embedded in a temporal grid. In this view, a temporal grid fulfills the . . . need for ordering events in a linear, cause-oriented series." (TSK, 81)

(2) "All going from place to place, experience to experience . . . actually occurs as a succession of 'timed out' experiences in the same 'spot'." (TSK, 151)

(3) "Time is neither linear nor sequential; in fact, there are neither moments nor successive movement, and thus no succession." (TSK, 136)

Statement 2 mentions a succession of experiences in the same spot, seemingly contradicting the spread-out linearity of statement 1; statement 3 apparently contradicts both linearity and succession. Is the initial TSK vehicle poorly conceived? Or do these statements describe different levels of time, and therefore refer to different domains within the circle of settings? Holding the three statements as hypotheses to be tested in the laboratory of experience allows us to pose and explore such questions. No matter what conclusions are eventually arrived at, persistent 'testing' of apparent inconsistency always seems to lead to greater understanding.

In an interview published in DOT, Tarthang Tulku suggests that apparent inconsistencies sometimes result from the attempt to address numerous different positions and conditions that need to be opened up (xlix):

Interviewer: Some people find *Time, Space, and Knowledge* itself to be so complicated that it seems to be conflicting at times.

Tarthang Tulku: The system of ordinary knowledge, which the book attempts to communicate with and open up, is very complicated and given to such a diversity of positions that, in order to speak to it and challenge it successfully, you have to try many different approaches and analyses.

The Initial TSK Vehicle Is Very Consistent

My attempts at rigorous comparison of apparently contradictory statements in TSK lead to two types of

165

resolutions. First, and most often, the comparison leads to insight, showing (as in the example above) that the statements describe different circumstances or levels of experience. Second, the comparison leads to the conclusion that terminology is being used in different ways, or in entirely novel ways.

When I started working with the initial TSK vehicle, past experience in testing the consistency of other vehicles led me to presume that a third type of resolution would occur repeatedly: the conclusion that the statements were in fact contradictory and confusing. Surprisingly, in almost twenty years of working with TSK, I have not found such contradictions. My testing has so far corroborated the following TSK statement (Tarthang Tulku 1977, 7):

> Theory, practice, all experiences, can become integrated on this path.

Effectiveness

The property of effectiveness addresses how well a vehicle functions to facilitate transformation of a certain domain of human experience—to what extent it moves us toward the center of the circle of settings. The properties of consistency and comprehensiveness discussed above are interrelated and important, but the property of effectiveness seems primary. Does the vehicle work, and if so, how well? Can its use produce undesirable side effects? Vehicles must, first and foremost, be functional.

Consider a vehicle containing this principle: "Loyalty to one's country unites a diverse people in a way nothing else can or ever will." How effective is this principle? Outside its nationalistic domain, it will have little effectiveness at all. Conceivably loyalty to one's country might have stopped the outbreak of civil war in the United States, but it would be unlikely to unite people in different countries. The domain of focal settings over which this principle is effective will be limited. And such limitation will obviously influence the effectiveness of any vehicle containing it.

A limitation in domain is only one aspect of ineffectiveness. If we believe that "loyalty to one's country unites a diverse people like nothing else," what do we do when our country follows an unwise policy? Do we surrender our intelligence and have faith that things will turn out well if we just remain loyal? If so, a side effect of adopting the "loyalty" principle is that we must cut off knowledge when it conflicts with our country's policies. If we agree that knowledge becomes more pervasive as the center of the circle of settings is approached, cutting off knowledge will restrict our ability to move toward the center. Thus, any vehicle containing the loyalty principle will be somewhat ineffective. In general, the most effective vehicles contain principles that produce the fewest such side-effects.

The Initial TSK Vehicle Leads to Greater Effectiveness

If we reflect on what makes the loyalty principle ineffective, we may decide the principle can be reformulated.

Perhaps whatever effectiveness results from use of the loyalty principle is due to a more fundamental principle, such as an appreciation or positionless knowing of one's fellow citizens. Side effects of using the principle may also result, because the principle itself does not address fundamental factors of time, space, and knowledge directly and in a balanced way.

As this example suggests, use of the initial TSK vehicle to inquire into effectiveness may help reveal harmful side-effects in any discipline that indirectly investigates these three fundamental facets of experience. As Tarthang Tulku says (DOT, xxvi):

> All scientific, religious, and psychological disciplines are confronting space and time, too—what else, at bottom, is there for them to explore? However, the problem with at least some of these other approaches is that they are investigating space and time very indirectly and unconsciously rather than directly and intentionally. Such an approach can yield insights and benefits for a while, but it is very slow, and capable of being exhausted. Since it's not aware of the real basis of its object of study, this approach can become frozen into artificial, static models.

Correspondingly, inquiry directed very precisely toward these central facets will tend to produce fewer side effects and to lead more quickly to a more expanded range of benefits (Tarthang Tulku 1977, 9):

> It puts you in touch with facets of reality that are truly *central* and wholesome, so that growth

is guided by something genuine. . . . Space, time and knowledge can ground you wherever you may find yourself, and can always point the way to new insight, because you are participating in something *alive* (Tarthang Tulku 1977, 9).

Precision Is Related to Effectiveness

If we generalize from the foregoing examples, we can say that the precision of inquiry afforded by a vehicle is closely related to the vehicle's effectiveness. Vehicles are heuristic systems that facilitate learning and change in a more or less precise manner. As with automobiles, we care not only whether a vehicle will go somewhere, but *how well* it will transport us. We care how precisely tuned the vehicle is.

Note that precision is not the same as truth or accuracy. The attribute of 'true' or 'false' is irrelevant to the functioning of a vehicle. The benefit of a vehicle whose purpose is to facilitate change and learning results from how well and how precisely it works, but not from whether it is 'true' in some sense. This inapplicability of the label 'truth' is confirmed by Tarthang Tulku's description of how TSK developed (LOK, xlvii):

Whether the new pictures and thoughts that formed as the old ones lost their hold were 'accurate' did not seem of primary concern; what truly mattered was the openness that allowed such new content to appear.

Though inapplicable to the initial TSK vehicle, the idea of truth does find its place *within* the vehicle.

169

Concern with truth and falsity, accuracy and inaccuracy, and dichotomous thinking in general is found primarily near the periphery of the circle of settings, where

> What appears . . . is . . . judged in terms of oppositions such as good and bad, right and wrong. The judgments in turn find expression in words and labels, and from this foundation come doctrines, traditions, customs, styles, and ideologies. (LOK, 44–45)

When we accept the shift from surface to substance, from appearance to realness, we look past the communiqué to accept the truth of the story being communicated (DTS, 23). In distinct contrast, higher knowing "does not depend on taking one position or rejecting another" (LOK, xli).

Conclusion

Many individuals have affirmed aspects of the comprehensiveness, consistency, and effectiveness and precision of the initial TSK vehicle. (See, for example, the essays in *Mastery of Mind* and *Dimensions of Thought*) For now, this scope, integrity, and direct efficacy of the initial TSK vehicle means at the least that TSK can serve as a forum or common ground for comparing principles and practices of other vehicles. "By focusing on time and space and on their interaction with knowledge, it may be possible to unify fields of learning that are now separate, and to bring together concerns that now seem opposed" (LOK, xvi).

In doing so, we should keep in mind that Tarthang Tulku challenges us to probe more deeply, looking for difference even as we explore connections, and not hesitating to challenge the vision itself (1983, 31):

> What's missing so far is the sense that people are challenging the vision itself. I would like to see them making comparisons with other teachings, looking for connections but also for differences; testing and probing to see whether the vision really works. My own sense is that the TSK book is really unusual, very different, but I don't find that reflected in people's reactions. When I look for clear, focused analysis and criticism of the vision, I don't find it.

That too will evoke clarity in our exploration.

NOTES

1. Although TSK says that at the third level, "one point is all points," I am assuming that third-level focal settings can still be represented by points in the circle. They might be better represented by a completely open center of the circle, a hole in the center of a disk. The different 'nature' of such a hole could signify a breakdown in the concept of focal setting at the third level: "The accommodating quality . . . is complete at precisely the point where the notion of a space, which to a greater or lesser degree allows or accommodates 'a' 'thing', collapses." (TSK, 15)

REFERENCES

Hobbs, Charles. 1987. *Time Power*. New York: Harper & Row.

Tarthang Tulku. 1977. "Time, Space, and Knowledge: Interview with Tarthang Tulku on his New Vision." *Gesar* 4:3, pp. 5–11.

Tarthang Tulku. 1983. "Time, Space, and Knowledge Today: Interview with Tarthang Tulku." *Gesar* 7:4, p. 31.

CREATIVE INQUIRY: FROM INSTRUMENTAL KNOWING TO LOVE OF KNOWLEDGE

Alfonso Montuori

In a recent discussion with my close friend John Lyons, strolling along the coast of the Monterey Peninsula, I found myself expressing my feelings of marginality in regard to the academic community, and also with respect to the general approach to knowledge in our time and culture. Although some of my work has been well received, the issues I am really interested in did not seem to resonate to the degree I had hoped. I thought I had articulated the main thrust of my interest in my work, but the responses were generally not to my overarching intent, but to specific aspects of my discussions. What was it, I wondered, that led my colleagues and my audience to focus on selected ideas, rather than on the larger issue I have attempted to address in all my intellectual "homes?"

As John and I spoke, I realized that I still need to clarify my own fundamental assumptions about what it is exactly that I am after. Recently I have put it this way: Even though the issues I have addressed are of great interest to me, I am ultimately more concerned with the very way we approach particular issues, rather than the issues themselves. I have found that the fundamental nature of the discourse about these issues, and indeed the way we think about them, is problematic. But this concern was not being communicated.

In this essay, I would like to explore whether this larger evolving passion can be expressed with the aid of the TSK vision, or those limited elements of the vision I have absorbed and integrated. My main interest is in exploring the way knowledge shapes, and in turn is shaped by, our understanding of the world. My sense (and this is what inspires me in the TSK vision) is that our whole understanding of knowledge, which presently is very much instrumental in nature, might be enriched by opening up to a more creative inquiry. To explore this possibility, I will look to a number of examples from my own personal experience. My aim is to use them to develop a more encompassing understanding of what knowledge is and might be.

Tools that Kill

Several years ago, my colleague Ron Purser and I consulted for a very large multinational, whose research division alone is made up of some 15,000 people all over the globe. Our area of expertise was creativity, and we had been called in because company management felt that their scientists were suffering from the "me too" syndrome, always catching up with innovations by others instead of generating new ideas of their own. What role were we to play? The senior executive who hired us explained to us what he wanted: "Tools," he said, "tools that kill!"

This incident has become a "defining moment" in my relationship with Ron. Nowadays we trot out the sentence "tools that kill" whenever we are faced with what we perceive to be a painfully instrumental, restrictive, and even absurd view of the richness of knowledge. Knowledge reduced to a deadly weapon! How does one approach and embody knowledge as a deadly instrument? What kind of practices, what kind of thinking and inquiry flow from such a "position?" Is this really the way that some people in our culture conceive of creativity and its uses?

Since this episode, Ron and I have tried to articulate a view which begins with a "love of knowledge" and uses that as a starting point for inquiry. We contrast this to the more instrumental view that begins with a "given," "objective" problem, and then raids a "knowledge-bank" in search of a solution.

One area where we have tried to do this is the field we call "social creativity." While there is a sizable literature on individual genius and the characteristics of the creative individual, there has until recently been hardly any research on creative groups, communities, and interactions (Montuori and Purser, 1995). Ron and I have written about this extensively, and developed a very strong interest in this area, fueled by our own experience as organizational theorists, and, in my case, as a musician. Many of my most memorable experiences of creativity occurred working in and with a band, with our creativity emerging out of the interactions of collective improvisation—sharing ideas, inspiring each other on the bandstand and off. But this kind of generative interaction was nowhere addressed in the research literature I found.

Despite a desire to understand the specific factors which lead to a group being creative, my own particular interest has been in understanding why creativity has not been viewed as a potentially collaborative phenomenon; why, indeed, "social creativity" is even sometimes viewed as an oxymoron. Why has there been little if any research or public interest in social creativity, at least until a decade ago?[1] What does that say about our culture, about academia, about our cultural research interests and strategies, about our thinking—about us? What can this blind spot (in our culture and also in business) tell us about our knowledge and our potential?

Reflecting on these issues has led me to question my own motives and interests more deeply. In a discussion with some colleagues recently I was asked if I have a "model" for social creativity. Sheepishly, with some feelings of guilt, I replied that I did not. Why not, I wondered? Should I have a model? What is so good about models? Models are certainly useful, and also intellectually appealing, but what is it about our society, and about social science, that leads us to think of models as the *summum bonum* of knowledge—or at least as a prerequisite for having anything to say as an "academic?" This set of questions challenged me to think about precisely what kind of "knowledge" our interest in social creativity offered or aimed at. What kind of knowledge were Ron and I generating in our own work? How did such knowledge match up with societal and academic expectations for "knowledge production?"

Trotting Out Methods

At a job interview a few years ago, I was questioned about methods and methodology. The university where I was applying for a position is known for its "alternative" approach to methodology, drawing from continental philosophy, qualitative approaches, and the like. "If you were to study this institution [meaning the university in question]," I was asked, "what method would you use?" I knew the "right" answer was to trot out some methodology such as ethnography, or action research, or any of a number of other approaches. But when I opened my mouth, I realized that an answer along these lines would only replicate the very problem alternative approaches had been designed to counteract; namely, the indiscriminate use of a method regardless of the context and of the "subject's" nature.

I tried to explain why I thought the question itself was problematic. Admittedly I was not very clear, and certainly not very diplomatic. I did not get the job, but I did get a "job" out of the question itself, one which has kept me busy ever since. Why was I so reluctant to give my interviewers what they wanted?

If I had given the search committee an "appropriate" answer, it would have shown that I "know" some of the current methods and when to apply them, and that I can pass this knowledge on to students. But that to me is profoundly unsatisfactory. Suppose one sets out to study a system and considers what methodology to adopt. For starters, without knowing why one is studying the system, or what the system is about, or, for that matter, for whom one is doing the research, can one really legitimately claim to know "how" to study it? What are the criteria for choosing one of the many methods out there, or, more interestingly, for observing the system in a "pre-methodological" context? Simply to impose a method—which (despite protests to the contrary) most likely will end up being the method(s) one is trained in and familiar with and therefore crowns as "right" and "appropriate,"—means jumping the gun in a very dangerous way. Furthermore, how does one investigate the very thinking which leads one to choose one method above another? How does one select among competing paradigms? Is there a way of addressing the larger context in which the discourse of method itself is situated—the nature of our thinking— rather than merely situating the method in a presupposed larger discourse?

I believe our "methodolatry" is a symptom of a pervasive, unreflective, instrumental approach to knowledge itself. In our society, information must be generated. Doing so in accord with one of the accepted methods legitimates that information as correct, and therefore as "true," or at least "error-free." It makes the results arrived at defensible, while also demonstrating the researcher's competence. Once the information generated is deemed correct, it can be used. At that point we are justified in calling it knowledge.

In TSK terms, I would put this approach to knowledge under the general heading of "technological knowledge." Tarthang Tulku illuminates its qualities and its limitations better than I could:

> Technological knowledge, with its emphasis on the objective realm, assigns primacy to knowledge of the 'already known'. The rule is put forward that knowledge must be based on the familiar: on labels, descriptions, and categories that are given in advance and serve as finite, discrete, and isolated 'counters' available for knowledge to manipulate. (LOK, 43)

> The limitations set up by the prevailing models turn knowledge into a 'commodity' and human beings into consumers rather than producers. The different systems of knowledge, each offering its own explanations and techniques, its interpretations and methods, leave open only the question of which system to adopt. (LOK, 253)

> The knowledge this first-level 'order' supports is knowledge of the already known—knowledge as technology, reflecting the limitations of first-

level time and space. Devoted to the need to cope, technological knowledge produces a steady stream of new facts, new theories, and new solutions. But it also perpetuates the patterns of need and not-knowing. Programmed mechanically in advance, it can make no sense of the prospect for a new way of knowing (KTS, 57–58).

Constructing the Creativity Toolbox

Today there is almost a fetish for generating information by applying current methods and models. Yet little attention is paid to the nature of information, and even less to the nature of knowledge itself—the knowledge of knowledge (Ceruti 1994). Different ways of conceiving knowledge, including new ways of knowing, tend to be ignored. The Laplacean belief still holds that "correct" ways of knowing, based on existing criteria and schemata, can give us complete information, and so let us predict and control the world around us (Ceruti 1994). This translates into an ongoing quest for instrumental knowledge—knowledge which can be immediately "put to work." Knowledge has an ordering and focusing function, allowing the self to "make sense" of the world, imposing a grid on experience that tells us what is going on and how to "handle" it, while at the same time eliminating all uncertainty, confusion, and ambiguity.

This instrumental approach clearly has an enormous range of applications, and has been very successful in many ways. But I do feel that viewing knowledge solely as a tool has some very serious implications.

These implications must be addressed, because they limit our approach to what we can know, and also limit what we can do.

The executive who wanted "tools that kill" provides a useful example of the dangers I have in mind. For this man, the issue of "innovation-deficit" was easily remedied by giving his scientists creativity "tools" in the form of processes such as "lateral thinking" or "bisociation." In this model, a scientist stuck for a new idea goes to the creativity "expert," who provides him or her with a creativity "toolbox." The scientist then rummages through the creativity "toolbox" and pulls out a creativity tool. The client "runs" the tool and comes up with the bright idea he or she needs.

Is this knowledge? Is this how creativity operates? More fundamentally, what kind of knowledge is it that makes us play out this model and accept this kind of thinking? What would happen if, rather than relying on the expert's tools, the researchers were encouraged to inquire into their own creative process, their assumptions about creativity, the actual nature of their practices, and so forth? These questions, which point at another level of knowledge, remain unasked.

The "toolbox mentality" that guides the ordinary approach to knowledge may be linked to the oft-noted pragmatic bent in the American character (Stewart & Bennett 1991). For decades the American "can do" attitude and no-nonsense practicality has been praised for its economic success. But the toolbox mentality that expresses this outlook is problematic, not necessarily because it is wrong, but because it is partial. For instance, today people tend to read books looking for practical advice on what they can do, preferably spelled out step by step. The "do-it-yourself," paint-by-the-numbers mentality, pioneered in such fields as home-improvement and *Reader's Digest* art or medicine lessons (the classic "I am Joe's pancreas" type article), has been transferred to a far wider domain that includes psychological and social improvement.

The "tools" that people want to learn how to use typically emerge as the final elaboration of a "model," which in turn is often a framework that divides a process into certain specific stages. A classic example in the field of organizational theory is the stages of group process that proceed through "forming, storming, norming and performing." Specific tools can then be developed for every stage. Models, once the currency of social science, have now filtered down to popular culture, where they seem to pervade our society.

Model-mania applies even to dealing with profound psychological issues (for instance, 12-step programs) or "enlightenment" (consider the progressive stages of insight in the popular New Age bestseller, *The Celestine Prophecy*, or Ken Wilber's [1980] more sophisticated structural-developmental model of the evolution of consciousness.) Paradoxically (given the individualism that shapes our culture), these books tell us how we can "do it ourselves" based on somebody else's framework. In other words, we can "do it," but we cannot "think about it." We are assumed to be incapable of inquiring into how we experience phenomena, or into their very nature.

What most people, and certainly most managers, generally have little time for is the theory that underlies a model. Theory is viewed as *a priori* dry and abstract, removed from real-life. It is the province of "eggheads" isolated in their ivory towers. Yet this dismissive attitude is quite dangerous. Every tool and every model is informed by a theory (loosely, a logically coherent set of descriptive and explanatory assumptions about the phenomena in question). Theorizing can drift into scholasticism, but it can also lead to a different level of inquiry. Put differently, eschewing theory completely means leaving unchallenged the underlying assumptions of any particular tool, model, or course of action.

Whether we know it or not, our actions are informed by a theory of the situation we are in, and that theory in turn is immersed in a larger "worldview" or philosophy of life, with a strong cultural component. To offer a model of my own (!), we might speak of a nested hierarchy going from the "smallest" element (perhaps "tools") through models, theories, paradigms (overarching frameworks for theories), and ultimately worldviews, which bring the full weight of our culture and history to bear on a larger interpretive framework for life and meaning. Without being consciously aware of this hierarchy, we will tend to shape our understanding of each new circumstance "as if" we were dealing with an objective situation. We will forget to check our assumptions about the world, testing them against our specific situation and noting how they shape what we act upon. Instead, we will treat them "as if" we were dealing with an objective situation. We will ignore the process of differentiation, of inclusion/ exclusion, that frames each perception and the distinctions it depends on. We will lose the opportunity to discover that there are many possible frames available, at many different "focal settings," each leading to very different understanding of "what is." And we will also lose the opportunity to engage in our own, full inquiry into the issues.

As an example, let us look at the popular creativity-tool called lateral thinking. Lateral thinking is based on an interesting model of creativity with roots in early research that settled on two distinct aspects of thinking, labeled convergent and divergent. Here a tool originates in a model that is based in a theory that grows out of the application of a specific scientific paradigm supported and generated by a specific (Western, modern, industrial/scientific, predominantly male) worldview. If we lose sight of this hierarchy, we fail to see that there are many different ways of conceptualizing creativity. We have no way to realize that there will be other ways of fostering creativity or "being creative." Our understanding of creativity will be limited by somebody else's fundamental assumptions, which we "buy into" unawares.

For instance, the lateral-thinking model leaves social processes and social context out of the picture completely. Theoretical assumptions are made that define creativity as a cognitive process, one in which affect and interpersonal relationships play no role. An exclusive focus on this one tool would thus place the emphasis entirely on internal cognitive processes.

Perhaps interests such as efficiency and speed are served in this way, and perhaps the scientific research behind this approach is impeccable on its own terms. But what of the factors left out of account? For instance what of the working conditions under which managers, researchers, and other employees work?

Suppose we wanted to address the issue of creativity education by looking at personal interactions, social constraints and possibilities, the environment of the researchers or educators, dynamics of power, or motivation. Suppose, more radically, that we wanted to explore the suggestion that creativity depends on a spirit of inquiry stimulated by a particular attitude toward the world around us. As long as we are using the lateral-thinking tool, we will have no way to do so. We will not know how to ask the right questions, or even suspect that broader questions about the relationship between creativity and our knowledge are relevant to our concerns.

Limitations on what can be known are not always innocent. There are clear reasons why management would endorse and encourage the cognitive and psychological approaches to creativity implicit in the use of the lateral-thinking tool. They range from widely shared understandings (the cultural myth of the lone genius, our cultural individualism, the reductionism of social-science methodology) to the unwillingness to explore the link between creativity in the workplace and the social, political, and economic factors that determine how organizations are structured. A more wide-ranging inquiry into creativity might well require a rethinking of such staples of the present business environment as hierarchy, control and reward systems, the bureaucratic propensity for order versus disorder, and the social and market forces that encourage a stress on predictability.

There are other issues at work here as well. Asking the scientists with whom our senior executive was concerned to whip out a tool when needed is a more reassuring approach to creativity than choosing to foster the holistic development of "creative persons," engaged in an ongoing, but potentially disruptive, process of creative inquiry. Our society is ambivalent toward creative individuals: the term "creative" has over- and undertones of "flakiness," unpredictability, disorder, and even madness (Whyte, 1957).

This ambivalence links a preference for tool-based knowledge with what I call "oppositional thinking." A polarization is at work; in this case, the polarization between "conformity" and "creativity," "ordinary" or "normal" and "wild," "abnormal," or "mad." The greater the polarization, the more the differences are dramatized. When the choice is seen as either/or, to the exclusion of a middle ground, the belief system itself generates a systemic blind spot, an issue the system cannot explore. The outright refusal and rejection of what is being opposed creates "black holes" in our knowledge, phenomena that can almost not be thought about, since they have no space in which to emerge.

Psychodynamically, we might call this an unconscious conflict. And where such a conflict is in operation, there will be a strong tendency to look away from the larger issues or domains in the hierarchy. The point in such a case becomes to offer individuals a tool while making sure that they can remain bound to the positive pole of the opposition that lurks in the background. Our scientists will remain "normal" people, who conform to what is expected of them by applying a specific tool or formula for being more creative. There is little risk that they will turn into potentially threatening "creative individuals." In this way, we try to turn creativity itself into something that can be standardized, controlled, and predicted.

Knowledge Goes to War

The senior executive who called us in for a "creativity consult" asked us for "tools that kill." The phrase implies that tools for creativity are in fact weapons. And whom are they designed to kill? The answer, of course, is that they target the company's competition.

The corporate scientists become warriors in the corporate battlefield. Here, "underneath" the tools, models, and theories (to use a spatial metaphor) is a deeper metaphor of war. The executive who hired us had made certain choices and needs informed by this metaphor, which shaped his knowledge more decisively than the theories he had in mind to support his views. This is precisely one of the reasons why metaphors can be illuminating: They make more apparent the affective component of thought. The theory remains, but the metaphor makes explicit implications that the theory itself might not illuminate.

The creativity tool is also directed at the process of creation itself, since the tool is supposed to generate creativity. But if tools must "kill" creativity so that it may be mastered, applied, controlled, measured, and made predictable, they defeat their purpose. Yet "living" creativity may be too unpredictable, even frightening, to behold and foster in the corporate context.

Is this metaphor of war "inappropriate," or even "wrong" or "bad?" At this point, I withhold judgment, although the reader has likely figured out my own proclivities. Yet I would certainly argue that the metaphor is limited and limiting. Just as was true of choosing to proceed by way of tools, when we proceed by way of metaphors, we are limiting ourselves to one particular approach, one attitude toward innovation and action that keeps other possibilities from emerging.

When we follow the war metaphor, we reduce creativity to a question of tactics—the speedy deployment of weapons to the troops. Time is of the essence in engaging the enemy, and the weapons must be dispatched immediately. A consultant dealing with a business executive guided by this metaphor will find it a real challenge to raise more strategic concerns. The constellation "war/tactics/weapons acquisition" accelerates the temporal dynamic, eliminating any possibility for certain kinds of creative education. In the heat of a battle-forged urgency, there is no chance to explore a wide range of options, to rethink the whole enterprise. Why would an executive on the attack want to waste time getting caught up in theoretical discussions about language, metaphor, and theory?

The Space of Creativity

Whether it has been brought on in part by the metaphor of "knowledge at war" or not, today a tremendous acceleration of knowledge confronts us at every level. Information is being generated with greater speed, transmitted with greater speed, and demanded with greater speed. This has helped lead to the feeling that Toffler (1973) described as "future shock." It has been addressed by those dealing with the "complexification" of the world in the "information age," who point out that knowledge is being fragmented into smaller and smaller distinct spaces (Morin 1994). The most obvious example of this is the phenomenon of interdisciplinary fragmentation, through which disciplines such as psychology, sociology, anthropology, politics, and economics slice the world up into so many different sections and spaces, generating ever more specialized ways of making sense of (and controlling) the world.

For understanding and creating our world, psychology, with its language of personality and the self, has become the most popular of these positioned realms. Our daily speech is permeated with psychological terms. The quest for "personal growth," "self-understanding," and "self-improvement," whether through weight-loss or through developing "personal power," has become a consuming passion and a big business.

From this perspective, the situation that Purser and I encountered when we went out to consult on creativity can be traced to the pervasive "psychologization" of creativity, so symptomatic of American culture. While in many ways a fascinating and important cultural development, psychologization is also problematic. With psychology in the saddle, social and philosophical understandings of life and of creativity are rejected or ignored (Stewart and Bennett 1992). American individualism, as many scholars have pointed out, has developed a view of the self that depends on what I would call an oppositional identity vis-à-vis groups and larger collectivities (Slater 1991; Ogilvy 1992).[2] The self defines itself in contradistinction to the group—to the other. It occupies a space and a position which is set against everything which it considers "not-self."

Similarly, knowledge inhabits "spaces" which are often opposed to each other. Thus, the humanistic psychology movement, which has strongly influenced the popular discourse of creativity, arose in reaction to behaviorism's stress on environmental stimuli as producing predictable "responses." Behaviorism's deterministic view left no room for free will or human dignity. In B.F. Skinner's words (1971), it would lead us "beyond freedom and dignity." Humanistic psychology reacted by stressing the role of creative individual agents, capable of making choices and of struggling against the oppressive forces of the conforming environment.

In turn, humanistic psychology, and psychology in general, have developed an "oppositional identity"[3] vis-à-vis sociology. To distinguish itself as a discipline or "field," a space of knowledge with hard boundaries, psychology has focused largely on individuals and their cognitive and affective processes, as opposed to groups and social factors—just as sociologists have generally sought explanations for human events at the level of the group and society. A clear indication of this is the absence of research into areas which uncomfortably straddle the personal and the social, such as the social aspects of creativity with which I am most concerned.[4]

I sometimes lecture in public about social creativity. I typically discuss the collaborative nature of musical performance and movie-making, among other activities. I note the social, political, historical, and economic factors that helped shape the lives and achievements of writers and painters, creative persons whose work we like to think is done "alone." I present the social constructionist argument or introduce the sociological perspective, discussing the role of "movements" in the arts, or the function of laboratories in science. In short, I invite the audience to broaden its understanding of the where and when of creativity. Inevitably, some in the audience will challenge this whole perspective, asserting that "ultimately" creativity is the lone act of a single individual. "Ultimately," in their view, none of the other "stuff" matters.

This hard-core belief, which in some circles would be described as a perfect example of the workings of "ideology," has multiple social, political, and historical roots (Montuori and Purser 1997). As an assumption about the nature of creativity, and about the isolated, autonomous nature of the self, it not shared by most other cultures around the globe, and even in the West it has only become prevalent in the last two hundred years or so. This does not make it necessarily wrong, but it does suggest that there is plenty of room for further inquiry. What is the "focal setting" that directs our inquiry into creativity into these channels? When we look for the sources of the creative act, in what space do we seek to locate it?

Since the focus of this article lies elsewhere, I will not try to review all the factors involved in the prevailing view of creativity. Suffice it to say that the focal setting at work here is "fixed" on the individual. Anything perceived as "outside" the boundaries of a very particular concept of the person, what Alan Watts (1966) called the "skin-encapsulated ego," is considered "epiphenomenal." To point to it either hinders the "project of the ego," or somehow diminishes the achievement of the individual by making it "dependent" on others. The "space" of creativity is inside the head (and, for humanistic psychology, the heart) of a single person— and that's that. As Tarthang Tulku suggests (LOK), a focal setting leads to a fixed position. To deviate from that position would clash with too many staunchly— and largely unconsciously—held assumptions.

Now, one response to this circumstance is to develop an alternative focal setting. Some of my colleagues have suggested to me that this is exactly what I should do with regard to the issue of social creativity. Show us how to do it, is their argument: Develop a model for what constitutes a socially creative setting and the characteristics of creative groups, and those who find such a model of interest will pursue it and reach their own conclusions. I can appreciate this position, and in fact I believe that this strategy would be successful. I am sure that within a few years there will be more "models" of social creativity than you can shake a stick at, all very useful, to be sure. Yet my interest ultimately lies elsewhere. As I see it, the effort to elaborate a new position through a new model will only direct our attention in a new way, only point us toward a new space. That is not my aim.

What interests me is the possibility of developing a different kind of discourse, a different form of inquiry into the whole process of creativity, one that can be transferred to other subjects as well. It is here that I find myself turning toward the TSK vision.

The Discourse of Knowledge in Space and Time

In the discussion so far, I have already been using fundamental concepts from TSK. Here are some additional points that I consider central to my concerns, drawn from *Love of Knowledge*:

> The restrictions on knowledge, which seem so absolute and final from the conventional perspective, can be analyzed in terms of 'positions' and 'conditions'. In the space-centered view of 'objective' reality, limitations on knowing are the consequence of positions. The self (to which the conventional view refers all knowing) occupies a place 'here' and lacks knowledge regarding something located 'there'. This lack sets up a basic tension, which generates momentum 'outward', activating the flow of linear temporality

that perpetuates the self and its constructs. From the time-centered view of the self, the same lack emerges as conditioning. Born into a particular setting and subject to a specific order, the self is shaped in its being and knowing. Its limited knowledge is the inevitable outcome of its circumstances, which define the self in its person and its potential. (263)

'Position' comes into play though 'opposition', active as the basis for identification and discrimination. It is dichotomies that define what is real. (265)

Each pole is a potential 'position' for the 'bystander' to adopt. . . . [T]he known world comes into being through the progressive marking out and 'owning' of such polar oppositions. (266)

Knowledge of Time and Space details how "positions" create "oppositions:"

The first level 'order' unfolds through polar concepts that are mutually interdependent. Language appears to give each member of the polarity a separate identity, encouraging us to give one side or the other greater value or importance, but the two sides are inseparable. When we choose happiness, we are choosing sadness, when we choose knowledge we are choosing ignorance. Each 'opposition' reflects a more fundamental and encompassing 'position'; when we let the 'order' communicated by language guide us toward choosing one side of each polarity, ignoring or rejecting the other, our choice will be incomplete and frustrating. (52–53)

Positions are defended in an adversarial style, because the positions are spaces occupied by the self—the self *is* its positions. Any challenge to those positions is viewed as opposition (another self's 'position') and a threat to the self's very integrity and existence. The characteristic mode of discourse for this way of understanding is debate. University debating teams aim solely to present one set of positions and oppose—ultimately, destroy—the positions of others. The highest form of discourse, our finest hour in the world of knowledge, involves not collective inquiry, but the defense of already existing positions, and the attack of any other discourse. Positions become impositions.

To be sure, positions may be altered as the result of a debate, but this tends to happen only on relatively minor points. As Thomas Kuhn (1970) famously demonstrated, fundamental paradigm shifts occur, not primarily through reasoned discourse, but because in time the "old-paradigm guard" literally dies out. For those who have invested a lifetime in a position, there is too much at stake in that position, academically, economically, in terms of prestige, even in terms of self-identity, for changes to be made. As Tarthang Tulku writes (1984, 69): "While we see ourselves as using knowledge, it may be more accurate to say that what we know is using us: We are drawn into responding to all that occurs around us."

When discourse and inquiry are confined in this unfortunate way, it leads to the frustration I have tried to describe above. For me, to present a new model of social creativity or a critique of an individualist/reductionist model, to establish a new metaphor or create a new tool, would do nothing to alter this fundamental mode of discourse. I would like to invite others to view creativity with me through different focal settings, exploring the times, spaces, and knowledge of creativity. But this is a fundamentally different enterprise than entering the debate arena. What I would like to present as an invitation is generally viewed through the adversarial lens of positions and oppositions. It then becomes a challenge to the existing position, an attempt to displace it with my view and invalidate the existing view. And that simply misses the point.

Dialogic Alternatives

With this underlying concern out in the open, let me describe the ways in which my colleague, Ron Purser, and I have been trying to invite a different understanding of creativity, one which does not depend on opposition. Without attempting to get at the underlying issues raised by TSK modes of discourse, but using the TSK language of "oppositions," we have sought to present alternatives to the standard opposition between "individual" and "social" views of creativity.

This approach starts by accepting what proponents of the romantic version of the individualist position often argue: Many a genius has been misunderstood and even reviled, forced to toil and struggle in a materialistic world that praises only money, fame, vulgarity, and so forth. The point meets with ready acceptance, for one does not have to be a misunderstood genius to appreciate that society can sometimes create obstacles in our path, and that it can create very large obstacles for those presenting radically new ideas.

Yet this is still another partial truth, another position based on an opposition. Geniuses—and "ordinary people" too—have also benefited from social intercourse, and the world around them does not have to be viewed as their enemy. Artists and scientists work in an existing field, whether physics or painting or music. They use the available tools, and they have colleagues, friends, teachers, and others with whom they exchange ideas, have arguments, and so on.

After all, for anything to be considered new or creative, it must stand out as "different" in the context of a tradition. And this relation between genius and tradition is complex. Even if the genius "breaks" with tradition, it is that very tradition which has allowed her to do so, by creating the "field" in which to operate, providing the context, the materials, even the inspiration. The romantic discourse of creativity, in tending to view tradition as nothing more than an obstacle for the true genius, misses this complexity.

The inability to conceive of "dialogical" relations such as the one I have just noted has been described by the French philosopher Edgar Morin (1994) with the term "disjunctive thought," an oppositional way of thinking that he finds to be "simple" rather than "complex." Not only is this "simple" or oppositional view of "what is" partial, but it closes off possibilities for "what could be" (for instance, working on creating a more generative, supportive, and "creativogenic" environment).

The more complex dialogical alternative replaces the mutually exclusive positions and oppositions created by technological knowing and disjunctive thought with a more generous understanding, one which recognizes that the dialogical dynamic that holds the two terms allows them to be not simply antagonistic, but also concurrent and complementary. For instance, the social forces of economics, politics, cultural trends, etc. can be antagonistic to, complementary with, and also concurrent with an artist's production.

Purser and I argue for the need to broaden our thinking with an approach that is dialogical, rather than disjunctive. Such an approach recognizes causal loops and mutual interrelation between, for example, the individual and society. We are in society and society is in us. Individual human beings cannot exist without society, and society cannot exist without individuals. If we attempt to "think" one without the other, believing that we must do so to avoid falling into a vicious circle, we will inevitably face frustrations and the opposition of positions, as described in TSK. If, on the other hand, we view the dialogical process as leading to a potentially "virtuous circle," we can embrace both terms, inasmuch as they define each other.

Another step in making this shift involves the recognition of a plurality of epistemologies or positions, each expressing knowledge in different times and space, each in different ways. All such epistemologies entail a certain focal setting, and each presents certain possibilities for knowledge and closes off others. For example, the possible approaches to creativity include the genetic, the personality-based, the cognitive, and the social-psychological.

As Ceruti (1994, 86) states:

In the classical epistemological perspective, which until very recently dominated the entire scientific-epistemological context, . . . concepts were always defined in reference to a privileged observation point to which it was believed all the various points of view could be reduced. The rejection of a fundamental point is exactly what characterizes the epistemological turning-point we are examining. What appears fundamental is not a single point of observation, but the narrative composed of various relationships. This narrative is continually defined and redefined between an irreducible multiplicity of observation and explanation points. Nature and the function of concepts such as information, chance, organization, etc., appear ever more clearly as being relative and intrinsic to the relationship among the system or domain considered, the methodological perspectives through which it is constituted, and the point of view, level, and subject of observation.

Such a pluralistic, dialogical, complex knowledge can express itself in dialogue rather than merely in debate: in open, creative inquiry rather than restrictive attempts at finding one right and true position to impose on the world. It invites us to entertain an idea, explore its edges, and explore the very knowledge which makes it possible, even as this knowledge explores its positioning and repositioning.

Creative Inquiry

In all this, our more fundamental goal is to promote a different spirit of inquiry entirely. We would like to encourage a way of going into the phenomenon itself, one which is more open to the different spaces and times, and the different knowledge, of creativity.

For instance, must we adopt or accept the popular focal setting that leads us to view the 'act' of creativity as a phenomenon which occurs in a lightning flash (time) inside the brain of a single person (space)? Or can we take into account the history of the person's inquiry into the subject and the role of interactions, friendships, arguments, etc.? Can we see our American, late-twentieth century view of creativity as the result of a specific interaction of knowledge in time and space, with the possibility that different time/space/knowledge interactions in different times and different cultures could lead to different discourses and practices of creativity? Here too I see our efforts as linked to the TSK vision. As Tarthang Tulku states (LOK, 13):

Reflecting on the vast array of knowledge that has already unfolded in history awakens an appreciation for what knowledge has to offer humanity. Our current way of knowing, rich and vivid as it is, may reflect only a single narrow wavelength of the full spectrum of knowledge.

The shifting flow of knowledge throughout history attracts little interest in contemporary culture, where the rapid rate of change makes past knowledge seem irrelevant. The resultant lack of historical perspective exacts a price. A narrow view of the past limits our understanding of the present and restricts our ability to foresee the future.

Indeed, broadening our knowledge of creativity as a phenomenon in time and space by drawing on understandings of creativity that have emerged in other spaces (Japan, Africa) and other times (pre-modern, modern, etc.) can challenge us to explore both the possibilities and the constraints created by our own discourse and practices.

My real question is this: As we conduct such explorations, can we engage in a collective dialogue, a collaborative inquiry that does not involve holding on to oppositional positions and developing oppositional identities, but allows us instead to entertain different positions and explore the very structure of oppositions? Having taken one position, can we then take other positions and see how they shed a different light on the phenomenon? Can we let go of our attachment to being "right," and explore what's left? Even if we do not agree with others, can we go beyond the desire to impose our position, and "entertain" other views? Can our knowledge cultivate the capacity for greater spaciousness, inclusiveness, and diversity?

What is needed here is a process of inquiry which involves the constant questioning of our assumptions and those of others, an inquiry which suspends immediate judgment, the exaggeration or obliteration of differences, and hierarchical classification. In the TSK mode, our aim is to approach all positions lightly and playfully, with an openness which permits ambiguities, complexities, and uncertainties, and allows the widest possible range of ideas to arise. For it is these very uncertainties, these ambiguities (which adversarial discourse would pounce upon as weaknesses), that seem to me the source of creativity.

As Morin (1994) has pointed out, complex thought is thought that does not reject, eliminate, or homogenize differences, ambiguities, uncertainties, and noise, but feeds on them. It views limits to knowledge as possibilities rather than obstacles. The TSK vision tells us that inquiry itself, proceeding in this way, can foster creativity by embracing the unknown. On the other hand, if one already knows the positions one wants to defend, the unknown will be seen as a fundamental threat to the rightness of our position—a failure to impose on others and also on ourselves. Surely in that case nothing new can come in. No innovation will be possible, apart from the kind of instrumental innovation which emerges as we find a new way of defending our position or challenging those of others. No dialogue is possible, and also no dialogical linking of ideas. This is the path of inquiry as war, and Tarthang Tulku has pointed to its consequences (TSK, 233):

[F]rom among the various criticisms made of ordinary knowledge, the most objectionable feature of the 'minding' and 'belief structure' trend [is that] it does not allow a meaningful and positive critique of itself to be made. Therefore, *it does not readily allow new perspectives to shine through.* Although there may be nothing wrong with beliefs and concepts in themselves, if they constitute the only way we know of being, they become a trap. They proliferate and interlock until no alternative to them is even visible. They amount to massive solicitations of our attention, keeping us 'tuned in' in a very constrictive way. [emphasis in original]

The TSK vision suggests a different approach to positions, conditions, and opposition (LOK, 271–72):

The labels and ideas that structure experience will naturally also shape and guide our questioning. But recognized as labels and ideas, they lose their power to confine the range of inquiry, and instead become elements available for investigation. . . . For inquiry to operate freely, it cannot be bound by the 'positions' that the 'bystander' adopts. This does not necessarily mean, however, that those positions must be rejected. Indeed, it is not clear that it would be possible to reject one set of positions without adopting another. Inquiry is free only if it allows for a way of knowing more fundamental than 'rejection'.

A position is the outcome of an act of positioning, which unfolds in time through discrete acts of distinguishing, knowing, and so forth. Seen in this light, positions are expressions of knowledge, rather than structures that limit it. Instead of accepting the viewpoint of the 'bystander', which insists on its fixed positions situated at a point off-center from an imagined origin, we could see in positioning the manifestation of a knowing that is not itself situated or specified.

The spirit of inquiry TSK invites is quite different from—and indeed shocking to—the predominant view of knowledge as instrumental (LOK, 306):

Inquiry can also proceed from an intention that has nothing to do with the 'needs' and 'concerns' of 'the one who questions'. The questions 'we' ask can arise out of wonder and the love of knowledge.

Intrinsic to this understanding is the recognition that

The attitudes we adopt in carrying out our investigation shape the attributes we find in the world we investigate (LOK, 307).

TSK invites a fundamentally different way of approaching knowledge:

Suppose that problems were understood as part of a global 'read-out' that expressed the result of a certain kind of knowing being in effect. Whatever its 'contents', as a read-out it would reveal this fundamental knowing as the source of a remarkable creativity (KTS, 262).

Knowing limits as limits, we know them also as knowledge. Aware of the mind as the one that affirms limits, we can ask whether mind too is knowledge. If so, knowledge becomes freely available in a previously unsuspected way. Self-sufficient, self-reliant, and dynamic, the mind expresses knowledge not as content but as capacity. (KTS, 327)

What does it mean to view knowledge as a capacity rather than content? Knowledge as content, the mode with which are familiar, comes in a variety of forms. It can be information, data, or facts and figures. In these various guises, knowledge is the "meat and potatoes" of our educational system. When we aim at this kind of knowledge exclusively, we wind up with what Paulo Freire (1973) has called the "banking" metaphor of education. Knowledge in the form of useful facts and so forth, is "stored" in learners, who then make a "withdrawal" whenever they need to use this information to perform a particular task. As we can see, this is not unlike the "tool" approach.

But knowledge as content is also knowledge as models, maps, and theories. At this level, the content of knowledge "shapes" the choice and use of knowledge. And it does so especially by insisting that knowledge is confined to content. Knowledge that knows knowledge in this way leads to a demand for knowledge that is pre-packaged and "ready-to-use." In the end, it gives knowledge as a tool, with all the limits we have explored above.

Now let us consider knowledge as capacity. Seen in this light, knowledge is freely available as the very essence of inquiry. When knowledge expresses capacity, we gain more knowledge through the ongoing inquiry into the very nature of the knowledge we are "using." As part of this process of inquiry, we can explore the way our knowing is shaped into content, with conditions, positions, oppositions, and impositions. Yet we do not have to invest in those positions; we do not have to "bank" on them.

Tarthang Tulku speaks of such a knowledge as the love of knowledge. He invites a knowing in which different understandings and positions are all viewed as expressions of knowledge, rather than as either "correct" or "incorrect" reflections of reality. Each such position involves certain constraints and certain possibilities—opening up a certain "focal setting," bringing certain kinds of knowing into focus while obscuring others. Notions of "correct" and "incorrect," "true" and "false" and "error" all take on different meanings. Instead of facing challenges, victories, and defeats, instead of deviating from our position or maintaining it, we find that each new situation becomes a source of knowledge, an opportunity.

Viewing knowledge as a capacity allows us to recognize our own capacity for knowing and inquiry without immediately having to reach for a model, tool, or theory. To use a musical metaphor, we no longer have to search for the right score, the right composition to play, the right model or theory to fit the object in front of us. Instead, we can improvise.

When we are always inquiring into the time and space of knowledge, subject and object unite in the performance. We can embrace each scale, all possible harmonies. They all become "licks." By taking our models and theories and tools "as if" they were "real," we can let go of them. Now we are free to explore them without attachment. In time we recognize that even when we thought we were following the score religiously, we were already improvising, but doing so unawares.

Improvising knowledge leads naturally toward collaboration as well. We steadily create possibilities for and with our colleagues, which in turn leads to choices which generate further possibilities, and also new constraints. Yet as we choose to go down one road rather than another, each new constraint can be the source of new inquiry, once more generating new possibilities as we explore its edges and the knowledge it embodies in space and time. In this way, an ongoing process of creative inquiry can be developed. Positions can be "entertained" together, explored and investigated in the knowledge that they are indeed positions, recognizing their oppositions as a further source of knowledge rather than an impediment to be removed. Creating a generative context for new possibilities, we express the challenge of a love of knowledge.

Perhaps I have come closer to putting into words this basic goal and project and the questions it generates. How can we foster a love of knowledge, and the conditions for the love of knowledge? What might the generative context be like that allows love of knowledge to shine through? How might an inquiry into social creativity itself be an example of social creativity? Perhaps at this point I could develop a model for doing so, but (no great surprise), that is not what I will do. Instead, let me close by suggesting that the inquiry itself will involve a plurality of narratives. These narratives are created in the telling—in the exchange created by listening, learning, and participating in the love of knowledge.

NOTES

1. Brainstorming, the closest thing we have to a social creativity "technique," involves keeping quiet while others are speaking, and not judging or critiquing their suggestions. The implication here is that in a group, we can be creative not through the interaction, but if anything by eliminating interaction. For an alternative view, see D. Bohm, *On Dialogue*. New York: Routledge. 1996.

2. This kind of oppositional thinking can become so extreme that it turns into what it hates, in what Jung called "enantiodromia." A humorous example is a recent advertisement for Coors beer which proclaims the drinker to be a "true individual," and then adds that 7 out of 10 drinkers who expressed a preference choose Coors. We end up with a situation where one can be an "individual" just like everybody else—indeed, precisely because one is like everybody else.

3. "Oppositional" identity defines itself in opposition to that which it is historically trying to differentiate itself from, and moves further and further away from the "opposing position." Any attempt at reconciliation—for instance, investigating creativity by taking into account both personality factors and social fac-

tors—is viewed as a challenge to the established position. Thus, when Purser and I published a piece on these issues in the *Journal of Humanistic Psychology,* we were immediately criticized as being "social determinists," despite our great efforts to state otherwise.

4.   This can also be traced to the specific fact that in American culture creativity has generally been assigned to the domain of psychology, with the result that little research on the subject has been forthcoming from sociologists.

REFERENCES

Ceruti, M. 1994. *Constraints and Possibilities.* [Il vincolo e la possibilitá. trans. from the Italian by Alfonso Montuori] New York: Gordon & Breach.

Freire, P. 1973. *The Pedagogy of the Oppressed.* In J. Ogilvy, ed. *Self and World,* pp. 438–51. New York: Harcourt, Brace, Jovanovich.

Kuhn, T. 1970. *The Structure of Scientific Revolutions.* Chicago: University of Chicago Press.

Montuori, A. and Purser, R., eds. 1997. *Social Creativity, vol. 1. Prospects and Possibilities.* Cresskill, NJ: Hampton Press.

Morin, E. 1994. *La complexité humaine.* Paris: Seuil.

Ogilvy. J. 1992. "Beyond Individualism and Collectivism." In J. Ogilvy, ed. *Revisioning Philosophy.* Albany, NY: State Univerisity of New York Press.

Skinner, B.F. 1971. *Beyond Freedom and Dignity*. New York: Bantam.

Slater, P. 1991. *A Dream Deferred*. Boston: Beacon.

Stewart, E.C., & Bennett, M.J. 1991. *American Cultural Patterns. A Cross-Cultural Perspective* (revised edition). Yarmouth, Maine: Intercultural Press.

Toffler, A. 1973. *Future Shock*. New York: Bantam

Watts, A. 1966. *The Book: On the Taboo Against Knowing Who You Are*. New York: Vintage.

Whyte, W.F. 1957. *The Organization Man*. New York: Anchor.

Wilber, K. 1980. *The Atman Project*. Wheaton, IL: Quest.

EPISTEMOLOGY IN PARADISE: THE SPATIAL EMBODIMENT OF KNOWLEDGE AND VALUE

Alan Malachowski

> *Sitting on the curbstone, looking at the sky, thinking: Where did it all come from? Why was I here? Epistemological questions. Of course that's how many philosophers nowadays like to handle such questions: essentially as childlike epistemology.*
>
> *Saul Bellow*

The Primacy of The Epistemological

Although the intellectual culture of the West currently enjoys an unprecedented wealth of knowledge, it is also burdened by what the philosopher Charles Taylor (1993, 208) calls "the primacy of the epistemological." By this he means "the tendency to think out the question of what something *is* in terms of the question of how it is *known*." This "pervasive feature of modern intellectual culture" is burdensome because, in putting the epistemological squeeze on traditional knowledge claims, it has generated an unhealthy, *skeptical* climate—one in which historically richer opportunities for intellectual growth and understanding have been stifled by 'subjectivism', 'relativism', and the like.[1]

Taylor maintains that the 'primacy of the epistemological' has produced particularly enervating results in the case of *morality*, where its relentless demands have precipitated a retreat into 'emotivism'—the conviction that evaluative judgements are nothing more than expressions of personal feelings.[2] There is now, he tells us, a "widespread belief that moral positions cannot be argued, that moral differences cannot be arbitrated by reason, that when it comes to moral values, we all just ultimately have to plump for the ones which feel/seem best to us" (1993, 208). Taylor has made concerted efforts to put epistemological considerations back in their proper (i.e. less dominant) place (cf. Taylor 1987). But perhaps even he underestimates the weight of the cultural burden they impose.

The tradition of 'epistemological primacy' Taylor alludes to operates by indiscriminately subjecting *all* knowledge claims to strict tests of *epistemological adequacy*. Claims which fail to negotiate these hurdles forfeit any right to play a substantial role in the culture of thought. Hence, epistemology comes to hold sway over ontology, and the public conception of 'being' shrinks accordingly.

Exact formulation of these 'adequacy tests' remains a matter of intense technical debate, but the main thrust of the sort of requirements involved can be expressed by saying that all knowledge claims must:

(a)   rest on a foundation of sound evidence which entails their truth (or else slot smoothly into an appropriate network of suitably supportive, evidentially relevant, claims);[3]

(b)   derive from clearly explicable mechanisms of knowledge acquisition.

Under this regime, a satisfactory knowledge claim has to come ready-packaged with good reasons for believing it to be true (The Evidence Requirement) and a perspicuous mode of cognitive and/or social access to its truth (The Transparency of Acquisition Requirement). Thus, for example, if someone claims to *know* that chemical C cures disease D, that claim will only be rendered epistemologically adequate by the provision of suitable evidence for its truth and an explicit account as to how its truth can be ascertained.

Although they appear to be eminently reasonable, such demands for 'evidence' and 'transparency of acquisition' can be very destructive. On the face of it, many deeply revered, traditional claims to knowledge fail to satisfy them, especially where values are concerned. Here we might think of the difficulties in specifying both strong supporting evidence and 'clearly explicable mechanisms of knowledge acquisition' for certain moral and religious claims, claims about the existence of natural rights, and so forth, as well as for innovative or

'non-ordinary' knowledge claims, such as those discussed in Donald Beere's article in this volume.

Those philosophers and kindred intellectual spirits
who have guided epistemology to its present com-
manding height tend to be sanguine about such
destructive consequences. In their view, knowledge
claims *need to be reflectively robust under conditions
of epistemological scrutiny*. That is just a brute fact of
modern intellectual life. If a traditional claim (e.g.
"God is the all-perfect creator of our world") fails the
adequacy tests, then so be it.

This epistemological ruthlessness now seems oblig-
atory. Once the genie of sophisticated epistemological
reflection pops out of the mind (so that when confront-
ed by a claim to knowledge it becomes *natural* for us to
press questions like "On what grounds *should* we
believe that?" and "How *do* we know that?") it is
impossible to put back. Under its gaze, any defense of
a traditional claim which flunks the tests for adequacy
is going to look like anachronistic special pleading.[4]

The Counter-Epistemologists

*Philosophy as it has long been practiced
in this culture . . . teaches or assumes that
human beings have become cut off from
knowledge, that knowledge must somehow be 'obtained' or 'recovered'. . . . Once
that structure is accepted, restraints
upon knowing multiply.* (LOK, 368)

Intellectual life, indeed culture in general, cannot thrive unless some traditional claims to knowledge are banished to the epistemological wilderness from time to time. Epistemological revision plants the seeds of progress and keeps the soil of thought fertile. However, there are those who challenge the circumstances through which modern theorists of knowledge seem fated to win out *whenever* they force otherwise respected traditionalists to play by the rules of the 'adequacy game'.

These thinkers—call them 'counter-epistemologists'—contend that the game is rigged. It is 'rigged' because it presupposes that the human condition is *inherently a condition of epistemological estrangement*. On their counter-epistemological understanding, the very attitudes which foster the creation and setting into place of the adequacy tests cut human agents off from traditional sources of knowledge and value, thus causing deep fissures in the web of their being. In other words, epistemological primacy is a significant 'cause of', rather than 'response to', estrangement.

Critiques of the 'estrangement presupposition' date back at least to Hegel. According to one prominent commentator (Solomon 1983, 286), Hegel believed it incorporated an insidious

> spatial metaphor [of] the mind as a mysterious realm in which there are experiences and beyond which are physical objects 'in themselves' [which gives rise to skepticism].

Later, but in a similar vein, Nietzsche criticized "the logical-metaphysical postulates" which foster the subject/object dichotomy at the very heart of 'epistemological estrangement' (Nietzsche 1968, 297):

> It is only on the model of the subject that we have invented the reality of things and projected them into the medley of sensations.

Following closely in Nietzsche's philosophical footsteps, Heidegger heavily satirized the thinking that "allows epistemology to command ontology" (Taylor 1990, 264), thereby engendering the 'epistemological gap' which leads to estrangement (Heidegger 1962, 89):

> The perceiving of what is known is not a process of returning with one's booty to the 'cabinet' of consciousness after one has gone out and grasped it.

A full account of the 'counter-epistemologists' would run on through Foucault to Derrida, Rorty, and Charles Taylor himself (cf. Taylor 1990). Some would argue that it culminates in recent feminist 'unmaskings' of 'masculine ideas' behind the knowledge-thin self of 'estrangement' (witness the 'epistemically-depleted' self that is left standing at the end of Descartes' famous voyage of epistemological doubt in his *Meditations*).[5] Others would insist that such a story needs to make significant detours—it might, for instance, cover the Dewey-James-Peirce pragmatist tradition, Feyerabend's 'epistemological anarchy', the 'critical theory' of the Frankfurt School, or the naturalizing projects of Quine and Wittgenstein.

The positions which emerge from this narrative of 'counter-epistemology' are too diverse to subsume under the banner of a single 'oppositional tradition', but one move does unite the figures who inspired these positions. In addition to attacking the conventional theory of knowledge, they all tend to accuse their counter-epistemological predecessors of remaining captive to the spirit of 'epistemological primacy'. Hence the tag 'counter-epistemologists' is doubly apposite.

The Epistemological Predicament

Although the counter-epistemologists have developed some well-documented and powerful lines of negative argument and critique, their positive conceptions of knowledge have not yet rescued the West from one of its primary epistemological predicaments: Epistemology is culturally annihilative, but unavoidable.[6] The *hygenic* conception of knowledge that epistemological primacy enforces goes beyond cleansing society of superstition and mistaken or fraudulent knowledge claims; instead, it tends to *sterilize the whole of intellectual culture.* For this reason, the epistemologists appear to have the upper hand. Despite dire counter-epistemological warnings that the 'primacy game' is rigged, it is difficult, when pressed, to find legitimate reasons for exempting knowledge claims from the adequacy tests.

The rationale for these tests seems compelling: Why *should* any claim to knowledge be excused from evidential support and/or be granted the premise of acquisitional opacity? Nonetheless, in many important cases the application of such tests causes total paralysis or, at best, epistemological inertia and a moribund ontology. This is why it was earlier intimated that perhaps even an astute and vociferous critic of epistemological primacy such as Charles Taylor underestimates its cultural burden.

Knowledge and Value Embodied

The objects of knowledge do not 'approach' us, nor must we journey 'somewhere else'. For it is in the nature of time, space and knowledge to be inseparable. As we come to embody space and time, knowledge is revealed as intrinsic to the nature of all being.   *(LOK, 368)*

Because Tarthang Tulku shows us how to dismantle "the prevailing model of 'bystander-self' experiencing 'outsider-world'" (KTS, xvii), it is tempting to view him as a counter-epistemologist, as one more thinker who accuses predecessors of remaining captive to the spirit of 'epistemological primacy', and who is liable to be similarly accused at a later stage in the history of ideas. But to reach this conclusion would be a gross misappropriation.

One of the features which makes Tarthang Tulku's work on the Time, Space and Knowledge 'vision' (henceforth: TSK) so fresh and exciting is the fact that it engages creatively with more conventional philosophical conceptions of knowledge while remaining aloof from the obsessively narrow concerns of recent Western theorizing. This combination of 'engaged detachment' can lift epistemological inquiry to levels where the predicament just described drops away into irrelevance, along with the entire debate between epistemologists and counter-epistemologists. Given the grip that both the 'predicament' and the 'debate' continue to exert, it is worthwhile trying to clarify just *how* Tarthang Tulku's 'visionary' approach to knowledge and values breaks new ground.

First, we need to be clear about what TSK does not set out to do. It does not seek to 'break new ground' by *refuting* or *replacing* contentions which are internally essential to the 'primacy' outlook on knowledge. TSK moves completely beyond the confines of such contentions. In this sense, TSK is akin to the radical 'revisions' advocated by the counter-epistemologists. But there is a vital difference. Despite their professed 'radicalism', the counter-epistemologists tend to compete with the epistemologists on their own territory. Hence they tend to share at least some of the assumptions underlying 'primacy'.

TSK appears to share none of these assumptions. It speaks the language of the 'epistemologists' and 'counter-epistemologists' not to 'refute', 'correct', 'modify' or even 'improve' their positions; it speaks in this way as a *benign gesture of communication* whereby it aims to draw attention to the beneficent opportunities for 'knowledge-and-value-beyond-estrangement' that it embraces.

The 'estrangement' that derives from epistemological primacy is a condition of *threefold* alienation:

(i) it removes us from many 'external' sources of knowledge/value which have sustained us in the past (mentors [voices of 'authority' and 'wisdom'], custom, ritual, art forms, etc.);

(ii) it obliterates many of the traditional 'internal' sources of knowledge/value (conscience, introspection, contemplation, dreams, visions, etc.);

(iii) it distances us from 'being' by narrowing down the ontological options to what can be relied on under conditions of estrangement.

We have already seen that the 'adequacy requirements' imposed by epistemological primacy drastically thin out the 'external sources', but they have an even more devastating effect on both 'internal sources' and 'being'. Take a fundamental example: human consciousness. Modern theory of knowledge considers consciousness to be 'radically non-epistemic'.[7] *In its own right*, consciousness has no epistemically important contents or capacities.

As to the contents of consciousness, these lack epistemic worth, because they become 'unstable' under the application of normal verification procedures. The argument runs as follows:

If consciousness suggests that something is the case *solely* on the basis of what it discerns in its own domain, how can consciousness know this to be the case without appealing to 'external resources'? (Suppose consciousness takes P to be true under the previously described conditions, how can it establish the truth of P without call-

ing up further mental representations or whatever? But, if it does appeal to additional mental
phenomena, how can it establish *their* epistemic
credentials?) 'Internal' (i.e. mental) verification
is thus either regressive or viciously circular.[8]

'Capacities' are likewise given short shrift, because
they yield no significant epistemic results: When human
beings reflect on, or in other ways *internally* examine,
their own consciousness, this creates no avenues of
'privileged access' to knowledge. By the same token,
consciousness is deemed to possess no special *ontological* status, and no unique connection with 'being'. On
this understanding, a person who attempts to take up a
stance of self-nourishment with regard to the native
contents and capacities of his or her own mind is
doomed to a starvation diet of self-deceit. Tarthang
Tulku expresses the ruling thought here (LOK, 39–40):

> With objective' modes of knowing active in the
> foreground, knowledge that is considered 'only'
> subjective is denied any ultimate significance.

By contrast, TSK invokes an epistemically-enlivened
notion of the human mind. It opens up what might best
be called 'the epistemic space within consciousness'
(Malachowski, forthcoming), and in doing so reveals a
tripartite antidote to the effects of estrangement:

New sources of knowledge

New relationships to knowledge

New kinds of knowledge

New Sources of Knowledge

When TSK 'opens up the epistemic space within consciousness', it does so *phenomenologically*. This is a controversial breakthrough. With its emphasis on 'public criteria for knowledge', its preference for 'objectivity' over 'subjectivity' and its radically non-epistemic perception of consciousness, the Western tradition excludes the very possibility of a purely *phenomenological solution* to its epistemological predicament. However, Tarthang Tulku's writings do not merely present philosophical arguments which encourage the reader to *believe* in the existence of new sources of knowledge that would thwart this exclusion process; rather, they enable the reader to *experience* those sources *by actually entering the appropriate space within consciousness.*[9] In *that space*, phenomena which are ordinarily credited no epistemic importance *as mental phenomena* (e.g. 'appearances', 'mental events', 'time', and 'space itself') do yield knowledge.

Each of these 'new sources' for knowledge receives careful, illuminating attention in the TSK writings. For present purposes, we will focus on the intriguing epistemic connections between the 'space-within-consciousness' and 'space itself'.

The concept of 'space itself' has become epistemically problematic in Western philosophy. On the whole, the problems concerned are unrecognized, glossed over, or ignored,[10] which may be just as well, because as things stand there appear to be no conceivable resources for dealing with them. Here is a brief example of how the concept of space causes problems:

(i)   Physical objects are 'space-demanders' (their existence requires an appropriate space);

(ii) (i) entails the temporal (and ontological) priority of space over objects;

(iii) Space is empty; *a fortiori* it is epistemically empty (it contains nothing for knowledge claims to get a fix on);

(iv) From (i)–(iii): the existence of objects in space is impossible to explain. Space is epistemically inert—hence there is nothing we can know about space to show how objects can enter it. Stuck at the level of epistemically stagnant space, our explanations can never reach the level which incorporates 'objects-in-space'.

Such fundamental difficulties suggest that the concept of space is *epistemically underdefined*. Moreover, when *consciousness* is brought into the picture, these difficulties increase. Leaving aside the 'verificationist' motivation mentioned above, the 'radically non-epistemic' interpretation of consciousness trades on an analogy with a non-epistemic understanding of 'space itself'. *Consciousness itself* is epistemically empty because *it is akin to space*, which contains nothing for knowledge claims to latch on to. Again Tarthang Tulku has put the latter point clearly (KTS, 149):

Space seems to lack all properties, so how can it be known? The activities of observation, measurement, and identification that knowing relies on have no application to space.

However, the concept of space cannot sustain such an analogy because, as the difficulties raised by (i)–(iv) in the 'space-demanders argument' above demonstrate, 'standard' space is an *underperformer* in epistemic terms. Moreover, the intensely problematic relation between 'mental space' and 'space itself' vitiates any *space-based* conjectures as to the lack of epistemic resources in consciousness. To point to a single issue, it is widely held that 'mental space' is not situated *in* space itself. This assumption not only raises the thorny question as to where mental space resides and how it *interacts* with a spatially-situated world, but, as Colin McGinn rightly observes (1995, 223), it also raises profound issues about the 'origin' and 'constitution' of consciousness:

> How could it (i.e. consciousness) have had its origin in the spatial world? . . . We seem compelled to conclude that something essentially non-spatial emerged from something purely spatial—that the non-spatial is somehow a construction out of the spatial.

The upshot of these unresolved issues is that current Western philosophical understanding of 'space itself' and its relation to consciousness needs a major overhaul. It is therefore in no shape to press home its instinctive *prima facie* objections of 'epistemic vacuousness' (to reiterate: consciousness is radically non-epistemic and space has no epistemic properties) against *TSK-inspired* exploration of the following innovative ideas (we leave aside discussion of any possible 'value counterparts'):

Consciousness itself embodies epistemic space.

Consciousness itself possesses epistemic capacities and properties.

Space itself has unrealized epistemic potential.

The epistemic space within consciousness can 'realize' the epistemic potential of space itself.

New Relationships to Knowledge

To activate we must envision, and to envision we must inhabit. Dwelling in knowledge, we counter the knowledge scarcity so characteristic of our time. We give knowledge access to our being, our actions, and our world. (VOK, 63)

When it manages to venture beyond the barriers of skepticism and accepts that knowledge is possible, the Western epistemological tradition vacillates between passive and aggressive accounts of knowledge acquisition. Sometimes it emphasizes the way in which the world carves knowledge into the mind with 'innate ideas' or 'sensory impingements'. Sometimes it stresses the way in which the human agent carves up the world in order to extract knowledge from it.

TSK brings into play a more even-handed approach. The process of 'coming to know' is an inherently dynamic process, but its 'dynamism' does not depend on aggressive acts of individual will, and it is balanced by a 'receptive gentleness' in overall approach. To enter 'the epistemic space of consciousness' and contact 'new sources of knowledge', it is necessary to set aside self-regarding epistemic ambitions and attempts to beat the 'external environment' into epistemic shape. TSK suggests that 'entry' requires more sensitive, *contemplative* methods. We can best enact these by starting from first base; that is by "fully inhabiting the situation we find ourselves in" (DTS, 211) and "looking with fresh vision upon our 'familiar' world" (LOK, 46).

When we take up 'residence-without-preconditions' in our present experiential situation, "we can loosen self-existence and open knowledge to presence" (DTS, 187). Then 'new', unforced and much 'closer' relationships to 'new sources of knowledge' are liable to evolve naturally. As we relax and feel more at home in all aspects of our present experience, *appreciation* of that experience tends to increase, even where its surface features are forbidding (as in illness, confusion, sorrow, or depression). Such appreciation unveils an 'appearance/reality' distinction *within experience* (e.g. 'pain' does not turn out to have the 'fixed essence' of the unpleasant 'sensation of pain'). This in turn, activates an *intimacy* with deeper epistemic dimensions of our being ("appreciation is the bridge between old ways of being and new possibilities" [VOK, 64]).

Ultimately 'appreciative dwelling' allows us to embody the 'epistemic heart' of being itself, while savoring its value *from the inside*. The ethical importance of this new ('insider's') *ontological take* on value has been recognized by Arnaud Pozin (MOM, 50):

In emphasizing the knowing dimension of reality, TSK invites us to restore respect and appreciation for reality as being. There are sound ethical consequences to this positioning. . . . We could say that the main part of 'human imposed' suffering comes from a failure to respect reality as being.

New Kinds of Knowledge

For someone who has not sympathetically explored TSK, the previous discussion of 'new sources of knowledge' and 'new relationships to knowledge' is unlikely to have raised more than the barest *theoretical* possibility that Tarthang Tulku's TSK writings have broken new epistemological ground. Hence, it would be gratifying, at this stage, to simply serve up a concrete example of a 'new piece of knowledge' which is uniquely 'TSK-derived knowledge'. However, the kinds of knowledge TSK invokes cannot be served up in this way. TSK-knowledge is not an 'end product' which can be viewed in isolation from the contemplative processes which enable us to 'embody' it.

This is not 'philosophical avoidance', nor 'sleight of hand'. TSK-knowledge appears to be *phenomenological in essence*. To a certain extent, it can be 'described', and we can be pointed in its direction, but its true nature is *non-propositional*. It *has to be experienced* (though, given that experience itself opens up beyond its normal surface 'felt qualities', this claim takes on a special meaning).

In *Dynamics of Time and Space*, Tarthang Tulku enhances the conception of knowledge depicted in the TSK writings by exploring the relationship between knowledge and light. The discusion is subtle, complex, and wide-ranging, but it can be divided into two parts. First, in a speculative mode, it muses on the prospect of discovering "a secret kind of biology of luminosity" (205) or even "a cosmology of light" (211). Tarthang Tulku's remarks in this connection are tentative, and because they are pitched at a high level of abstraction and generality, they are difficult to square with more orthodox notions of 'biology' and 'cosmology'. Nevertheless, they furnish a tantalizing hint of the kind of 'knowledge-as-light' which might accrue from a future TSK-instigated 'science-beyond-science'.

The second significant part of this discussion provides some evocative—at times almost poetic—descriptions of the "self-luminosity of awakened awareness" (207) that emerges when knowledge and value are 'embodied'. These descriptions of "luminous inward knowledge"—"knowledge that reveals the luminosity of being [and] bears within itself its own luminous shining" (215)—give *some* 'taste' of *what it is like* to "become light—a vastness light without words or names" (213)—and thereby embody TSK-knowledge. They also show why the embodiment of TSK-knowledge brings in its wake a deeply *appreciative* connection to the intrinsic value of all being.

Tarthang Tulku paints a familiarly haunting picture of life which *fails* to embody 'knowledge-as-light':

As thought stumbles along in the darkened arena it has constructed, making guesses as to what must be so, it only manufactures more darkness. Out of the lengthening shadows, a

host of voices emanates, mumbling and com-
plaining, accusing and explaining, chattering or
rambling, or making shrill demands. Untraceable
and unowned, their steady murmur becomes the
background of our being (DTS, 210).

Nevertheless, he acknowledges that to contrast this
'dark life' with a 'light-informed' existence may cut little ice with those who have no experiential inkling of
"what it means to embody light" (205). They may
question the 'realism' of the TSK rhetoric:

Perhaps this sounds like words without substance, descriptions cut loose from experience.
What does such light have to do with the light
we awaken to each morning? (205).

Tarthang Tulku replies with a straightforward practical suggestion. For when words fail to convey the
nature of TSK-knowledge, we can be guided back to the
source of that knowledge:

The answer will not come on the level of ideas.
The best reply is: Mind is available. Look directly there, without preconception or precon-
ceived limitation (DTS, 212).

The 'knowingness' that TSK engages does not
negate or provide a substitute for 'propositional knowledge'. It can, however, help dispel the philosophical
mystique which surrounds this sort of knowledge. For
the 'propositional craving' so characteristic of the
Western epistemological tradition is largely a product
of the philosophical hallucination of 'estrangement'.
Western culture's response to this imagined state of

exile (i.e. from knowledge) has been to invest virtually all its intellectual resources in what Heidegger aptly called 'calculative thinking' (*rechnende Denken*). This thinking deploys information-based knowledge (i.e. propositions *about* reality) to extract and control the scarce resources of nature in the service of individual desires (cf. Foltz 1995). In his discussion of 'technological knowledge' (DTS, 169; 159), Tarthang Tulku echoes Heidegger:

> Space is filled up with the structures adopted by technological knowing. . . . Intent on manipulating its world, the self relies on methods for knowing that promote a sense of mastery: logic, measurement, rhetoric, machinery.

However, TSK allows us to inhabit dimensions of knowing within which the frenetic, self-centered concerns of calculative/technological thinking pale into insignificance. When knowledge and value are embodied, all forms of scarcity vanish. In the whole-hearted dance of the light of being, an epistemology of paradise unfolds. Manipulation of oneself, the environment, and others is no longer necessary or desirable:

> Manifesting in the contact of heart to mind and being to knowledge, light gives freedom of mind beyond all imagination. Immaculate and indestructible, diamond light offers universal illumination, communicating the wholeness of love and compassion. The gods can only be jealous.
>
> (DTS, 208)

NOTES

1.   Unfortunately, Taylor does not resist universaliz-ing what is characteristic of modern *Western* culture. One 'pervasive feature' of the epistemological tradition in that culture is the tendency to hide the parochial nature of its concerns beneath the rhetoric of 'univer-sal concerns'.

2.   Cf. MacIntyre 1981, 11–12: "Emotivism is the doc-trine that all evaluative judgements and more specifi-cally, all moral judgements are nothing but expressions of preferences, expressions of attitude or feeling."

3.   These conditions cater for both the 'foundational-ist' and 'coherence' approaches to knowledge which now exhaust the options for 'Western epistemologists'.

4.   For penetrating observations on the destructive consequences of theoretical reflection, see Williams (1985). And for some interesting remarks on whether reflection can destroy knowledge, see Altham (1995). Finally, consider this semi-lighthearted remark by David Lewis (1996): "Maybe epistemology is the culprit. Maybe this extraordinary pastime robs us of knowledge. Maybe we do know a lot in daily life; but maybe when we look hard at our knowledge it goes away."

5.   Cf. Nicholson (1990; esp. Part One: "Feminism As Against Epistemology"); Anthony and Witt (1993).

6.   This claim is intended to leave open the question as to whether the counter-epistemologists actually have the resources to 'come to the rescue' here.

7.   The phrase is Ruth Millikan's (1993, 207), but it presumably derives from Hilary Putnam's characterization of truth as radically non-epistemic (Putnam 1983).

8.   This is a quick précis of Wittgenstein's influential objections to the very idea of 'private knowledge' (Wittgenstein 1968).

9.   The various 'exercises' Tarthang Tulku has devised for the TSK writings enable the reader to progress beyond the 'propositional link' (of 'belief') with new sources of knowledge. I do not discuss these here, but I hope to examine some of their philosophical implications on another occasion.

10.   For a notable exception, see McGinn (1995).

REFERENCES

Altham, J. "Reflection and Confidence." In *World, Mind, and Ethics: Essays on the Ethical Philosophy of Bernard Williams*. ed. J. Altham and R. Harrison. Cambridge: Cambridge University Press.

Anthony, L. and Witt, C., eds. 1993. *A Mind of One's Own: Feminist Essays on Reason and Objectivity*. Boulder: Westview Press.

Foltz, B. 1995. *Inhabiting The Earth: Heidegger, Environmental Ethics, And The Metaphysics Of Nature*. New Jersey. Humanities Press.

Heidegger, M. 1962. *Being and Time*. Oxford: Blackwell.

Lewis, D. "Elusive Knowledge." *Australasian Journal of Philosophy*, 74:4 (December 1996).

MacIntyre, A. 1981. *After Virtue*. London: Duckworth.

Malachowski. "The Epistemic Space Within Consciousness". *World Futures* (forthcoming).

_____. "Contemplative Reality." Forthcoming.

McGinn, C. 1995. "Consciousness and Space." *Journal of Consciousness Studies* 2:3.

Millikan, R. 1993 "Metaphysical Antirealism?" In *White Queen Psychology and Other Essays for Alice*. ed. R. Millikan. Cambridge, MA: MIT Press.

Nicholson, L., ed. 1990. *Feminism/Postmodernism*. New York: Routledge, Chapman and Hall.

Nietzsche, F. 1968. *The Will To Power*. Vintage: New York.

Putnam, H. 1983. *Reason, Truth, and History*, Cambridge: Cambridge University Press.

Solomon, R.C. 1983. *The Spirit of Hegel*. Oxford: Oxford University Press.

Taylor, C. 1987. "Overcoming Epistemology." In *After Philosophy*. ed. K. Baynes, J. Bohman and T. McCarthy. Cambridge, MA: MIT Press.

_____. 1990. "Rorty in the Epistemological Tradition." In *Reading Rorty*. ed. A.Malachowski. Oxford: Blackwell

_____. 1993. "Explanation and Practical Reason." In *The Quality of Life*, ed. M. Nussbaum and A. Sen. Oxford: Clarendon Press.

Williams, B. 1985. *Ethics and the Limits of Philosophy*. London: Fontana.

Wittgenstein, L. 1968. *Philosophical Investigations*. Oxford: Blackwell.

TURNING INWARD OUTWARD: TOWARD A PUBLIC SELF AND THE COMMON GOOD

Jack Petranker

The problem is always: How shall we understand ourselves as simultaneously both private and public beings?
Hanna Pitkin (1981)

We live in a world where the private self stands at the center of all experience and all possible ways of knowing. In some sense it has always been so, but today we seem committed to playing out the full consequences of such a view. The result is the problems that underlie the daily news: a social fabric torn to ribbons; tensions that foster hostility and escapism; a culture whose prevailing modes of discourse are consciously shaped to encourage what is superficial; and personal experience marked by anxiety, frustration, and a sense of emptiness.

The dominant responses to those troubled by these symptoms tend to fall into one of three camps. The first challenges the privileged position of the self, arguing that there are more fundamental sources of knowledge and values (for example, the shared values of a community or a tradition, the claims of classical rationalism, or the authority of revealed truth). Those who hold this view see their path clearly marked out before them; however, they have little to say to others who do not share their fundamental premises, and in a culturally diverse society their calls to restore (or create) a fixed set of values or way of seeing the world are inevitably met with distrust.[1]

The second approach affirms the continuing value of privileging the self. This is the conventional wisdom: 'liberalism' in a social and cultural sense rather than as a political stand. Taking the lack of transcendent or foundational knowledge as a given, liberalism maintains that we can aim no higher than to maximize the opportunity for each individual to pursue his or her own values; to seek out a personal version of what is true and meaningful. Without dismissing the importance of making such opportunities available, I think it fair to say that this view is precisely the one that leads to the dead end described in the opening paragraph.

The third approach agrees that we lack all access to any form of final truth, but rejects the search for such a truth on either the public or private level. Pointing to the dangers of oppression and domination that result whenever doctrines are affirmed at any level, it invites us to make of our lives a more playful project. The act of creating one's own world—provided one does not take the undertaking too seriously—offers the best hope for finding meaning and value.

Despite their strong differences, these three alternatives—let us call them communitarianism, liberalism, and postmodernism—seem to me to share a fundamental assumption: that the self is private in its very core. It is this assumption I question in the present essay. I will suggest that—despite our deeply ingrained beliefs to the contrary—the self does not have to be private at all; that it can learn to be public in its innermost way of being.

To situate the self in its own private realm is to make claims about how the self appears in space, acts in time, and comes to know. In the argument that follows, I will challenge these claims, arguing that the self can appear differently, act differently, and know differently. But for this to happen, we must call into question the very distinction between 'public' and 'private'.

PART I: BEING IN PRIVATE

[T]he condition of man . . . is a condition
of war of everyone against everyone.
    Thomas Hobbes

The first thinker to put the self at the center of his philosophic system, René Descartes, did so with the intention of founding a new basis for knowledge. Descartes determined to doubt whatever could be doubted, hoping in this way to arrive at that which could not be doubted. In short order, he doubted away the evidence of his senses, the reasoning of his mind, and the authority of the past. What he could not dismiss was that he was engaged in such a doubting. In this way, Descartes arrived at the famous *cogito*: I think, therefore I must exist.

The I that emerges from this course of doubting stands frail and unaccommodated, naked and alone— without a trustworthy identity, reliable knowledge, or defensible guides for conduct. It is born into the thinnest of thin air, suspended over the pit of nihilism and dark ignorance. To arrest its plunge into the abyss, Descartes offers three kinds of support. The first is the prevailing moral standards of the day, which Descartes adopts provisionally at the outset of his inquiry. The second is the rules of reason (which can guide all further inquiry, but only after they have been rendered immune to the corrosive acid of doubt). The third, and most important, is the self-evident existence of a beneficent deity, whose goodness assures that the self is not deceived in its fundamental perceptions, value judgments, and mental operations.

In the centuries following Descartes, the three legs of this tripod were each kicked away. Conventional morality, never more than a temporary accommodation to the need for guidance in how to act, collapsed of its own accord when asked to stand up to critical reason. The existence of God (more generally, the avail-

ablity of any source of ultimate truth and values)
seemed self-evident and indisputable to Descartes, but
not to later thinkers, and given the nature of the
Cartesian enterprise, to raise the doubt was enough to
destroy the certainty.

As for the role of reason, those who followed
Descartes found that when they turned inward to
investigate their own nature, they discovered a self
guided not by reason, but by desire. Following the logic
of that discovery, they put desire at the center of their
world, restricting the role of reason to an advisor offering clever counsel as to how the self's desires might
best be achieved. The point was made definitively by
David Hume in the century after Descartes: "Reason is
and ought only to be the slave of the passions."[2]

Sheltering the Self

If the self emerges into the world with no supports, it
must see to its own shelter and make its own order. A
few decades after Descartes, Thomas Hobbes addressed
this need. Since Hobbes accepted as fundamental the
desiring self intent on satisfying its own needs and
wants, he concluded that the natural state for human
beings was one of conflict, with each man out to
achieve his own aims. To rescue humanity from this
state of anarchy, he proposed creating Leviathan, the
great machine of government.

Both Hobbes' analysis of the human situation and
his solution to the difficulties it creates continue to
guide us today. Responding to the threat posed by the

self's unmoderated desires, modern states are founded on the principle of setting competing interests against each other, so that they cancel one another out (Wolin 1960, 388–93). Whether deliberately set in place (as in the checks and balances of government) or simply encouraged to operate (as in state-moderated capitalism), the conflicts fostered in this way ensure that no one group can gain sufficient power to impose its will permanently on others. With each force or interest competing against every other force or interest to have its way, the outcome is relative stability and some measure of civil order. Against this backdrop, the private individual is free to pursue privately determined ends and values.

The attitude toward the self which such arrangements reveal reflects a strange ambivalence. On the one hand, the chief purpose of creating such constructs as government is to safeguard and maximize the rights of the individual; on the other hand, the mechanisms for doing this are based on the felt necessity to neutralize the power of the individual. We celebrate the freedom of each member of society, but at the same time we regard one another with a sense of wary mistrust. Liberal democracy as an ideal is mingled with liberal democracy as the counsel of fear.

The distrust of the individual at work in such a model is clear to see in the dominant contemporary formulation of liberal democratic theory, John Rawl's *A Theory of Justice* (1971). Rawls suggests that the individuals who come together to form a society and establish its rules should operate from behind a "veil of ignorance." That is, they should structure society and its rules without knowing who they will be in the society after it has come into existence: what status or attributes they will possess and what role they will play. In effect, when they enter the legislative chambers, they leave their private selves parked outside. And this is the whole point. Ignorant of who they are and what they desire, they are forced to legislate for the good of all, and particularly for the welfare of the least privileged members of society.

This willfully chosen ignorance operates not only with regard to 'my personal qualities', but also with regard to what beliefs I accept. My moral or religious convictions, my values, my most cherished assumptions about what is true and false: All these are rejected as valid matters for consideration when it comes to framing the structures of a just society. For unless I am willing to profess ignorance regarding my beliefs as to what is true, I will inevitably seek to impose those beliefs on others, and this is precisely what liberal political thought aims to avoid.

Of course, the intention here is that excluding issues of truth from the sphere of public debate leaves individuals free to pursue and act on their convictions in private. Yet the consequences of imposing public ignorance with regard to such matters cannot be so easily restricted. Once ultimate truths and values are rejected as fitting topics for public discussion, their very legitimacy becomes suspect. As Tarthang Tulku has written (LOK, 33): "[When] issues of value and meaning fit into the subjective realm, they recede from view as possible subjects of knowledge or topics of public discourse. In such circumstances, what is meaningless comes to the fore by default."

Triumph of the Private

The strategy of willful ignorance that liberal democracy adopts with regards to questions of what is true or has value has today become a guiding principle—a truth of its own—in virtually every sphere of conduct. In our 'postmodern' age, we learn to maintain an "incredulity toward metanarratives" (Lyotard 1984, xxiv). No matter where we turn, there are simply no absolutes—not in religious matters, not in lifestyle, not even in the laboratory. The view that truth is made rather than found is woven into the very stuff of popular culture, repeated endlessly even in entertainments made for children. For better or worse, most of the leading forces that shape our culture, from multiculturalism and relativism to consumerism, hedonism, and escapism, can be understood as responses to this perception of the way things are.[3]

One consequence of the postmodern rejection of ultimate truths is that virtually every area of life become politicized, in the sense that all interactions are understood in terms of competing private and group interests. Critics of the established order find evidence of domination and power struggles in every human relationship. We learn to regard the foundations of society—tradition, authority, religion, and so on—in the same way we have come to regard political institutions: as artificial devices used by society to prevent anarchy by imposing a particular order, one that will inevitably favor some interests over others.

The result is to affirm in all realms of human concern what the political realm has long considered true in its own domain: Meaning, value, and conduct are strictly a matter of private choice, and action is shaped by personal desires and convictions. In such a world, tolerance becomes the dominant social virtue, for I have no right to impose my own (ultimately arbitrary) values and beliefs on others (Rorty 1989). Claims for a more embracing set of values, founded in something more fundamental than the self, provoke only skepticism and suspicion, for as a private self I am intent above all on not being made to play a role in someone else's drama.[4]

The triumph of this politicized way of thinking makes the demand for freedom into the ultimate value in virtually every aspect of life. When our frame of mind is positive, we celebrate this new freedom as the greatest achievement of our time. Like actors who write our own scripts, we can do as we will, knowing that tomorrow we may do otherwise. My values are my own concern, and if they express nothing more meaningful than my own desires—my own personal pursuit of happiness—so be it. I need not justify my commitments—or my betrayals—to you or anyone else.[5]

It seems easy to point to an inconsistency here. When I choose in favor of my own private values and virtues, I am relying on cultural values that privilege individuality. When I claim the right to enact my own drama and fulfill my own desires, I am relying on the culturally determined notion of a separate, independent self. Why accept these claims as valid: Why privilege the self? In doing so, have I not smuggled in an absolute after all?

Postmodernists respond to this charge with a shrug. Richard Rorty, an adept at the postmodern way of thinking, acknowledges freely that the self is a construct, a "tissue of contingent relations, a web which stretches backward and forward through past and future time[; it is not] a formed, unified, present, self-contained substance, something capable of being seen steadily and whole." The self is constructed out of its own beliefs and desires, and is nothing more than those beliefs and desires (1989, 83–84).

To point to this limitation, however, does not amount to challenging the centrality of the self; rather, it is a way of naming the situation that we face as contingent individuals. We should "be content to think of any human life as the always incomplete, yet sometimes heroic, reweaving of such a web." The task of the individual is the task of the poet: to "make a self for himself by redescribing [the cultural] impress in terms which are, if only marginally, his own." And the postmodern hope, in Rorty's version, is "that culture as a whole can be 'poeticized' rather than as [for] the Enlightenment [the] hope that it can be 'rationalized' or 'scientized'" (1989, 41; cf. 43, 53).

The postmodern victory of the private self presents itself as a triumph of intelligence over domination, freedom over conditioning. Yet to live in the postmodern condition seldom evokes the joyous feelings we might expect when good has prevailed over evil. As postmodern selves, we tend instead to feel that we have somehow been cheated. Busily weaving our web of private truths and concerns, we complain of being powerless, fear being manipulated, and experience our lives as insignificant. Uncertain how to give our lives meaning, we feel anxious, incomplete, and strangely hesitant. Bereft of any knowledge we can count on, we feel agitated, resentful, and trivialized. Whether we respond with cynicism or defiance, with politics or poetry, with a retreat into the haven of the family or the pursuit of small pleasures, we know in our hearts: This is not a good way to be.

Private Space and Private Time

The problematics of the private self are linked to the fundamental way we have of understanding who and how we are. As the one that knows and that owns its experience, the self occupies a domain separate from what is known. The world that has the self at its center has been split in two, with the realm that the self occupies cut off from the rest of reality. This split-off, private realm is wholly inaccessible to knowledge, for the self knows by directing its senses and its activity outward (LOK, 264):

> In this model, knowledge results from *the projection of a knowing capacity out into an unknown world*. The self appears as separate from the events it knows—a 'bystander' that extracts knowledge from experience. . . . The resulting division between the source of *knowing*

and the source of *knowledge* establishes a 'gap in knowledge' as basic. [emphasis in original]

When knowing is understood in this way, the self and the private realm are ultimately unknowable:

"Knowledge is understood to apply only in the objective realm; in the subjective realm of desires and feelings, knowledge has no role to play. . . . While the cultural conditioning of the self, the modification of the self's identity over time, and similar issues are all open to inquiry, the 'fact' of identity itself, to which all knowledge is subordinated, is inaccessible to knowledge." (LOK, 33–34)

This analysis might seem at odds with our conviction that we know our own existence more intimately and undeniably than we know anything else. But that is because the existence we call our own is not actually linked to the ultimately inaccessible private self at all. Such a self, precisely because it is inaccessible to knowledge, can possess none of the characteristics that we think of as constituting ourselves (in philosophical terms, it is "deontological" [Sandel 1982]). Instead, the identity we proclaim as being ours is constructed through narrative. True, the narrative can come into being only because the self is available to take on the role of narrator. But the identity of the narrator is likewise the outcome of a story, one of a variety of roles that the self can take on (LOK, 171–76):

The stories told by the narrator-self are about the needs, desires, feelings, experiences, pro-

246

jects, and understandings of the self. . . . The narrator's stories unite [the self as] owner, actor, and objective self, bearing witness to their existence and persistence 'over' time. The central narrative structures—"I am; I feel; I experience; I want; I act"—are the self-authenticating truth of every story. The narrator thus asserts the self by telling another story—a founding story that makes possible all other stories.

The ongoing persistence of a unified self appears to the mind as a self-evident truth. . . . Established prior to all questioning, the founding story is 'self-perpetuating'. . . . All knowing is directed toward points after the flow of self-centered experience is already in operation. . . . Each new experience is assigned a place within a web of needs, interests, situational patterns, and emotional reactions. . . . In committing to the narrative, the self finds the basis for asserting its identity. . . . Self and objects are placed on the same 'objective footing', with the self at the center and objects as 'useful' adjuncts. [emphasis omitted]

The private self thus proves to be a complex entity. In terms of space, the self is the inaccessible owner of knowledge and experience that inhabits the private realm and reaches out to bridge the gap between its own being and the world. In terms of time, the self is "radically situated" (Sandel 1982, 21), its identity (including its existence in the unknown private realm) shaped through ongoing narratives that have as their unifying theme the founding story. It is a part of the founding narrative that these two selves are in fact one and the same entity.

I shall return below to the self's spatial restrictedness; for now, I want to focus on its temporal constitution. Here a difficulty emerges: A narrative-centered way of being inevitably binds the self to its own past conditioning, for narrative depends on taking hold of what has already appeared and making sense of it (LOK, 149). At the most fundamental level, then, the self's identity is centered on the past (DTS, 84–85):

> If time consists of moments that arise in succession, each specified by the lineage of moments that have preceded it, each recorded in turn, then *all of time is past time*. . . . [W]henever we try to take hold of the present, to comprehend it so that we can respond to it, what we actually discover is the immediate past. . . . We could put it this way: Although what appears now or will appear in the future has not yet happened, it has already 'happeneded'. . . .
>
> Caught up in identity, defining and assigning, recording and playing back, we found our lives on this pastness. As we occupy successive segments of time, we enact an identity determined in advance, shaped by what has already 'happeneded'. As inhabitants of the past, we can only take up what has been passed down. We are like a piece of music that has already been conducted: There is no chance to act or create anew.

Because this temporal conditioning is central to the private self's identity, the very possibility of freedom proves illusory (LOK, 188):

> When the narrative is in operation, . . . the creative power of time is interpreted exclusively in terms of the recreation of the old. The narrative is governed by old stories and by the accumulated memories of personal and collective descriptive knowledge. The dynamic that emerges from creation so interpreted will assure a future based on similarities to the past.

Bound to the past, the self is not at all what it claims to be (DTS, 90):

> At stake in this silent battle for the being of time is whether we are truly alive. The recordings of the past have no vitality to offer us, yet we seem to have no alternatives available. It is as though we have built our lives on an impossibility, insisting that we can create life out of what has already passed away. Each day, each moment, we perform an ongoing miracle to make the impossible possible. Yet deep within, the suspicion festers that the 'miracle' is really a hoax; that the claims on which we found our lives are profoundly inauthentic, even fraudulent.

On the one hand, the inauthenticity of the private self helps explain the sense of incompleteness that often steals over us as consumer of a postmodernized reality. On the other hand, however, it suggests that an alternative to the private self might well be possible. I turn now toward that possibility.

PART II: BEING IN PUBLIC

Men, though they must die, are not born
in order to die but in order to begin.
            Hannah Arendt (1959)

For the self to emerge from the private realm, it must transform its ways of being in time and space. For a first take on how this might be possible, I turn to the thought of Hannah Arendt, the great mid-century political theorist who analyzed the distinction between public and private along just such spatial and temporal dimensions.

A Public Realm of Action

To understand Arendt's conception of public or political action, we must start with her distinction between action on the one hand and work and labor on the other. When human beings labor (to survive), or when they work (to produce goods), they are expressing and responding to the contingencies of their existence. Work and labor grow out of our need to have to shelter, food, and clothing, as well as our wish to make use of the objects of the world to satisfy our needs and desires. Action, however, brings a different dynamic into play. "In acting and speaking, men show who they are, reveal actively their unique personal identities and thus make their appearance in the human world" (1959, 159). To appear in this way allows human beings to free themselves from their ordinary conditioning, to transcend their own limitations and achieve greatness.

In the modern world, writes Arendt, action has lost its power to let human beings appear, for it has been banished into the private realm (the realm appropriate to labor and to work) (1959, 45). Nowhere is this more true than in the modern realm of politics, where the public space of the *polis* (the Greek city-state) has given way to the *social* realm. As a strange hybrid of the private and public, "society" reshapes the political community into a kind of giant household (28). By focusing on "social" concerns (for example, the eradication of poverty), we assure that the private will extend its reach into all political arrangements; that "private interests assume public significance" (33).

This development, which corresponds to the triumph of the private described in the first part of this essay, destroys the opportunity for individuals to achieve greatness: "This enlargement of the private, the enchantment, as it were, of a whole people, does not make it public, does not constitute a public realm, but, on the contrary, means only that the public realm has almost completely receded, so that greatness has given way to charm . . ." (1959, 47). Since "no activity can become excellent if the world does not provide a proper place for its exercise" (45), the triumph of the private means that the opportunity for freedom through action in public has been lost.

Why is it that action can take place only in public? Arendt's answer is that public action is special in allowing the actor to communicate the uniqueness of who he or she is. "Because of its inherent tendency to disclose the agent together with the act, action needs for its full appearing the shining brightness we once called glory, and which is possible only in the public realm" (1959, 160). Only in public, in taking a formal stand before others, does the self *appear*, and thus come to be. When we put ourselves at risk by disclosing ourselves in "the simultaneous presence of innumerable perspectives" (1959, 52), we bring light to the dark unknowns of private existence.

The contrast between the private and the public realms is thus precisely that in the private realm the self, cut off from the world, is not fully real. "World alienation, and not self-alienation as Marx thought, has been the hallmark of the modern age" (1959, 231; footnote omitted). When we reveal our "unique distinctness" through public action (175–76) we overcome that alienation; we enter the world and become fully real. "To be deprived of [appearance] means to be deprived of reality, which, humanly and politically speaking, is the same as appearance" (1959, 178; cf. 1965, 94–95). For this reason, "action is entirely dependent on the constant presence of others" (24).[6]

Beginning Anew

Public action is also Arendt's solution to the past-centered temporal condition that characterizes the private realm. When we disclose our own unique being in action, we bring something new into the world. "To act in its most general sense means to take an initiative, to begin. . . ." (Arendt 1959, 157). It is through this beginning, this breaking free of linear time, that human beings achieve their destiny: "[T]he faculty of freedom, the sheer capacity to begin, . . . animates and inspires all human activities and is the hidden source of production of all great and beautiful things" (1963, 169).[7]

As an eruption into linear time, action in effect creates its own time, one that intersects with conventional time but leads in the direction of freedom. It does so by creating a narrative: "[T]he related faculties of action and speech . . . produce meaningful stories as naturally as fabrication produces use objects" (1959, 212). However, the narrative that Arendt invokes here differs both from the aesthetically inspired "weaving of the web" through which the postmodern self affirms its own significance, and from the founding story of the private self depicted in TSK. The political actor creates a narrative by *enacting* it. Only when it is publicly enacted does the narrative of action escape the determinism of linear time: "[The capacity to begin] develops fully only when action has created its own worldly space where it can come out of hiding, as it were, and make its appearance" (1963, 169).[8]

Because it breaks with conditioning, manifesting a kind of perfect spontaneity (1963, 166), action can seem miraculous (1963, 169):

Every act, seen from the perspective not of the agent but of the process in whose framework it occurs and whose automatism it interrupts, is a "miracle"—that is, something which could not be expected. If it is true that action and beginning are essentially the same, it follows that a capacity for performing miracles must likely be within the range of human faculties. This sounds stranger than it actually is. It is in the very nature of every new beginning that it breaks into the world as an "infinite improbability," and yet it is precisely this infinitely improbable which actually constitutes the very texture of everything we call real."

Such improbabilities will come to pass only for a few individuals, and then only in those rare circumstances (e.g., the Athenian *polis*) or moments in history (e.g., the American Revolution) when the old can truly be put at risk and the new can manifest (1963, 4–5).

In summary, then, Arendt offers two fundamental suggestions for how the self can emerge from the private into the public realm. First, it must appear in public, which means that it must disclose itself to others. Second, it must create time anew, which it does by enacting before others its own unique narrative. With these alternatives in mind, we are ready to look at the very different opportunities for emerging from the private realm offered in the TSK vision.

From Glory to Decisive Creation

Let us start with temporality. Like Arendt, TSK offers as an alternative to the past-centered time that the private self inhabits a time that begins anew. In LOK, the point is made in terms of knowledge : A knowing that did not belong to the self could emerge "only if the 'first moment' itself were transformed, so that it no longer maintained its character as the initial instant in a linear sequence" (LOK, 391)." What Arendt refers to in this context as the 'miracle' and 'infinite improbability' of action is similarly described in TSK an ongoing mystery (DTS, 159):

> Only ordinary understanding is mystified by this 'ongoing' mystery play that enacts and informs our being . . . ; only the structures of consciousness insist on covering over the mystery with the familiarity of the prerecorded. . . .

If we abandon the linear temporal structure of 'from' and 'to' (VOK, 24; LOK, 410), and turn toward the 'unknown' time of the 'prior' (DTS, 141-42; 187–88), we are no longer bound by the past, but instead can inhabit the present. However, while Arendt's actor accomplishes this by enacting a narrative that discloses his uniqueness to others, in TSK, the self gives up its uniqueness. Instead of creating itself, it allows time to create appearance (KTS, 480; 484):

> The point at which the vastness of potential knowledge embodies in the actual is the 'point of decision', . . . prior to all distinctions and characteristics. . . . For the 'decisive point' to be decisive, it cannot be a point of origin, a 'source from' or a 'pointing to'. . . . The very possibility that knowledge can develop cannot be said to originate *within* a temporal order. Instead, the knowledge available within the 'point of decision'

is its own source. The point 'reads-out' its own appearance; enacts its own decision. . . .

As in Arendt, to make such a move is to put conventional structures at risk (KTS, 484): "In this ongoing emergency, all that is is invariably at stake."[9]

From Appearance to Openness

TSK also differs from Arendt in its approach to freeing the self from its isolation in the space of the private realm. Whereas Arendt relies on a public realm constituted by the presence of others, TSK suggests that the self can actually 'loosen' its private way of being; can come to be differently. It does so by giving up its claim to be the owner of experience—the one who knows—and acknowledging that knowledge is available *within* what appears (DTS, 144):

> In each moment, we can choose and cherish knowledge in all appearance. We can awaken our sensitivity and react newly to what arises; can cut each instant rejection of knowledgeability and inhabit what is happening.

When the self lays down the burden of being the owner of experience and knower of knowledge, it no longer has to distance itself from what is known in order to know it, and accordingly the distinction between private and public no longer has to be maintained in the same way. The self can 'come into the open', exchanging the privileged private realm for direct presence to experience (DTS, 178):

We do not need to speak for time and space, for if we know how to listen, time and space speak for themselves. We do not have to proclaim our portion, because we are already inseparably related to the whole. . . . [W]e can let go of the knowledge that we possess and merge with a knowledge that transcends all positions. We can embody this knowledge in ways that are concrete and specific, showing time, space, and knowledge in operation.

As the self emerges *out of* the private realm in this way, it becomes a public self. Of course, a self that is public in this sense may not act in public in Arendt's sense, for in the reading I am giving it here the term 'public' need not involve the presence of others at all. Still, the public self stands in opposition to to the private self in just the ways Arendt suggests: no longer isolated and cut off; no longer fraudulent or less than real.

Inhabiting the World

From a TSK perspective, Arendt's prescriptions remain too closely bound to the usual conceptions of the private self. The political actor who enters the public arena puts on a public 'persona' (as Arendt notes [1965, 102–104], the term refers to the mask put on by actors in the Roman theater, and referred in Roman law to the legal identity that gave the actor standing to assert claims in public). Yet behind that mask the private self is still at work, appearing to other private selves and enacting a narrative that remains bound to the self-centered structures of linear time.[10]

We could put the point this way. Arendt's political actor enters the public arena as an act of self-aggrandizement. Through such action, the self 'comes into its own', seeking its own glory and greatness. In TSK, by contrast, the 'greatness' that opens when the private realm is left behind does not belong to the self, nor can it be possessed by the self. While Arendt's political actor enters public space in order to appear in his "unique distinctness", the self in TSK yields its pride of place to "the universal unique" (DTS, 146).

This is not to say, however, that entering the open arena of presence (in TSK terms) mean leaving the self behind. "'My' knowledge and positions form a part of the emerging whole, and so remain available" (DTS, 178). Indeed, the private self *must* be the starting point of any inquiry and all action (DTS, 142):

> The knowledge that gives conducting form cannot belong to a self, for the self is a creature of conducted time, and its world is a conducted world. Yet if we reject the self, with its emotions, its claims of identity, and the pain it inflicts in deceiving itself and others, we will close the only gateway through which a founding and conducting knowledge can emerge. To arrive at the prior, we must first inhabit fully our presenting world, whatever its content and obscuring patterns.

Rather than rejecting the self, TSK invites us to 'inhabit' the self *as* we inhabit the world, making 'the-world-we-inhabit' a unitary, knowledgeable whole.

The objection might be made that a public self that we inhabit rather than identify with is an impossibility. First, the private self seems unknowable in its essence (LOK, 194–96). If the self does not occupy the same space as objects in the world (LOK, 104); if the 'I', like the eye, cannot see itself, how can it ever emerge into being, 'alongside' of everything else? Second, a self that became available in this way, while it might not be an *object* of knowledge, would also no longer be the *subject* who knows. But is knowledge without a subject even conceivable? The project of bringing the self into the public domain seems to depend on authenticating a way of knowing that could stand as an alternative to the past-centered and subject-based narratives of the private self. If such an alternative does not exist, we will remain bound to the private realm after all.

The short answer to the first of these objections is that the self is *already* present in the world, before all claims to ownership or narrative accounts. Whenever we make sense of the world that the self knows and acts on (and we do this in every moment), the ways in which the self conducts such a making sense are directly available to us. Since the self is the one that formulates knowledge, makes evaluations, and has experience, these very activities reveal the self in action. By first turning inward to focus on the way that the self conducts its knowing projects, and then turning this inward outward (DTS, 112–13), we can succeed in bringing the self into the open.

This same approach holds the answer to the second objection as well. As we turn the inward outward, a new form of knowledge becomes available. This new knowledge, which I shall call 'the knowledge of the whole,' is certainly not separate from the self's conventional ways of knowing. But, as we shall see, it does offer a powerful alternative to such ways of knowing.

PART III: THINKING IN PUBLIC

Every thinker puts some portion of an apparently stable world in peril and no one can wholly predict what will emerge in its place.
            John Dewey (1958a, 222)

In the first part of this essay, we saw that once the self withdraws into the private realm, reason becomes a tool for achieving the aims of the self; in Hume's deliberately provocative phrase, that "reason is and ought only to be the slave of the passions." In this model, reason and desire work at cross purposes to one another; put differently, the self as the one who desires becomes the enemy of rationality. It follows that—even though it is the self that is thinking's active agent—for rational inquiry to work well, it must be carefully shielded from the self:

> The technological way of knowing is aware of this limitation on the knowledge it presents, and tries to counteract it . . . by adopting measures to *cordon off* technological knowledge from the bias that unexamined claims of identity and

territory would otherwise introduce. The scientific method, which insists on elaborate safeguards against 'subjectivity' in its attempts to arrive at the 'objective' truth, is perhaps the fullest expression of this concern . . . (LOK, 38; emphasis in original).

Like Arendt's political actor, the scientist (as the model rationalist) is the private self with a mask on—in this case, the mask of neutrality and dispassion. To put on this mask has consequences similar to what happens in the Rawlsian retreat behind the veil of ignorance: The private self as such—the self as thinker and knower—is cordoned off from inquiry. Precisely because it is not publicly accessible, the private domain simply cannot be investigated using the methods of available to science. In effect, then, despite its commitment to open-ended inquiry and hostility to the authority of received opinion, science builds into its methodology (and thus makes unquestionable) the claim of the private self to be the one that knows.[11]

While this structure does not bar inquiry into properties of the self, it does suggest that if we wish to look at the private self in operation, we must rely on ways of knowing that are not scientific in nature. A scientist might reply that rejecting a scientific, rational approach delivers us into the hands of irrationality and emotionalism, but that would be true only if the dichotomy of rational and irrational exhausts all possibilities for how to exercise the human capacity for knowledge. To show that this is not so, I turn now to consider the ways in which we human beings think.

Modalities of Thinking

Thinking as conceived of in science involves thought that reasons from premises to conclusions or generalizes from examples: thinking as deduction or induction, or more broadly, thinking as logic or rationality. Such thinking is not cognitive in nature; that is, while sensory data gives us knowledge of the world, thinking does not. As Arendt puts it (1978, 187), thinking does not know objects; it only thinks *about* them.

A different kind of thinking comes into play when we address a problem or concern in order to deal with it or make it go away: thinking as problem-solving. This pragmatic sort of thinking is what we have in mind when we descrive reason as a servant of the private self and its desires. It might be considered to encompass the first kind of thinking, or else to make use of it to accomplish its aims; alternatively, it might be described just as well as the application of rationality to practical concerns.

A third kind of thinking, though well known to everyone, generally escapes the notice of those who focus on rational forms of knowledge. This is thinking as it operates in the background of our waking activities: commenting on what experience presents, going over past memories, making plans, worrying, fantasizing, and so on. Such ongoing thinking is for the most part trivial and repetitive, and does little to advance our interests or increase our knowledge (DTS, 51):

[Thoughts] recycle the same themes and images, call up the same memories, dwell on the same concerns. They react to whatever stimuli present themselves, leading nowhere in particular. As we go about our day, thoughts cycle through our minds like the background hum of an appliance or a nervous gesture that we repeat almost unconsciously.

This third mode of thinking relates to a fourth. As we move through or 'have' experience, we shape it into meaningful structures. We do this in part by telling ourselves stories, narratives that string together and organize an ongoing series of thoughts, perceptions, and images. But we also structure experience simply in labeling it from moment to moment. In the dual sense that it is ongoing and that it establishes the framework for experience, this fourth and most comprehensive kind of thinking might be called "global thinking."

Even though it may not crystallize as fully formed thoughts, global thinking is active whenever we identify or even acknowledge some aspect of experience. For instance, as Arendt notes (1978, 171), each individual word we use (for example, the word "house") can be considered a "frozen thought," passing on the outcome of previous acts of thinking. In this sense, we depend on thinking and its products whenever we automatically identify the objects or relationships that make up our world. Insofar as they rely on manipulating thoughts in accord with fixed rules, the first two types of thinking noted above could be said to make use of the products of global thinking as well.

The "active naming and identifying" that comprises global thinking structures our reality. "Just as breath sustains the body, so thinking sustains the world that we inhabit" (DTS, 51–52). This theme is developed by Tarthang Tulku at some length:

> First thought constructs the frame; then it fills in the specific features and characteristics that confirm the identity of what is experienced. As identities are assigned, their mutual co-referring confirms the whole. A world is set in place. . . . (DTS, 19)

> Thoughts structure experience by 'building up' reality. Together with their content, they communicate the *substantiality* of that content. . . . The pronounced content of the thought refers to and affirms other related content understood as being situated 'elsewhere': the content of the previous thought, the existents present in the preceding moment, the preceding moment itself; in fact, the whole lineage of the present arising. Patterns of engaged images yield familiar projections, which are pronounced into daily life. (DTS, 53–54)

When we rethink thinking to include such labeling and identifying, we realize that whether we are solving problems or fulfilling our desires on the one hand, or simply engaging experience as it presents itself on the other hand, we are always thinking.

Thinking vs. Thoughts

When thinking takes hold of experience and 'makes sense' of it, it turns that experience into the content of thoughts. This is another version of the dynamic noted in the first part of this essay: As we name and identify, abstract and generalize, we do not actually engage what is happening; instead, we lived in the past-centered world of the 'happeneded'.

We could put this same point in terms of space. When thought identifies experience and turns it into the content of what is happening, it strips away the space in which that appearance 'takes place'. 'Actual' experience differs from 'thought-about' experience precisely in that the latter has been 'despatialized'.

Thought despatializes experience in another, more fundamental sense: by 'filling up' space completely with the content of what thought names and identifies, so that space 'as such' disappears (DTS, 52):

> As each thought arises, its content is located or assigned in terms of past experience and future concerns. . . . In this world of substance and identity, there is no possibility of gaps.

Now, it might seem that this way of operating is inescapable, for we are always taking hold of experience and making sense of it through thoughts and the stories that thoughts help generate (LOK, 257–60), always reaching out from the private domain of the self to discover and make use of a world (LOK, 102–104). Bound to the structures that thoughts and stories establish, we move in a world that is predetermined. "However we approach the search for knowledge, in the end we seem restricted to a limited set of thoughts, images, concepts, and meanings" (LOK, 259).

The usual answer to this dilemma (for those who regard it as such) has been to insist on the availability of alternative forms of knowledge that break out of the closed circle of thoughts and their labels (DTS, 21):

> One possibility for cutting through the limita-tions of a verbal way of knowing is to turn to experience directly, inviting its immediacy to open our senses to a deeper knowing. Methods are available for activating a different kind of awareness, in which we note qualities, charac-teristics, and interactions without assigning them back to objects that possess them. . . . At a more subtle level, we could even allow [the] naming tendency to operate, without accepting its conclusion as final.[12]

Yet such an approach has severe limitations. On the practical level, meditative realization (or parallel expe-riences evoked by art) is rare and difficult to achieve (DTS, 21–22). More fundamentally, it is likely impossi-ble for the self confined to the private realm. "When the self emerges as already active within time and space in a characteristic way, 'how' and 'where' will it contact new prospects for knowing?" (LOK, 263–64). Even the most immediate sensory experience is condi-tioned by constructs (DTS, 22); even the prospect of a 'no-thought' realm is itself a thought (DTS, 55).

The alternative, more accessible approach is to turn from our preoccupation with the content of thoughts to focus instead on the activity of thinking. For thoughts are themselves an active and vital arising. Although in the first instance "stories transform the knowing aliveness of their own dynamic into the affirmed solidity of what is told" (DTS, 61), their aliveness is not thereby used up. Within each thought and each experience, the thinking that constructs the thought or experience remains available. *Thoughts* do distance us from experience, but the global *thinking* that creates and manipulates thoughts and frames the whole is *an inseparable part of* each experience. Once we look away from the substance of what is thought and turn to the activity of thinking, we rediscover the present aliveness that thoughts take away. We could put it this way: What distances us from experience is not that we are always thinking; it is that we are always 'thoughting'. And while thought isolates the self, as thinker, from the content of what is thought (LOK, 99–106), thinking—once we learn to enter into its aliveness—does not.

Thinking that retains its aliveness is the gateway through which the self can emerge from its private realm to join with the rest of what appears. For it is precisely the move away from thought as an experience and into the substance of what has been thought (which is also the move away from the present and into the past) that confines the self to its private domain (DTS, 62):

As substance takes form, . . . [i]dentity moves to the center of what appears. Space becomes zero and disappears; mind becomes zero and withdraws. Knowledge also becomes zero, vanishing into the domain of subjectivity.

In other words, as mind withdraws, it proclaims the substantial identity of the private self as the one that thinks and knows. Each new thought, once it has been established, confirms this structure. Still, this is not the final word. To think does not commit us to the private realm of the self at all. Even when the self has already swung into action, we can think and be present, thinking the self *along with* whatever the self knows. This is what I mean by thinking in public.[13]

Thinking as Presence

Each new thought that comes into the mind—whether it takes the form of an image, a concern colored by emotionality, a narrative, a logical proof, or a simple sense of being present in a particular situation (with all the attributes of that situation variously available)—has implicit 'within' it a particular spatial structure. The content of the thought, on which we normally focus our attention, is one pole of a bipolar spatial structure: At the other pole is the thinker. The distance between these two poles defines a space.

This 'mental' space is charged with various kinds of meaning; from a slightly different perspective, it is populated by various entities. For instance, when an image of someone I care for comes to mind, it may be accompanied by an emotional reaction, memories, or future-oriented concerns. I may be aware of these inhabitants of the thought-space established between the image as content and myself as thinker, but more likely they flicker on the edge of awareness, ready to be engaged. Other kinds of mental events, not thematically related to the image, also help shape the space. They solicit attention or subtly color my experience, in somewhat the way that external events or bodily sensations are incorporated into the substance of the dream that engages me while I am asleep.[14]

If we turn from a single-minded focus on the content of what is thought to inhabit this space of thinking, we discover that the private self is present in this space as the thinker, in precisely the same way that the content of the thought is present. Viewed in the light that illuminates the space of thinking, the private self is neither privileged nor isolated; it does not stand apart from everything else. To use TSK terminology, the self is 'given together' with all that appears. (TSK, 82).

Of course, the self understood in this way no longer has substance in the way we usually imagine. Instead, it is constituted in the same activity of naming and labeling that creates the content of what is thought (LOK, 194–95):

> [H]ow can 'I' establish my own existence? . . . In knowing, 'I' observe, categorize, and characterize; 'I' apply names and labels. This activity seems to be what 'I' label as 'I'. . . .

In other words, when we think the whole, the self is part of what is thought: " [It] is only a part of what we are calling the 'output' of the focal setting. It has no special status" (TSK, 82).

To challenge substantiality in this way may seem jarring (though a postmodernist sensibility will presumably take such a prospect in stride), but it actually does not depart all that far from our ordinary ways of experiencing. Just as we never encounter 'the world' as we go about our existence, but rather use the concept 'world' as a way of making sense of experience, so we do not experience the self directly, but rather use the construct 'self' to organize experience in characteristic ways. And while we do experience the self as separate from what it observes, in the space of thinking this 'perception-of-the-self-as-separate' is just another 'inhabitant'.[15]

As a way of questioning the perception that either the self or its relations to what is thought or observed have solid, independent status, DTS suggests that we imagine 'flattening' space (42–44):

> If we flatten an object, we reduce its dimensions from three to two. But this is a flattening that takes place within space and depends on space remaining as it is. To flatten space as such would be entirely different. Here is one way to think about it: In a flattened space, each point in space would be flattened, so that it no longer supported extension in the dimensions of height or depth or width. Since standard geometry defines a point as occupying zero dimensions, we might say that such a flattened point would become less than zero, or 'zeroless'. . . . A zeroless world would offer neither blockage, restrictions, nor borders. In the interacting of appearance, there would be no occupancy or possession, and hence no interruption. There would be no point at the center and no point that encompasses the whole; no structure that would support such distinctions as 'center' and 'periphery'. There would be no properties to be owned and no structures founded on ownership.

In a flattened 'space of thinking', the properties that we ordinarily take for granted and that shape experience (such as the distance between self as knower and what is known, or the sense of continuity that accounts for the identity of the self) would simply be present as part of experience (DTS, 58):

> [When thoughts become] the agents of zeroless space [the] dimensionalized structure they proclaim is flattened in a quite specific sense: *What appears and the operations to which we attribute its appearance arise side by side, together with the dynamics of their interaction.* We see that established dimensionality simply 'pops up' together with each arising thought. [emphasis in original]

The 'established dimensionality' that pops up in this way is more than the three-dimensional world of 'physical space'. It is the structured-out world shaped by the founding story, in which the self stands at the center of experience, so that all experience is 'mine'. Flattening *this* 'thought-out space' means making 'zeroless' the structures through which the self constructs and proclaims what is so, including 'ownership of experience', 'cognition by a subject', and 'self as owner'. And this in turn means that while such claims persist, their shaping, ordering capacity becomes open for questioning. Together with the dynamic it evokes, that capacity now stands "side by side" with what it shapes. Everything is content, or nothing is; assumptions, identities, and predispositions are all 'juxtaposed' (another significant TSK term). In such a world, "thoughts no longer exert a gravitational pull capable of shaping appearance into substance" (DTS, 58; for a more extensive discussion, see DTS, 254–56).

271

The effect of such a transformation is to turn the world of the self inside out, in the specific sense that the private realm is no longer privileged. If one imagines the content of thoughts and the objects of perception as pictures mounted in a gallery, then the structures we use in making sense of our private selfhood are simply more portraits on the wall. Looking at experience, we encounter not only the content of experience, but also the structures and claims that put the self at the center of a known and experienced world (cf. LOK 173–74). But these claims no longer refer back and authenticate a closed-off, private realm in which the self is the only inhabitant. Because they have been flattened, they do not refer to anything at all. Every claim with regard to the self and its uniqueness is 'out there', alongside every other element of experience. Freely available to be known in all its manifestations, the self has entered the public realm.

Is such a transformation possible? Among the many ways that TSK offers for activating new ways of knowing, let us look briefly at two with this question in mind: multidimensionality and cracking thoughts.

Multidimensionality

The momentum of the founding story that places the self at the center leads to 'single-minded' knowing (LOK, 175): "As the narrative flows along, one observation identifies on specified quality; one subject takes in one point; one knower makes one judgment, resulting in one conclusion that is immediately linked to the next." Such a single-minded rush to judgment restricts the range of what is possible to what has been presupposed.

The alternative is to cultivate appreciation for "the multidimensional interplay at the heart of the ever-presenting field of human possibilities . . . undetected layers of ordering [that] operate in unanticipated ways" (DTS, 63–64). The vehicles for doing so include speculation, imagination, and analysis, which share a capacity to "cut through the sameness of what is thought" (DTS, 66). In addition, multidimensionally also comes to the fore whenever we let the conceptual focus on the content of thoughts merge with the sense of being an embodied and engaged human being.

The fruit of multidimensionality is a different way of thinking: "Once they come alive to the multidimensionality of transitional construction, thoughts invite radiant possibilities." (DTS, 66). As KTS puts it (324–25):

> The multiple range of opportunities, the countless ways of seeing and being, allow for wonder and delight. These possibilities are themselves knowledge. Their availability reveals the self-concern of 'what matters to us' as the outcome of a particular 'focal setting'. . . . Without giving up reason as a starting point, we can see 'into' the reasonable and into our responses to what is not bound by reason. We can glimpse within appearance the shadow of 'something else'.

When we looks multidimensionally, past and future become available as present projects and regrets, while the thinker becomes the one within each thinking who feels, reacts, identifies, and embodies, or who withdraws and disappears. Specific thoughts, expressing specific concerns, may manifest a momentum that sweeps us up and carries us away, yet at the same time we remain anchored in other dimensions of reality, all of which are equally co-available. Such a multiplicity does not contradict the 'flattening' of space described above; rather, a flattened space, because it imposes no structures, allows appearance to reveal unexpected—even boundless—depths.

Cracking Thoughts

We have already noted the stream of situated and situating thoughts that flows through experience: positionings, assumptions, 'idle' thoughts, daydreams, recollections, and so forth. At times we also shape our thoughts more consciously, in order to make a plan or arrive at the solution to a problem. In both cases, thoughts offer a particular opportunity. If we first engage their content on the basis of our interest and concern, we can use the energy of our involvement to crack open the solid structures of the thought. In effect, we are thawing the frozen thought to release the thinking that has given it shape. The resul can be a burst of energy that immediately generates a stream of insights. The process may actually feel something like small explosions in the mind.

The key to cracking open thoughts is to turn from an exclusive focus on the content of the thought, but without cutting off our involvement in that content. Once we have some experience in doing this, we find that we can direct our inquiry in numerous ways. For instance, we can note and track the thinker active in each thinking, or else the emotional tone or related bodily sensations that accompany a thought. When a thought comes complete with an image, we can turn our attention to the perspective from which that image is seen, or we can ask whether there is someone 'within' the thought who is doing that seeing. Again, there is the dynamic of one thought arising, followed by the next, and so on: a dynamic that the exercises in the TSK books investigate in depth.

Still another possibility for cracking open thoughts comes when thinking that has focused on a problem or concern directs awareness so strongly that we break through our ordinary perspectives to discover new knowledge. We have all had such experiences: times when a thought that we have carried around with us for days or even years as a frozen construct suddenly melts, reshaping the whole with which are engaged at that moment, opening a new dimension, or flattening space directly.

When thoughts move out of the restricted domain of conceptual understanding ("thoughts that I am having"), they release the more fundamental energy active in the shaping and structuring activities of global thinking. Similarly, when a story I have been casually involved in engages me more fully (without, however, triggering the mechanism of identification) the founding story itself becomes more fluid and dynamic, and I come more fully alive. Something like this may be what happens when the words of an author we are reading take hold of our imagination or transform our ordinary perception, so that we see things in a new way. It may help explain our powerful reaction when a close friend comments perceptively on a pattern we have been playing out unawares, or asks a question that 'brings us up short'. It may also be related to the ability of poetry, philosophy, humor—or simply an unexpected juxtaposition—to reshape our world, at least for a time. Unlike content-centered acts of communication, in which I pass on preformed thoughts to you as I might give you my telephone number, what is communicated in such instances seems to be the transforming, generative thinking from which thoughts—and the founding story itself—arise.

Thinking the Whole

Even more fundamental than the founding story, in TSK terms, is the 'logos', understood as a 'second-level knowledge' within which ordinary knowledge arises. The logos embodies knowledge in a different way, as "a process, a 'knowingness' that expresses itself in the activity of knowing, free from projection or identification" (KTS, 420).[16] TSK suggests that when we drop our automatic identification of (and with) the private self as the one who thinks, we open up the possibility of thinking the 'logos' as a whole (KTS, 421):

> As an active knowing, inquiry converts the first-level opposition between knowing and not-knowing into a partnership. Instead of being exhausted in pointing 'to' or 'from', knowledge is left free to *know itself* as the *context* of lower-level knowing and not-knowing. . . . To know in this way, *through* the knowledge of the 'logos', is to 'embody' an all-pervading knowledge that strips the first-level structures of knower and known of their claim to ultimate significance.

This 'knowledge of the whole' allows the space within which the knower and what is known arise together to open naturally. We see that thoughts have an I and the I has a world; that 'reality' as the self knows it has the structure of a thought, of something already thought out. When the knowledge of the whole is active, we continue to think the content of our thoughts, including the fundamental, structuring thoughts of the founding story, but thinking is not reduced to that content. Within the logos, self and world, thinker and thought arise together. In the "differently dimensioned" knowledge of the whole (DTS, 65), the self emerges effortlessly into the open.

The idea that thinking can open to presence in this way may seem surprising. Often nowadays we regard thinking as the tool of a technological, dominance-centered form of knowledge, and react against it. This "rage against reason" (Bernstein 1992) is valuable when it leads us to question the structures that thought sets in place, but it can become a hindrance if it prevents us from understanding that thinking has its own power (and beauty). And it seems vitally important to recover this other dimension of thinking, for whether we acknowledge it or not, thinking is ever active in shaping and structuring our world.[17]

I hope I have shown that by rethinking thinking—entering its present space and time—we create the opportunity to break down the structures of thought that ordinarily make the private a privileged realm. If so, the prospect of a public self may no longer seem either inherently contradictory or unimplementable. I turn now to consider the implications of a self so constituted for the pursuit of the common good.

PART IV: ACTING IN PUBLIC

*I think that I am one of very few Athe-
nians, not to say the only one, engaged in
the true political art, and that of the men
of today I alone practice statesmanship.*
Socrates, Gorgias (521d)

The first great political thinkers of our tradition, Plato
and Aristotle, agreed that democracy is naturally allied
to tyranny, for the tyrant rules solely for the sake of
fulfilling his own desires, and it is in democracy that
desire gains the upper hand over reason. At the same
time, desire itself is a kind of tyrant, forcing us to do its
will without regard to our own welfare.

True to this insight, the form of democracy we practice today has tyranny as its shadow side. In the liberal
democratic state, individuals are tyrannized by their
desires; in turn, they are perceived as potential tyrants,
ready to impose their will on others to obtain what
they want.[18]

In this respect, the controls that characterize our
political systems (popular elections, the rule of law,
individual rights, a government of checks and balances,
etc.) are one-sided. Although they address in detail the
danger that the private self could become a tyrant, they
ignore (or even foster) the tyranny of desire (enshrined
in the American psyche as the "inalienable right" to
the pursuit of happiness). The veil of ignorance, discussed in the first part of this essay, can be understood
as the theoretical counterpart to such practical mea-

sures, forcing the individual to give up the rile of tyrant by artificially depriving her of all knowledge of who she is or what she wants.

I have argued for a more radical solution, one that addresses the issue of tyranny in both of the aspects just mentioned. Exposed to the light of knowledge, engaged in the act of thinking, present to what appears, the public, 'inhabited' self stands in a different relation to its desires, and is able to stand up to their tyranny.[19] By the same token, it no longer stands at the center of experience, asserting its own tyrannical claims. Instead, it is available in a way that renders those claims questionable—available "as a particular patterning in space and time: thought and mind distributed out in rhythms that lead to a sense of shaping and possessing, of me and mine" (VOK, 142).

Perhaps it is because he offers a similarly radical solution that Socrates, who had little use for politics in the conventional sense, proclaims himself in the *Gorgias* to be the only true statesman in all of Athens. In his dialogues, Socrates does something analogous to what I have been urging here. By asking the most fundamental questions, he invites the self of his dialogic partners out into the open, where it can join with others. Those whom he questions gain the opportunity to know the who of who they are; to befriend themselves, and thus to become friends to others. In all these ways, Socrates lays the foundation for a differently constituted political order, one inhabited by public selves.[20]

To follow up on this Socratic possibility, I offer below some tentative thoughts on how a public self might act as a member of the body politic. I do so in terms of a (clearly incomplete) set of political virtues: knowledge, conversation, forgiveness, and resolve.

Knowledge

The private self is cut off from knowledge by the un-bridgeable distance between the private and the public realms. "As bystanders, we start from a position of not-knowing and never really advance beyond it. Situated at distance from what needs to be known, we cannot really bridge the gap" (DTS, 173). The practical expression of such a not-knowing is a reliance on models and concepts. Instead of attempting to know directly, we depend on knowledge at a distance, like a mechanic whose first step in repairing a broken piece of equipment is to read the repair manual (VOK, 167). Speaking in more political terms, we could say that knowledge grounded in the pre-established separation of self and world manifests as the rule of law: a set of injunctions meant to approximate a more direct way of knowing.

When we rely on laws and other rules, we are less concerned with what is right or true in a particular situation than with establishing a system that will give us acceptable results across a wide range of situations. We aim at this result for a variety of reasons. First, it is assumed that rule-based decision-making will reduce conflict, streamline decision-making, and allow rational planning in situations where individuals hold or might hold competing views of what is true or right (as a simple example, consider speed limits on highways). Second, rules are often meant to incorporate communal values, and to assure that those values will be upheld in cases where individual actors choose not to respect them (for instance, in defining and then punishing criminal conduct). Third, the application of rules is meant to eliminate opportunities for bias (an example is the various rules of procedural due process imposed on government officials) Such advantages are thought to outweigh any lack of precision or potential injustice that results from applying rules in particular cases; i.e., from the fact that rules are at best an *approximation* of the knowledge of what is right to do in any specific circumstance.[21]

The application of rules also has a distinct disadvantage. By encouraging individuals to stake out positions based on the conceptual dichotomies that rules impose, they actually lead to greater conflict (DTS, 175):

> Our spontaneous actions must be harmonized with the code of ethics in operation; our demands for justice advance one claim in opposition to another. Our declaration of rights confirms the existence of wrongs; our struggles for peace assure conflict and frustration; our calls for reform prove that someone else is in control. Each question becomes a claim, each claim a battle, each battle a question of power.

When the self becomes public, rules lose much of their justification, because a knowledge of the whole becomes available. Unlike the private self, which acts precisely in order to fulfill its desires (LOK, 34–35), the public self encounters desires as a part of the public landscape. Rather than being so many tyrants intent on imposing their will, the desires I automatically designate 'mine' are simply an element that comes into play.

Once we "stop insisting on the unique importance of our concerns [and] personal needs" (VOK, 172), we can arrive at "the still and silent place at the center of our being where knowledge is freely available" (VOK, 165–66). At this point, rule-based approximations of knowledge may no longer be the preferred approach in many cases where we routinely apply them today. Instead, we might find that we can trust a more direct and immediate form of knowing, based on being present in time and space. The famous story of King Solomon acting as judge in the Old Testament illustrates this distinction: When two women both claimed to be the mother of a baby, his proposed solution (dividing the baby in half) revealed to everyone the limits of rule-based thinking, while the response of the two women could be seen as reflecting in exaggerated form the different positions of the private and the public self.

Conversation

Democracy has always been thought to depend on a free flow of information and the opportunity for debate and discussion. The leading contemporary theorist in this field, Jürgen Habermas, argues for allowing respect for our partners in communication to guide us toward rational discourse, in which the distortions that enter communication when we seek only to advance our own interests can be overcome. (Bernstein 1983, 195).

This view is wholly consistent with liberal democracy. It aims to control or modify the self's tendency to pursue its own interests, while suggesting that the basis of political discourse is persuasion that appeals to such interests.To take a specific example, one rationale for increasing the penalty for a crime in this model might be that such an act informs the potential criminal of the grave consequences of breaking the law, and thus encourages him to refrain from the criminal act in order to best satisfy his own interests. The difficulty is this: When political actors focus only on achieving their own well-being, it is open to question how much communication can ever truly take place. As Peter Euben frames the issue (Euben 1994, 211–12):

> [The *Gorgias* shows] how the "founding" of a dialogue, even among fellow citizens, involves interest and power. The question, of course, is whether this is ever *not* the case: whether there can be a discourse that provides a common ground while acknowledging the contestable origins of that ground, or whether we are left with more or less disguised tyrants and mute contests of force, in spite of all our talk.

The answer to that question will differ if the self becomes public. Where the private self communicates to get agreement on what it has already established to be so (KTS, 472–74), the public self calls its own positions into question. It brings into view the mechanisms through which "[each] 'gesture' of knowledge [becomes] the 'posture' of a knowing self—an 'imposter' who appropriates what has no owner" (KTS, 54).

In appropriate circumstances, the public self may still communicate its positions in order to persuade or even compel. But unlike the private self, it has another alternative available. In communicating its beliefs and values, it can also communicate itself, holding nothing back as privileged. As Tarthang Tulku comments (DTS, 257):

> The focus is no longer based on asserting our claims in opposition to someone else's, but on speaking to mutual concerns. We think less in terms of 'I' and more in terms of 'I and you', of 'we' or 'you and they together'.

With nothing excluded from the conversational arena, the public self can join with its conversational partners in a truly creative exchange. This is all the more so because the public self engages a way of thinking that does not insist that things are a certain way, but instead remains present to all that is: a thinking that always begins anew. Ready to put everything at stake, it 'converses' in ways that allow new knowledge to emerge.[22]

Forgiveness

One of the preconditions for political or communal interaction is trust. As a basis for trust we might look to such factors as the other parties' good will, rationality, intelligence, truthfulness, or reliability, to values that the parties share, or to the procedural constraints governing the interaction. When such factors break down or prove inadequate, agreement and interaction become impossible. Here I want to consider another basis for trust that operates when the self becomes public:

the capacity for universal forgiveness as a foundation for starting over.

By looking to forgiveness, I am returning once more to Hannah Arendt. In discussing what constitutes political *action*, Arendt includes forgiveness as a particular kind of *reaction*: "Forgiving . . . is the only reaction which does not merely re-act but acts anew and unexpectedly, unconditioned by the act which provoked it" (1959, 216). To allow for the possibility of forgiveness is to be open to the past, in the sense that one is ready to recreate that past and start over.

Arendt argues that forgiveness is intrinsically limited by our inability to forgive ourselves. For to forgive is to pardon the what for the sake of the who, but the who that we are, sealed off in the private realm, is never known to us (1959, 218–19). For the public self, however, this same restriction does not apply. By knowing inward outward, we can come to know ourselves, and this means that we need not be bound by our past. In fact, forgiveness is the natural response to a past that has not been turned into the position of a private self, for what is not owned cannot be judged.

Universalized in this way, forgiveness allows for interactions that truly start anew; that make each moment a decisive creation. In forgiving all that has come before, I start from no foundation. I do not have to hide from the past and the circumstances it transmits forward to the present (as in the enforced and artificial 'starting over' of the veil of ignorance, which Rawls [1971] in this context calls the "original position"). I need not set aside who I am, for the structures that emerge from the past neither shape nor determine who I shall be.

Forgiveness in this sense offers a political equivalent to TSK's invitation to free ourselves from the 'from-to' structures of a linear temporality: "Rich in knowledge but lacking in substance, the past cannot bind us" (DTS, p. 311). The power to forgive suggests the possibility of a democracy whose citizens can tell their individual stories without turning those stories into concealed claims for domination. It also offers a foundation for equality, for when we are always beginning anew, what basis is there for discrimination?

Forgiveness serves as the foundation for trust by assuring each participant in an interaction of being heard and being valued, of not being treated as an adjunct to the other party's private concerns. Through its unflinching presence to the past, forgiveness makes possible an unbounded presence in this moment. Able to embody its own past without making it into a position or having to defend it, the public self is free to face without presuppositions the future it shares with others, and to act for the welfare of all.

Resolve

If forgiveness brings the past into the present, resolve does the same for the future. By resolve, I mean the intention to act into the future by steadily recreating a freely chosen present. We could take as its defining instance the vow. I would argue that the private self cannot make a vow in this sense, for its promises are made and kept in the dark unknowns of the private world, where nothing definite can ever be established.

In looking to resolve, I am guided once again by Arendt, who puts the promise at the center of political structures (1959, 219–20). However, the promise and the vow are fundamentally different. The promise has political significance precisely because the private self, hidden from public view and thus unknowable, cannot be trusted. In the promise, this self binds itself to be tomorrow as it is today (or pay the penalty), thus creating an island of predictability in a sea of uncertainty (*Ibid.*). In this sense, the promise is yet another device for binding the private self, as one might build up the banks of a river to prevent flooding.

In contrast, the vow grows out of the public knowability of the self. Once the self is available to be known, it is also available to be created, and that is just what I do through taking a vow. Having entered the open space of presence, I shape through my resolve my own being, which means that I shape as well the whole of the world I inhabit. And since I am guided in my shaping by the knowledge of the whole, I can be trusted to direct such a shaping toward the common good.

Leaving aside religious vows and other special cases, the vow could be seen as an intensely private undertaking, standing in sharp contrast to the promise, a mutual agreement among private selves. Yet this initial understanding is misleading. The promise is a tool or device manufactured and set in place in the empty space between isolated private selves. The vow, on the hand, shapes directly the space in which the self appears with others, engaging self and others equally. It is also for all time: not in the sense that it continues forever, but in the more fundamental sense that through my resolve I start time anew—an act of creation that I renew from moment to moment.

Resolve comes to completion in action. Here we come at long last to a meeting ground between the public as the realm where all is in principle knowable and the more usual understanding of the public as the realm where individuals interact. The space in which the public self appears, where I can know with the knowledge of the whole, remains a space that only I can know. But when resolve leads me to act on that knowledge, it propels me into the space we all share. What is more, it assures that I will give up the fruit of my action (whether it be fame or gain or pleasure), for as long as I am acting as a public self, I have no claim to be the separate enjoyer of that fruit. Brought to fruition by such a giving, public action seals the decisive moment and clears the way for the next act of decisive creation.

CONCLUSION

The prime condition of a democratically organized public is a kind of knowledge which does not yet exist.
John Dewey[23]

Because we have learned to live in a way that privileges the private, we consider it right to let our own values, beliefs, and desires guide our conduct and our dealings with others. What I do in private is my own concern, just as what you do in private is yours. It is in private, as a private self, that I seek meaning and fulfillment.

Accustomed to this 'self-centered' way of being, we find it difficult to realize that the private self is cut off from knowledge in the most fundamental way. First, it does not know itself, for the private realm is inaccessible to inquiry. Second, it cannot gain access to the world it seeks to know and act in, but must rely on past-centered constructs (thoughts and pre-established identities) to make sense of what is happening.

Faced with such a lack of knowledge, the self makes do with what it has. Like someone forced to live in total darkness, it establishes a well-ordered, predictable environment, then marks out pathways through it, moving from one carefully identified place to another. "In one unified action it takes a position, posits a situation, and imposes meaning" (LOK, 147).

The machinery of government and the institutions that shape the social order are tools for creating such an environment. We might say that they *simulate* knowledge; from a slightly different perspective, we could call them substitutes for knowledge. Thus, capitalist theory tells us that when individuals are allowed to pursue their own private interests, society benefits, *as if* guided by the invisible hand of a being that knows how to achieve the common good. Again, the system of checks and balances in government or the operation of political parties, by setting one faction against another, is designed to *mimic* the outcome were political actors motivated by a disinterested concern for the public welfare. In the same way, the judicial system invites claimants to tell their own versions of reality, assuming that the truth will emerge from competing falsehoods.

In the not too distant past, traditional ways of doing things, traditional values, and traditional beliefs were thought to embody knowledge more directly than this. Today, however, that belief has largely broken down. Truths once seen as binding on all are now challenged as personal or social constructs. Calls to serve a higher ideal are regarded warily, as invitations to be manipulated. While reason and rational inquiry offer a certain degree of guidance and frame the rules for discourse, claims of objective analysis are increasingly seen as just another cover for individuals intent on furthering their own private interests. As for public discourse, when I speak in public, it is either to rehearse the positions I already hold, or else to persuade you by appealing to your privately held concerns and values.

In such circumstances, not knowing becomes a public virtue: a safeguard against claims to knowledge that might be imposed on others or bias inquiry. When I join the debate on public affairs, I don the veil of ignorance, *pretending* I have no private positions to maintain. When I take the role of scientist and search out facts that can be publicly verified, I make sure my studies are 'double blind'. When I discharge administrative or judicial responsibilities, I likewise insist that justice must wear a blindfold.

In this essay, I have argued for an alternative to these restricted ways of being and knowing. The public self has no greater claim to know 'the truth' than the private self, but its presence in public does give it access to a different knowledge. First, it can know itself; second, it can be present to experience directly, rather than relying on past-centered constructs; and third, it can know with the knowledge of the whole. The knowledge that arises on this threefold basis, bound neither to claims of truth or factual validity, is wholly reliable—wholly indestructible.[24]

When the self lives out its life in public, it is naturally present to others. To say that I am 'out there', along with everyone else, is another way of saying that we are here together. To acknowledge such a solidarity certainly does not tell us how to decide any specific political or social issue. But it does set the conditions for what might be a different kind of politics, or rather, a different way of acting for the common good.[25]

Throughout this essay, I have been using the word 'public' in a specific and rather unusual sense. The public self remains private in the sense that it has experiences inaccessible to others. Since I have argued for focusing on the nature of precisely such experiences, it might seem that I am actually inviting the self to withdraw even further into its own concerns. For instance, if my response when a friend comes to me with a problem is to focus on my reaction to that situation, rather than on solving my friend's problem, I am only feeding an obsession with the self.

This objection remains too closely tied to an understanding of the self as private. If our aim is to invite the self into the open, a focus on the 'interior' experiences of the self will be our natural point of departure. But as the self learns to accept this invitation, we can gradually 'forget' the self as the focus of our concern. As we cultivate an "inward knowing outward,"[26] we arrive at a knowledge not owned by the self, and we come to frame our concerns in terms of the needs of all. To put it another way: Having turned inward to enter public space and time in the sense I have been presenting, we can turn outward to enter—for the first time—the public realm, where solidarity obtains naturally.

It would be naive to imagine that such a way of knowing—and being—could replace conventional politics or the rule of law. Government today engages in a kind of social engineering, shaped by a politics that thrives on discord. Whether and how the public self joins the fray is not my chief concern. My point is that another kind of public engagement is possible. In the absence of consensus, with truth a casualty of contingency, we can still find ways to come together.

Such possibilities for conversation (in the broader sense of citizenship) are closed to the private self, which "lives in the world like a permanent alien, always afraid that if it stirs up trouble its papers will be revoked and deportation proceedings initiated" (LOK, 226).[27] But when the self can *be* in public, it can also be at home. This, it seems to me, is a precondition for a true public realm to come into being. For our present alternative—an 'intersubjective' public realm where private selves interact—is not really public at all.[28]

The artificial public realm we presently inhabit is shaped by substitutes for the structures that might grow from a true concern for the public good. In place of knowledge, we have rules; in place of forgiveness, working relationships. In place of mutual resolve, we have contracts; in place of friendship, tolerance.

Such artifice may well be necessary, but we do not have to accept it as the final limit of our possibilities. Beyond the private self, in the realm where Kant once placed the sacred (cf. Pangle 1992, 35; 39), a different knowledge—a different basis for interacting with one another—is available.

In an era when intellectual pursuits are viewed as eccentricity, and faith or commitment to great causes strike many as unintelligible, the path of action for the common good remains open. In a time when discourse increasingly turns incoherent, we can still speak of our collective welfare in ways that makes sense. In such a conversation, the possibilities of the public self are too precious to be lightly dismissed. If even a few individuals could come to take it seriously, interacting with one another on this basis, a different paradigm for being and acting might emerge.

Convinced that he had a sacred duty to pursue truth *in the company of others*, Socrates chose to give his life rather than withdraw into the private realm (Apology 37e–38a). His example suggests that we have much to gain by turning from the private to pursue a more public way of being. I cannot say where such a pursuit will lead. But in the end, what more can we ask than to see before us a possibility that takes us beyond ourselves?

NOTES

1.   Among those who challenge the self in this way, communitarians at present command the most attention. Communitarians hold that society must be based on a sense of shared values and mutual concerns, and that a self cut off from fundamental knowledge and mutually accepted values is impoverished at the deepest level. See e.g., Barber (1990), Sandel (1982), MacIntyre (1984), Taylor (1989), and Bellah, et. al. (1985); for a good survey of communitarian views and other alternatives, see Digeser (1995). Yet the communitarians have no ready answer to the argument that society as a whole no longer possesses such shared values, and that to call for their reinstatement amounts to "terminal wistfulness" (Stout 1988). The question is how to go beyond liberal 'privatism' without relying on communal forms of knowledge that either do not exist or seem increasingly powerless to guide us. This essay could be viewed as a response to that question.

2.   Descartes was not unmindful of the role of desire in the human psyche, but once he had restored God to his rightful place in the universe, he had no difficulty in making desire subordinate to reason. Later thinkers, unable or unwilling to put the divine order to such use, tende to accept the centrality of desire as an existential truth of human nature. As John Dewey put it, "to be a man is to be thinking desire" (Dewey 1906, 100 [quoted in Westbrook 1991, 129]).

3.   The views summarized in this paragraph go by a variety of names, including postmodernism, decon-

structionism, and genealogy, and are widely discussed in intellectual circles. For additional comments on this and several of the other themes raised by this essay, see the essay by Nichol in this volume.

4. A strong commitment to the self and to privacy might seem to foster libertarian political views, but matters are not that simple. For instance, if I hold that freedom to choose is meaningless without the resources to enact what I have chosen, I may seek an aggressive redistribution of social goods. If I fear the destruction of goods I hold dear—clean air and water, wilderness, cultural diversity, individual initiative—I may seek laws that preserve them. Nonetheless, a thoroughgoing 'postmodern' view does seem on the face of it to conflict with the degree of commitment needed to support any strongly activist political stance.

In linking the tendency for the social construction of reality to collapse in on the self with postmodernism, I do not mean to suggest that individualism is a postmodern development. In 1840, De Tocqueville wrote in the second volume of *Democracy in America*: "Democracy ceaselessly draws one toward oneself alone, and threatens finally to shut one up entirely in the solitude of one's own heart" (2.2.2). Earlier in the same volume he had written, "America is . . . one of the countries where the precepts of Descartes are least studied and are best applied. . . . Everyone shuts himself up tightly within himself and insists on judging the world from there" (2.1.1) (De Tocqueville 1959). Postmodernism, at least in some of its aspects, can be seen as the farthest extension of such an individualism.

5.   Expanding the range of freedom in this way paradoxically reduces the significance of politics as such. In
an earlier age, Americans tended to regard their political system as the source of their freedom, and assigned
it almost religious significance. Today government is
seen as just a complex device, and one that seems
rather sordid and unpleasant in its workings. Still, the
lingering sense remains that politics ought to function
differently, that political actors should be able to rise
above self-interest for the sake of the public good. The
contrast between that ideal and the perception that politics is "a dirty business" still has the power to evoke
feelings of bitterness. Occasionally the result is outrage
that provokes a political response. More often, however, it is cynicism and disengagement.

6. The fact that private experience, no matter how
intense, can never be wholly real (Arendt 1959, 46), is
rooted in the inaccessibility of the private self, which
Arendt acknowledges: "The moment we want to say
who somebody is, our very vocabulary leads us astray
into saying *what* he is . . ." (1959, 161).

7. John Dewey makes a similar point: "Genuine time,
if it exists as anything else except the measure of
motions in space, is all one with the existence of individuals as individuals, with the creative, with the
occurrence of unpredictable novelties" (Dewey 1960,
241–42 [quoted in Kaufmann-Osborn 1991, 257]). In the
course of writing this essay, I have been struck by the
relevance of Dewey's thinking to many of its major
themes. I will note some of these connections at the
appropriate points as markers for future research.

8.   The triumph of the private in recent times can perhaps be traced in the progressive loss of any sense that public action in Arendt's sense has unique significance. First the need for action is stripped away: The drive to 'get on television,' to have one's 'fifteen minutes of fame', suggests the possibility of appearing in public without having to 'do' anything. Next the public is eliminated as well: One can appear to oneself; for instance, by starring in one's own videos or photo albums. Ultimately even the recorded and publicly available image proves superfluous: My actions become real not because I do them, but because I remember doing them. As a current billboard advertisement for whiskey reads, "Make memories now, sleep later." In privileging past over present, this final move renders even the *idea* of public action meaningless.

9.   For a light-hearted but insightful presentation of what it would mean to give up a self-centered linear temporality in favor of always beginning anew, see the film *Groundhog Day*. There the protagonist discovers that when time is 'pointless' and narratives make no sense, freedom comes through choosing to participate in time's decisive creation. The film suggests that such creation is overwhelmingly positive.

10.   It might prove fruitful to compare more carefully the notion of a private self speaking and acting through the public persona with Rawl's political actor, seeing (and not seeing) through the veil of ignorance.

11.   In all these respects, science is the natural ally of liberal democratic theory. As Thomas Spragens, puts it (1990, 178), there is a "profound similarity between the

procedures that govern successful acts of inquiry and the procedures that govern humane and civlized political regimes." Spragens attempts to rescue the merits of scientific inquiry for democratic theory in the face of a postmodern critique. In his view, democracy can dispense with the need for shared values and also take a skeptical view toward reason itself, yet still use the scientific model to structure a political discourse governed by an "open textured theory of the good" (120). The following quote suggests some of the key elements in his argument (248):

> "What provides practical reasoning with its disciplinary force—with its objectivity—is not some putative transcendence of all historically contingent human desires, interests, and limited perceptions. Its disciplinary power inheres instead in the way it compels its participants toward the general and away from the particular. . . . [It] forces us toward the attainment of a common point of view and toward the understanding and appreciation of the general interest."

This approach concedes that private concerns will continue to be dominant, but argues that they can be forced to put on a public face. Compare Kaufman-Osborn (1991, 133): "A true concept, then, is one whose excision of specific points of view ensures that it can be shared by all who engage in formally identical practices of rule-governed observation and reasoning." I would argue that such an approach, while it may be fruitful, can at best yield a *facsimile* of knowledge that is not owned by a self.

12. Tarthang Tulku seems to be referring here to specific meditative techniques used in the Buddhist tradition. A similar view underlies one characteristic Western understanding of art. More generally, the Romantic strain in Western thought maintains that if we could cleanse our perception of the activities of the thinking mind, we would arrive at a more deeply satisfying way of being. See, for example, Robert Frost's "When I Heard the Learned Astronomer."

13. The possibility that thinking can 'come alive' in this way has its parallels in the work of numerous thinkers. To mention just a few: In *Life of the Mind* (1978), Arendt approaches thinking much as she had earlier analyzed action: By creating its own space, thinking can break out of the mold of conventional time that confines the private self. John Dewey takes a different approach, distinguishing thinking from experiencing. For Dewey, as soon as we experience, we also begin to distinguish this from that; in particular, to separate subject from object, so that the subject can make use of the world that it experiences (Dewey 1958a, 19; 22). When we take this latter activity as fundamental, we are led to a "spectator theory of knowledge" ("STK"), which radically restricts what we can know. However, we also have the option of relying on experience directly, and when we do so, the distinction between public and private tends to break down. See, for example, Dewey (1958a, 82): "Empirically, things are poignant, tragic, . . . splendid, fearful; are such immediately and in their own right and behalf. . . . These traits stand in themselves on precisely the same level as colors, sounds, qualities of contact, taste and

smell." For a clue as to how one might proceed in analyzing thinking in a Deweyan vein, see Kaufman-Osborn (1991, 22): ". . . the conduct of thinking takes its cues from and remains deficient until re-fused within the unreduplicable contexts of noncognitive experience from which it is ultimately derived." Similarly, Martin Heidegger's ties thinking closely to presence. See, for example, his reflection on what it means to stand in the presence of a tree (1968, 44):

> When we think through what this is, that a tree in bloom presents itself to us so that we can come and stand face-to-face with it, the thing that matters first and foremost, and finally, is not to drop the tree in bloom, but for once to let it stand where it stands. Why do we say "finally"? Because to this day, thought has never let the tree stand where it stands.

In *Thought as a System* (1994), David Bohm explores the significane of thought's dependence on the past, and offers an alternative approach.

14.   The model I sketch out in this paragraph, while necessarily condensed and simplified, is meant to point toward an aspect of thinking that is wholly left out of the more usual model that sees thinking as a string of words or thoughts that unfolds in a linear fashion. Once we look at thinking as an ongoing activity that accompanies and shapes all our experience, we quickly realize that the 'string of words' model is grossly inadequate. The 'stream of consciousness' model found in some modern works of literature (most famously, in the "Molly Bloom Soliloquy" in James Joyce's *Ulysses*)

is more convincing, but still falls short of what I shall refer to below as the multidimensionality of thinking. Of course, many thoughts take form through words or (perhaps more accurately put) have a verbal dimension. This seems to be because, as suggested above, words can be viewed as summaries of previous thoughts and thinkings. In this sense, words are like the clothing thoughts put on when they want to appear before the mind. "Dressed up" in this way, thoughts offer a second-order labeling of experience, one that abstracts from the original richness of experience and allows experience to be more readily manipulated for the purposes of the self. My sense is that Western students of various meditative traditions who speak of cutting off discursive thinking often have primarily this second-order labeling process in mind.

15.   From this perspective, self and world are intimately related and interdependent: "The self's fundamental desire is to know and establish a world into which the self can emerge" (LOK 149; cf. 173). The outcome of this effort to establish a world for the self to know is the founding story, which places the self in the world ("Here I am.") See the discussion at p. 247, above. Note that to say that the self and its world are part of an ongoing story does not begin to say that they are unreal in the sense of being a 'mere' mental fabrication, any more than the paradoxes of the observer in quantum physics means that atoms and their components 'parts' are unreal. For a cogent discussion of this point, see Heidegger (1962, para. 44[c]). A useful summary of a similar analysis by Dewey can be found in Westbrook (1991, 129–30).

16.   In addition to the logos and the founding story, TSK refers to the underlying structures of experience in terms of 'field', 'temporal order', 'read-out', and 'field communiqué'. John Dewey (1958b, 194 [as quoted in Kaufmann-Osborn 1991, 192]) identifies a similar sense of the whole: "The undefined pervasive quality of an experience is that which binds together all the defined elements, the objects of which we are focally aware, making them a whole. The best evidence that such is the case is our constant sense of things as belonging or not belonging, a sense which is immediate. . . . The sense of an extensive and underlying whole is the context of every experience and it is the essence of sanity."

Compare in this regard Richard Rorty's concept of a 'final vocabulary' (1989, 73). In advocating an "ironic" approach toward one's own final vocabulary, Rorty seems close to TSK. Yet Rorty's ironist does not extend her irony toward the deepest claims of the self; she is only ironic with regard to claims made after the founding story is in place. A related limitation is that Rorty's ironist is open to alternative final vocabularies, but not to understandings–and influences—that go so deep they cannot be put into language at all. For a related critique, see Bernstein (1992, 286–87).

More generally, while Rorty and other postmodernists make an attack on the substantialist claims of the self part of their stock in trade, they seem oblivious to the privileged private realm as the most fundamental of such claims. Thus, their attempts to "decenter" the subject (Bernstein 1992, 328) seem strangely ineffective. Just as the Copernican revolution has not kept us from observing that the sun rises and sets each morning and evening, so each revolution in ideas that claims to depose the self ultimately leaves it set firmly in its place. Cf. Taylor (1989).

17.   Today thinking is also active in shaping new worlds—virtual realities constructed in cyberspace by a thinking dedicated to turning the ciphers of computer code into human habitats. When we enter virtual space, we allow thought to cut us off from reality not once, but twice. If we do not understand how thinking operates, we lose the ability to ask just what this second-order space of thinking leaves out of account: What we leave behind as we log on. For a fuller discussion, see the article by Nichol in this volume.

18.   This is not to say that such wants will necessarily be selfish: It may be that the self numbers among its desires the welfare of others. For a clarifying discussion of this point, see Sandel (1982, 147–61).

19.   In emphasizing that the public self escapes the tyranny of desire, I am taking a position related to both communitarianism and classical rationalism. Communitarians argue that the desires of the self must be subordinated to values shared by the community as a whole, while classical rationalists argue that desire must be subordinated to reason. Both positions are discussed in depth in Digeser (1995), who summarizes their concerns as follows: "Communitarians charge that [the liberal] regime fosters fragmented, atomistic, emotivist, shallow, instrumental, disengaged selves. . . . [C]lassical political rationalists [say that] our culture disorders and impoverishes our souls" (1995, 4). See

also the sources cited in note 1, *supra*. My own view is that both positions fall short; first and primarily because they continue to accept as given the fundamental structures of the private self, and second, because the solutions they propose are not viable in the context of present-day society.

20.   This way of approaching the matter was suggested by my reading of Peter Euben's discussion of the Gorgias (1994). The following passage (211–12) in particular is related to the ideas in this paragraph:

> [Callicles' ongoing attempt to fulfill the desires of the masses] deprives him of any identity of his own. Without such an identity, Socrates is not talking with "Callicles" but with some simulacrum or momentary representation of "him." For Socrates to talk with *someone*, he must detach Callicles from his love and unite Callicles with Callicles' own self. Only when Callicles is a friend to himself can there be friendship between Callicles and Socrates.

21.   This description is of course oversimplified. For instance, the common-law judicial system does attempt to deal with the particulars of each situation and to establish what is true. The working assumption is that when two sides, each standing in the position of a private self, are adversaries, truth can emerge by allowing each to present its own competing, and presumably distorted, version of the truth. Political debate is sometimes described in similar terms: When ideas are allowed to compete in "the marketplace of ideas," the idea with the most merit will prevail.

22.   In using the word 'conversation' (rather than the more usual term 'discourse') to describe the communication of the public self, I mean to suggest several points. First, discourse is usually understood to take rationality as its ideal, while 'conversation' suggests a broader range of possibilities. Second, discourse suggests division, whereas conversation stresses what is shared (compare the two terms 'discord' and 'concord'. Third, discourse is related to discursive thinking, which to some extent presupposes the private self. Fourth, the etymology of the word 'conversation' suggests being involved with ("turning with") others, and at one time was used with this meaning in a sense that suggested citizenship. (See, for example, Paul's "Letter to the Phillippians" in the King James version of the New Testament (3:20): "Our conversation is in heaven.") Finally, conversation allows for the possibility of intimacy. We converse with our beloved, and perhaps with the divine in our prayers. Both these examples might be thought of as ways of *transcending* the private self. In contrast, consider the formalized 'discourse' of the law court or the academic journal: both attempt (often unsuccessfully) to *restrain* the private self by confining it within a narrow, 'objective' domain.

23.   Dewey (1927, 166; in Westbrook [1991, 310]).

24.   I owe this last point to Alan Malachowski.

25.   I do not mean to suggest that the understanding of what it means to act in public is entirely without consequences for the standard range of political issues. For instance, if we stand on a footing of equality with others, we may wish to support measures to give more

equal access to the political system, such as the reform of campaing financing. We may come to understand differently our relation to the past and to future generations (an issue, as DeTocqueville pointed out, that has always been problematic for democracies), or our relation to our sheltering earth. We may see work as an arena that offers special opportunities to engage the public self (cf. Kaufmann-Osborn 1991, 251–52). More fundamentally, we may wish to reconsider the terms in which we frame political debate, looking for a vocabulary that does not proceed from either rights or interests (the watchwords of the private self) and is instead more consistent with a public way of being.

26.   This phrase comes from DTS, which names such a knowing "eknosis." (See DTS, 39; 159–69).

27.   A strikingly similar analogy, in a very similar context, can be found in the work of John Dewey: "The self becomes not merely a pilgrim but an unnaturalized and unnaturalizable alien in the world." (Dewey 1958a, 30; quoted in Westbrook [1991, 326]).

28. If we liken the artificial public realm of the private self to the restricted space we ordinarily inhabit, then the repeated invitation found in the TSK vision to restore the openness of space could be seen as a potential blueprint for restoring the public realm (DTS, 33–34):

> In space that has been restored to wholeness, forms appear but do not take birth; they exhibit but do not take up the conditions they portray. . . . Appearance shares in the 'no identity' of space,

'taking form' without a body, accepting what is given. . . . If this way of being seems beyond our present capacities, it is because of the confinements imposed by our ways of knowing, which sever our connection with the boundless capacities of space. Awakening to space inaccessibility, we see our task before us: to bring space forward, to allow it appear, so that it can offer its abundance freely.

To begin to reflect on how this analogy could be understood in a political context, consider the workings of a jury. Jurors at trial are asked to being anew: to let go of their personal identities and preconceptions. Although they have no ties to their fellow jurors, they are asked to create a community that can arrive at consensus. And apart from their resolve to do justice, they have no stake in the outcome.

REFERENCES

Arendt, Hannah. 1959. *The Human Condition*. Garden City, NY: Doubleday Anchor.

_____. 1963. *Between Past and Future: Six Exercises in Political Thought*. Cleveland: World Publishing.

_____. 1965. *On Revolution*. New York: Viking Press.

_____. 1978. *The Life of the Mind*. San Diego: Harvest/HBJ.

Barber, Benjamin. 1990. *Strong Democracy: Participatory Politics for a New Age* (4th ed.), Berkeley: University of California Press.

Bellah, Robert, Richard Madsen, Wm. Sullivan, Ann Swidler, and Steven Tipton. 1985. *Habits of the Heart.* New York: Harper & Row.

Bernstein, Richard J. 1983. *Beyond Objectivism and Relativism: Science, Hermeneutics, and Praxis.* Philadelphia: University of Pennsylvania Press.

_____. 1992. *The New Constellation: The Ethical-Political Horizons of Modernity/Postmodernity.* Boston: MIT Press.

Bohm, David. 1994. *Thought as a System.* New York and London: Routledge.

De Tocqueville, Alexis. 1959. *Democracy in America.* Vol. 2. tr. Henry Reeve. New York: Vintage.

Dewey, John. 1906. "Beliefs and Existences." Quoted in Westbrook (1991).

_____. 1927. *The Public and Its Problems.* New York: Henry Holt.

_____. 1958a. *Experience and Nature.* NY: Dover.

_____. 1958b. *Art and Experience.* NY: Capricorn.

_____. 1960. *On Experience, Nature, and Freedom.* ed. Richard Bernstein. Indianapolis: Bobbs-Merrill.

Digeser, Peter. 1995. *Our Politics, Our Selves? Liberalism, Identity, and Harm.* Princeton: Princeton University Press.

Euben, J. Peter. 1994. "Democracy and Political Theory: A Reading of Plato's *Gorgias.*" In *Athenian Political Thought and the Reconstruction of American Democracy.* eds. J. Peter Euben, John R. Wallach, and Josiah Ober. 198–226. Ithaca: Cornell University Press.

Heidegger, Martin. 1962. *Being and Time.* tr. J. Macquarrie and E. Robinson. New York: Harper and Row.

_____. 1968. *What is Called Thinking.* tr. J. Glenn Gray.New York: Harper and Row.

Kaufman-Osborn, Timothy. 1991. *Politics/Sense/ Experience: A Pragmatic Inquiry into the Promise of Democracy.* Ithaca: Cornell University Press.

Lyotard, Jean. 1984. *The Postmodern Condition: A Report on Knowledge.* Minneapolis: University of Minnesota Press.

MacIntyre, Alasdair. 1984. *After Virtue* (2d ed.). Notre Dame: Univ. of Notre Dame Press

Pangle, Thomas L. 1992. *The Ennobling of Democracy: The Challenge of the Postmodern Era.* Baltimore: Johns Hopkins University Press.

Pitkin, Hanna Fenichel. 1981. "Justice: On Relating Private and Public." *Political Theory* 9:3, 327–352.

Plato. 1961. "Apology," tr. by H. Treddenick; "Gorgias," tr. by W.D. Woodhead. In Edith Hamilton and Huntington Cairns, eds., *Plato: The Collected Dialogues.* 1961. Princeton: Princeton University Press.

Rawls, John. 1971. *A Theory of Justice.* Cambridge: Belknap Press.

Rorty, Richard. 1989. *Contingency, Irony, and Solidarity*. Cambridge: Cambridge University Press.

Sandel, Michael J. 1992. *Liberalism and the Limits of Justice*. Cambridge: Cambridge University Press.

_____. 1996. *Democracy's Discontent: America in Search of a Public Philosophy*. Cambridge, MA: Belknap/Harvard Press.

Spragens, Jr., Thomas. 1990. *Reason and Democracy*. Durham: Duke University Press.

Stout, Jeffrey. 1988. *Ethics After Babel: The Languages of Morals and Their Discontents*. Boston: Beacon Press.

Taylor, Charles. 1989. *Sources of the Self*. Cambridge, MA: Harvard University Press.

Westbrook, Robert B. 1991. *John Dewey and American Democracy*. Ithaca: Cornell University Press.

Wolin, Sheldon. 1960. *Politics and Vision: Continuity and Innovation in Western Political Thought*. Boston: Little Brown.

BRACKETED BODIES, PIVOTAL BODIES: TRAJECTORIES OF THE POSTMODERN SELF

Lee Nichol

At the Banff Center for the Arts in Alberta, Canada, Amethyst First Rider is using DVD three-dimensional software to create trickster stories. Amethyst is a member of the Kainai Nation, part of the larger Blackfoot Confederation. Her stories are not her own, but rather variations on recurrent themes, given to her by her people, and by her relations—rivers, trees, and crows; stones and sand; wind and time. These are Napi stories, crafted yet again to convey the meanings of a world to coming generations.

Amethyst is being assisted by fourteen-year-old Wabanakwut Kinew, an Ojibway from Lake of the

Woods. Owing to his special skills at the terminal, Wabanakwut is known as 'the wizard'. Wabanakwut's father is Tobasonakwut Kinew, former Grand Chief of the Treaty Three Ojibway, and is a member of the *Midewiwin*—the Grand Medicine Society. In the early phases of Midewiwin training—the first four or five years—one studies rocks. I have sometimes heard Tobasonakwut say, in the presence of mountains, "If you have the eyes to see, those mountains are not still. They are moving, like waves on water."

I have for some time been discussing the cultural impact of computer technologies with Tobasonakwut, and with Amethyst's husband, Leroy Littlebear, director of Native American Studies at the University of Lethbridge and a practicing lawyer. Our conversations keep coming around to the same essential point. Modern civilization has created a technology that can simulate and in some cases even replace 'reality', but it comes up short on the requisite perspectives needed to comprehend and guide this technology. Given this lack, there are good reasons for regarding with skepticism and caution the reach of digital systems into virtually every aspect of contemporary life. Yet here are Amethyst and Wabanakwut, immersed in cutting-edge programming. I thought I had grasped the 'native perspective' on these issues, but now everything had been turned upside down.

The Blackfoot have an interesting response to my confusion. From their perspective, the use of computers by Native cultures and the use of computers by Western cultures are two very different things. By and large, they see us Westerners as young children. Enthralled and hypnotized by our apparent ability to predict and control the universe, we fail to recognize that our most fundamental perceptions have been loosed from their moorings in the natural world, resulting in a mind that sees increasingly limited aspects of its own projections. Digital technologies serve primarily to accelerate this tendency, confining the mind ever more strongly to sharply restricted forms of perception and meaning.

By contrast, Native cultures are seen as 'grounded', in the most literal sense. When the Blackfoot boots up a computer, the moorings to the world have not been cut. Perceptions and values, tens of thousands of years in the making—*the mountains are like waves*—are brought to bear in the interface between human and machine. The underlying ethic is different: not prediction and control, but rather an ongoing need to comprehend and renew all of human experience in its relation to the surrounding world. If digital technologies can be used to this end, all the better: the program becomes a prayer, cast into the flow of time for the benefit of generations past and present.

Does such a view hold any answers to the current problems of western civilization? I cannot say. Yet I find something radically important in the Blackfoot/Ojibway perspective on technology. I summarize this perspective as follows: First, wisdom and knowledge must be central to the functioning of any healthy culture. Second, there are orders of mind beyond the rational that can inform the actions and technologies of

313

civilization. Third, the knowledge related to such orders of mind is a living thing, linked to an active willingness to test the boundaries of all that is held to be 'true' and 'real'.

Although Western society has its own traditions of knowledge and wisdom to uphold—corresponding to those that guide Amethyst First Rider and her people—these traditions, with their inherited meanings of the true and the real, are today doubted and discarded. Amidst the strains of the upheaval our society is currently experiencing, the spirit of questioning behind this doubt could potentially bring genuine knowledge alive. Yet we are so practiced at doubting and questioning ("Question Authority" is now a bumper sticker) that these arts of the mind have become largely reflexive. Ironically, the very spark that could move us toward wisdom may itself be going the way of mechanism.

Perhaps our questioning has become reflexive because it has run headlong into a serious conundrum: True questioning is total, not restricted to the 'out there', the external authority. Total questioning involves *the authority of my own experience*. It will inevitably penetrate my values, my identity, my very sense of reality. Such an assault may seem unbearable; to shirk its implications natural.

Reacting to the possibility for radical questioning in these ways, however, is neither useful nor necessary. Questioning is not intrinsically hostile or self-destructive, but simply open. Nor must it be relativistic, leading inexorably from the premise that everything can be questioned to the conclusion that nothing has any inherent meaning or value. To the contrary, true questioning remains open to the possibility that some perceptions of reality may be more whole, more coherent than others.

It is my position that in order to inquire into deeper knowledge, we need to recover our *capacity for total questioning,* and to engage *a willingness to enter fundamentally new terrain.* In taking that view, I find myself attentive to two cultural movements that are currently in great vogue. The first, related to the issue of questioning, is commonly referred to as deconstruction, a central element in the broader movement sometimes known as postmodernism. Initially a technique of literary criticism focused on authorship and linguistic hegemony, deconstruction and its variants are today widely used to cast doubt on the essential unity of any structure, be it text, value, or self.

The second, which involves the exploration of new terrain, proffers the domain of cyberspace as civilization's new frontier. This perspective holds that digital technologies, with their striking capacity to accommodate 'deconstructed' identities, have the potential to transform our old ways of knowing and being.

Persistent doubts lead me to question the meaning of both these postmodern movements. While deconstruction may *perhaps* augment total questioning, and entry into cyberspace may *perhaps* augment transformation, I see a contrary tendency at work: that deconstruction and 'virtual realities' more often serve to obscure and dissipate these very capacities. In particular,

315

they obscure what it would mean to explore and challenge the self.

In the first two sections of this essay I will highlight the nature of these obscurations, focusing first on deconstruction and then on cyberspace. In the third, I will examine the manner in which Tarthang Tulku's TSK vision and David Bohm's work with proprioception offer a more radical perspective on comprehending the nature of the self.

PART I: PLATELETS

Even in death, the subject will exist through hypertalia: 'I am—dead'. The vampiric subject, what a horror! It is precisely in this sense that the decline of the subject in contemporary social theory remains haunted by a resurrection and return of the repressed.
Marcus Doel (1995)

The term 'postmodernism' denotes a nexus of cultural trends and theoretical perspectives that has emerged in the industrialized Western world in the latter half of the twentieth century. It refers to the disintegration of definitive guiding principles, or 'metanarratives', in many fields, including literature, history, psychology, art, and science. Postmodernism calls into question the reliability of authorities who can define 'how things are.' It throws up for grabs implicit guidelines for negotiating the intricacies of daily life. The net effect is a sense of pervasive fragmentation at the cultural level, and for many at the personal level as well.

Numerous theorists have interpreted and fueled the evolution of postmodernism, among them Jean Baudrilliard, Gilles Deleuze, Michel Foucault, Fredric Jameson, and Jean-François Lyotard. Perhaps the most influential is Jacques Derrida, originator of the term 'deconstruction.' A brief examination of deconstructionist theory as it figures in his work will aid in developing the themes of this essay.

Central to Derrida's perspective are two terms: *logocentrism* and *différance*. Logocentrism refers to the notion that there is a one-to-one correspondence between words and things: that a word accurately captures or reflects the essence of the thing it refers to, whether the thing is 'cat', or 'love', or 'god'. Derrida's position (and that of many others who predate deconstructionism) is something like this: Not only do words *not* reflect the essential qualities of things, but there *are* no such essential qualities. Our sense that a cat, or an abstraction such as 'love', possesses any essential qualities whatsoever is an intersubjective linguistic artifact, not a quality inhering in the 'thing itself'. Deconstruction therefore posits logocentrism as a fundamentally flawed philosophical stance.

The term *différance* carries a double meaning, pointing to 'difference' (spatial) as well as to 'deferral' (temporal).[1] The meaning is more or less the following: Consider three aspects of experience: the outside world, the concepts formed about that world, and the sounds (words) that match the concepts. We begin by leaving aside the outside world, as its immediacy is considered to be at least once removed from us. We are then left with our concepts and the words that represent them, or in linguistic terms, the signifier (sound/word) and the signified (the concept). Our ongoing experience, therefore, is constituted by (a) the (rather simple) matching of words and concepts and (b) the (rather complex) relations among the concepts themselves. It is Derrida's position that there is no such thing as a concept that stands on its own (a 'transcendental signified'), but that all concepts are *relational*—they take their meaning only in relation to their difference from other concepts.

The source of any emerging meaning is thus the 'play of differences'. But because this play of differences is 'limitless', 'infinite', and 'indefinite,' meaning is always *deferred* to a time that never arrives—because at that time, the same play of differences will be at work. This leads to a final conclusion: Since actual, independent referents are found neither in concepts nor in the world, *there is only discourse*, or language, and nothing else of essence. Or, given Derrida's contention that writing is more fundamental to language than speaking, *there is only the text*, the 'text' being any event or object as constituted in a language system.

Arcane as some of these formulations may seem, they translate rather handily to a more practical level of application. The perpetual shifting of meaning implied by *différance* has, for deconstructionists, a radical implication: Not only is no reading of a (conventional) text final, but no particular reading can have more meaning or relevance than any other. This is so for two reasons. First, any reader is operating from a relative, unstable set of meanings, as this is the nature of the 'meaning-system' (language) itself. Second, the author herself is operating within the constraints of that very same system. There is, therefore, no *original* meaning for the reader to apprehend, even if he could. Nor can there be.

It is unclear whether the deconstructionist trajectory as it traces beyond these basic tenets is specifically Derridean, or if its adherents give it a life of its own. In either case, a pair of strategies, each infusing both academic and popular culture, flow from the underlying scheme put forth by Derrida. One of these strategies is overtly political in nature. It asserts that just as no text can have a fundamental, or 'privileged' meaning, neither can social events or configurations have privileged interpretations. Long-standing political and historical values are consequently to be deconstructed, revealing their ideological foundations and paving the way for the (theoretical) reconfiguration of power relations.

The second, more general strategy involves the critique of unexamined assumptions in any field. In this sense it brings to the surface and accelerates subterranean currents at work in postmodernism for many years. This more generalized version seems often to take on a reckless and superficial aspect. The activity of questioning becomes an end in itself, carried on with no intention of uncovering value or meaning. Indeed, to have the intention to uncover meaning would violate a basic theoretical premise of deconstruction: that intrinsic value or meaning does not exist.

Further, since questioning is expressly prohibited (through a rejection of 'the metaphysics of presence' [Derrida 1991b, 11–14]) from addressing either questions of *being* or any possibility of extra-linguistic experience, it remains at the surface. Indeed, the surface—the text—is all there is. A kind of reflexivity is thus set in motion. Questioning (a circular process with no resting point) is all there is to do. A cynical relativism emerges, and the circuit is closed by a refusal to turn the questioning back on the model itself.

The failure to question such questioning finds cultural expression in a tendency to assume that all values, all choices are of equal validity. In working closely with adolescents over a period of fifteen years or so, I have seen this tendency grow from year to year. I have even contributed to it, for I have spent considerable time and energy encouraging young people to develop critical perspectives that call into question claims of objectivity or absolute truth. But the questioning of absolutes does not necessarily result in the position that everything is relative. It may be that everything is relative, but it also may not be. To mechanically insist that all is relative can itself be an absolute position, a closed system that orders and dominates any particular question brought within its purview.

In many respects there is an odd symmetry between adopting a relativistic view, and the actual state of fragmentation in the world. The two seem complementary, and a participant in the modern world may find respite in the coherence between her view of things as relative, and the chaotic jostling of events in the world itself (as abstracted, for instance, in rapid-fire CNN-style news reports or the pastiche-aesthetic of MTV). But what are we able to conclude from this symmetry? N. Katherine Hayles, observing the relationship of post-modern theory to postmodern culture, suggests (1990, 285) that "[i]ssues become energized in theories because they are replicated from and reproduced in the social." In other words, a theoretical position (or a news report) may derive from actual observations of conditions in the world, but the theory (or report) then feeds back into that world, creating new perceptions. The theory is active, not simply reflective or interpretive.

Deconstruction and other postmodernisms have just such cultural reverberations. They are inexorably reinjected into the culture, often in diluted or popular-ized form. The deepening fixation on relativism at both the university and secondary-school levels—precisely where habits of inquiry are formed and practiced—reflects such a reinjection. Of course, deconstructive relativism is still in stiff competition with a series of absolutisms, but it has carved out a very significant position as a heuristic device in contemporary culture.

My aim in raising these issues is not to dismiss the validity of the deconstructionist enterprise. Its applica-tion to regimes of power is both incisive and useful, and its analysis of language and meaning, while far from novel, provides grist for fruitful inquiry. It seems to me, however, that deconstruction is a very limited form of questioning, insufficient for fostering the kind of knowledge or intelligence that might warrant the designation 'wisdom.' As the primary emergent mode of questioning within the culture—whether recognized as such or not—reflexive deconstruction, with its pull into relativism, moves toward the structural closure of mental horizons. What passes for perceptive deconstructive analysis not only 'crowds out' any deeper questioning; it overtly dismisses such questioning as 'metaphysical' and thus illegitimate.

The way that deconstruction functions to close off questioning, even while affirming its importance, can be seen quite clearly in its consideration of the self, or 'the subject'. Here again we can see the double nature of social theory at work, both mirroring and reproducing a set of historical circumstances. On the one hand, such theory reflects the historical evolution of a disoriented and fragmented self, a self whose condition is due to the disintegration of a coherent social context. On the other hand, such theory actively contributes to this phenomenon by proffering a recurrent deconstructionist strategy: the structure in question (in this case, the self) was never what it seemed to begin with. It was always a fragile social construction, and disruptions and alterations in the social fabric simply bring this to light. Therefore, like all other reified structures, the self must be deconstructed. Our lot is to witness the 'end of the subject'. Marcus Doel frames the issue thus:

> Indeed, one can already discern the outline of a dominant motif: the subject as a catastrophe site, accompanied by a rapidly ossifying consensus: the dynamism of the subject has finally

exhausted itself and is now fated to disappear through a terminal decline. For many, there is a conviction that the catastrophe has already occurred, and that we are living in a dead zone, or waiting period, haunted by the death of the subject.[2] (1995, 226)

What can it mean, this death of the subject? Is it the termination of a particular literary device? Is it the breakdown of a social role? Is it the disintegration of the individual self, the ego? Certainly, the role of the subject as a literary phenomenon has been the focus of much attention,[3] but it is the subject as social role and individual self that concerns me here.

For a clue as to what deconstructionists mean by the death of the subject, we can look to the language with which this 'death' is described. In his analysis of the fate of the postmodern self, *The Saturated Self*, Kenneth Gergen suggests (1991, x):

Rather, like concepts of truth, objectivity, and knowledge, the very idea of individual selves— in possession of mental qualities—is now threatened with eradication.

In this version, it is the 'very idea' of the self that faces eradication. But what does it mean that the *idea* of the self is eradicated? There seem at least two possibilities, one of which Gergen actively pursues, and which I will presently address. First, however, I will outline the other. The designation 'idea' suggests an abstract conception of some thing or some activity, apart from that thing or activity itself. I can, for instance, have the *idea* of water-skiing. I can share this idea with others, and entertain their ideas about water-skiing. None of this, of course, is the actual activity of water-skiing. The same applies to the idea of the self, or the subject. We might say, "The idea of the self is suffering greatly in the postmodern milieu," meaning that our formulations of what a self is are undergoing great change. We might even suggest that the idea of a self is being eradicated. But just as our conversation about water-skiing does not affect people who are actually skiing (at least not initially), so the *idea* of the self may be altered, even 'eradicated', yet the concrete activity of the self carries on undeterred.

Unlike water-skiing, the activity of the self is more or less universal, and it is assigned rather high value. Consequently, if theories about its death become ubiquitous, this self is likely to take note. Even—or especially—among those who proclaim its death, if the self has not undergone an actual rather than a theoretical death (and it almost certainly has not), it is certain to reassert its presence. Hence Marcus Doel's perceptive notion of the 'vampiric subject,' cited in the epigraph to this section: a creature whose death is proclaimed in theory, only to return ever more forcefully in actuality. From this perspective, the *idea* of the death of the subject seems deeply problematic.

Gergen pursues at length a second possibility. This is that the self, as a socio-linguistic construction, is capable of massive restructuring, depending upon the milieu in which it is situated. In this version, the self *as idea* is equivalent to Derrida's 'signified': a shifting concept that can take its meaning only in relation to other concepts (Gergen 1991, 110):

> For the deconstructionist, language is a system unto itself, a cultural form that owes its existence to a collectivity of participants. . . . Thus, individuals are not the intentional agents of their own words, creatively and privately converting thoughts to sounds or inscriptions. Rather, they gain their status as selves by taking a position within a pre-existing form of language. 'I' am I only by virtue of adopting the traditional pronoun in a culturally shared linguistic system. A language without the pronouns 'I' and 'you' might fail to recognize persons as having individual selves.

All this translates directly into daily life (1991, 150):

> The ideal of authenticity frays about the edges, the meaning of sincerity slowly lapses into indeterminacy. And . . . one is simultaneously readied for the emergence of a pastiche personality. The pastiche personality is a social chameleon, constantly borrowing bits and pieces of identity from whatever sources are available and constructing them as useful or desirable in a given situation. If one's identity is properly managed, the rewards can be substantial—the devotion of one's intimates, happy children, professional success, the achievement of community goals, personal popularity, and so on. All are possible if one avoids looking back to locate a true and enduring self, and simply acts to full potential in

the moment at hand. . . . Life becomes a candy store for one's developing appetites."

This in turn paves the way for the 'relational self':

As the moorings of the substantial self are slowly left behind, and one begins to experience the raptures of the pastiche personality, the dominant indulgence becomes the persona—the image as presented. Yet as all becomes image, so by degrees does the distinction between the real and the simulated lose its force. At this point the concept of the true and independent self . . . loses its descriptive and explanatory import. One is thus prepared to enter a . . . final stage, in which self is replaced by the reality of relatedness—or the transformation of 'you' and 'I' to 'us'. . . . As self-constructions cease to have an object (a real self) to which they refer, and one comes to see these constructions as means of getting on in the social world, one's hold on them is slowly relinquished. (1991, 156)

Two aspects of this scenario warrant attention. The first involves the manner in which the 'pastiche personality' inhabits both space and time. There appears to be a kind of gliding through space at work here, from children to goals to intimates to community—a frictionless malleability that derives from the (purported) absence of an enduring self. Yet this is difficult to envision; whatever cultural conceptions of self we may have (or not have), friction is a recurrent aspect of our daily life. This friction—manifesting in a certain sandpaper-like quality—is a fundamental aspect of our experience largely *because* of the existence of a self, however it might it might be conceived.

In Gergen's scenario, all one needs to do to escape this point of friction is to 'avoid looking back to find a true and enduring self.' The problem is, of course, that whether you 'look back' for the self or not, it will tap you on the shoulder and remind you of its presence— its enduring fears, its habits, longings, and so on. The avoidance of 'looking back' amounts to little more than a repression of the self's habit patterns. In a Derridean scheme, concepts ('signifieds') may slip past one another like lubricated platelets in the bloodstream, but this seems much less likely in the realm of daily life.

At this point Gergen makes a parallel assumption about the self in time. He tells us that the pastiche self 'simply acts to the full potential of the moment at hand.' Apparently, 'not looking back' creates a perpetual 'moment at hand,' a perpetual present. Such a framework of experience, however, seems fundamentally unrealistic. It is eerily reminiscent of that inhabited by Chauncey Gardener, the protagonist of Jerzy Kozinski's *Being There* (1970). Chauncey's world was created from naiveté—a blissful ignorance devoid of any real comprehension of the flow of events around him, or of his responsibility within that world. There is no small irony in the fact that a scenario which Kozinsky offered as a wake-up call for mindlessness is now put forward as a viable model for conducting our lives.

A further problematic aspect of Gergen's proposal is the suggestion that a relational culture entails the "transformation of 'you' and 'I' into 'us'." Here Gergen seems initially to point toward an attractive model substantiated by our growing knowledge of other cultures. If different linguistic structures can generate different realities, such differences may well extend into the realm of identity structures. At one level, various Asian cultures, particularly in their more traditional aspects, manifest 'relational' phenomena, where the group—indeed social process in general—is considered more fundamental than the individual. And in Native American cultures, whose languages are almost universally verb-based rather than noun-based, relationality is quintessential: not as social theory, but rooted in perceptions, meanings, ceremonies, and language, passed along within a culture for hundreds of generations.

Yet what can we make of such models as alternatives to the self as we experience it? In my own limited contact with native peoples, I have come to sense very different orderings of reality from those inherited in a Euro-American context—a quality of concrete relatedness between such people and the living world quite unlike, and in crucial respects superior to, Western experience. But it is not my experience that native people are without self, without ego. Their self may be configured in very different—perhaps healthier—ways than that of a Westerner, *but self there is*. Indeed, the ancient cultures of India and Tibet—relational by any measure— developed perceptions and analyses of the self that to this day are unparalleled in their scope and subtlety.

These reflections suggest to me that the dynamic that generates the self is more fundamental than either language or culture. Postmodern theories of the self, for all their perceptiveness, seem ultimately misleading. While they do subtly delineate the self's machinations —even positing a certain self-lessness—they in no way account for the self's tenacity and universality, much less the nature of its generating dynamic. Concerned with the self as *idea*, such theories seem to slip too quickly past the self as embodied experience. In doing so, they leave the impression that apprehending and addressing the problems of the self is ultimately a matter of acquiring the correct theoretical perspective. But to package and dispense with the self in this way, as Doel points out, is to assure its perpetual recurrence.

To the extent that the self is actually threatened by the fragmentation of postmodern culture—and theoretically threatened by postmodern discourse—it will inevitably search for new foundations. We could imagine that it would do so by turning toward the prospect of apprehending its actual nature. But before we seriously consider this alternative, we must look at the major alternative that is presently advanced so vigorously in certain parts of our culture: the notion that the self can reinvent itself, opting for new life in the non-contingent domain of cyberspace.

PART II: BRACKETS

In the Mirror of the Cyborg, anxiety about identity centers not on lack, but on informational patterns that must cohere for continuity of the subject to be assured.
    N. Katherine Hayles (1993, 186)

With the explosive growth of the Internet and the World Wide Web, we are witnessing the convergence of postmodern theory and daily experience. Cyberspace has become a moment-to-moment testing ground for 'decentered' selves, 'distributed' selves, and 'multiple' selves. Gergen's 'pastiche personalities'—Derrida's 'signifieds'—have become ubiquitous in the realm of digitized communications. It is suggested that "[T]he mode of interaction that this milieu fosters—congeries of personae whose greatest commonality is a single physical substrate in which they are loosely grounded, collective structures whose informing epistemology is multiplicity and reinvention—makes transformation as reflexive as it is transitive" (Stone 1992, 621).

Before the celebrations begin, however, it is well to ask what has happened to Doel's 'vampiric subject'. At the conclusion of *Life on the Screen*, her survey of identity structures in cyberspace, Sherry Turkle raises this question directly (1995, 267):

"In cyberspace, hundreds of thousands, perhaps already millions, of users create online personae who live in a diverse group of virtual communities where the routine formation of multiple identities undermines any notion of a real and unitary self. Yet the notion of the real fights back. People who live parallel lives on the screen are nevertheless bound by the desires, pain, and mortality of their physical selves.

Dwell as one might in the domain of the virtual, it seems there is always 'home' to come back to—for food, sleeping, and other inconveniences. The sandpaper is still there. Suppose I leave the terminal, go out for milk, and am insulted by the convenience-store clerk. Surprise! That nagging self of old, the one with the body, is back. 'Distributed' as the self may become, it still has an active, non-digitized locus, one with lungs, heart, adrenaline, emotions, defensive posturings, reflexive insecurities, and most of all, an embedded history—a phylogenetic coding so complex as to reduce the computer's filiations to the status of a fruit fly, if that.

In the second part of this essay, I will argue that one aspect of this complex coding—what I will tentatively call the 'primordial' self—is unlikely to terminate simply because social theory, or practice, has changed. To the contrary: the subtle dynamism of this coding is likely to be suppressed, obscured, and thereby strengthened through acclimatization to cyberspace. This is so for two reasons. First, subscribing to the illusion of disembodiment—a basic tenet of the aesthetic of cyberspace—deflects attention from the body's phylogenetic coding. To ignore this coding, and its intimate link with whatever conception of mind we may hold, is to perpetuate our subjection to the coding's dynamic principles. Second, emergent popular assumptions of a decentered, groundless self are moving toward a trap: the theoretical relegation of a complex phenomenon into the "I know that already" category, leading to the collapse of true inquiry.

I will first outline what I see as an essential difficulty in properly conceiving the meaning of cyberspace. A heated debate is afoot as to whether our allegiance should be with 'real reality' or digital realities, be they chat groups or full-immersion virtual reality. At the extremes, we hear from 'neo-Luddites', who variously argue against quick cultural acceptance of digital technologies and emphasize the importance of 'the real'; and from 'techno-evangelists' who attempt to demonstrate the practical and evolutionary benefit of such technologies.[4] If these were in fact the parameters of choice, I would go hands down with the neo-Luddites, preferring to err on the side of caution and careful examination. But this spectrum of argument must be understood as a sub-set of a larger question. What neither side in this debate brings to the table—at least, not in a manner that is shared with the reading public—is a careful assessment of the fact that our sense of the 'real' is itself a kind of construction, or as Tarthang Tulku might say, a focal setting. (TSK, 3–5)

Various scientific and philosophical disciplines posit the constructed nature of reality, not simply through language, but through the formation of perception itself. Neurobiologist Humberto Maturana, physicist Heinz von Foerster, and anthropologist Gregory Bateson figure prominently in the emergence of this 'constructivist' view of reality. The essence of this view is the contention that the visual/ auditory/kinesthetic images of the outside world that we experience from moment to moment do not mirror reality 'as it is.' Rather, the images we experience are both highly selective and in large part reflexively predetermined.

This selectivity and reflexivity occurs well before our conscious apprehension that, for instance, "a dog is walking across the street." The conscious impression "dog walking across street" may have a rough, practical correspondence to something occuring in the world. But this impression can in no way qualify as a mirror of reality, because (a) it automatically—and necessarily—leaves out a vast amount of activity and information that is simultaneous with "dog crossing street" and (b) even within the domain of the selected information, we only make a *best working guess* about what is seen. Our guesses are often right, but sometimes not. The 'dog' may be a wolf.

Further, my 'perfect husband' may be a cheat, my 'stable career' may disintegrate due to downsizing, my 'home' may be threatened by hostile assault or revolution. When any such event occurs, we generally experience a sense of unreality. We may even think, "This can't be happening; this is not real." Such a reaction or sensibility is consistent with the constructivist contention that the majority of our waking experience is very much in the nature of a dream, with few marking points in what we usually think of as objective reality.

The foundational tenets of a constructivist view are aimed not at the conscious, or even unconscious, subjective/psychological level, but rather at the generic formation of pre-conscious perception. While a constructivist view may shed much light on the nature of psychological tendencies, it is this constructivist insistence on the selective and reflexive nature of perception itself that is both radical and unsettling.

Three examples may help to demonstrate elementary aspects of the constructivist perspective:

Hold the book with your right hand, close your left eye, and focus on the star with your right eye. Move the book slowly forward and back along your line of vision until the round black spot disappears—about 12 to 14 inches. By keeping the star well-focused, the spot should remain invisible even when the book is moved parallel to itself.

To this experience, von Foerster comments (1989, 42–43):

> This localized blindness is a direct consequence of the absence of photo receptors (rods or cones) at that point of the retina, the 'disk,' where all fibers leading from the eye's light-sensitive surface converge to form the optic nerve. Clearly, when the black spot is projected onto the disk, it cannot be seen. Note that this localised blindness is not perceived as a dark blotch in our visual field (seeing a dark blotch would imply 'seeing'), but *this blindness is not perceived at all, that is, neither as something present, nor as something absent*: Whatever is perceived is perceived 'blotchless'. [emphasis added].

While the 'blind spot' demonstrates lapses in the visual field—as well as the lack of awareness of this absence—the 'illusory contours' diagram below demonstrates the reflexively constructive nature of visual perception:

Even if one attempts not to see the white triangle, it nonetheless appears. And this holds true even when one breaks down the components of the illusion:

Perhaps even more telling is a third experiment. Glance at the diagram below, then cover it and draw what you have seen:

Neuropsychologist Robert Ornstein comments on this experiment (1991, 178):

Because we unconsciously dream up a sem-
blance of the world, our experience "cleans up"
information and "straightens it out.". . . You
probably drew the slanted ellipse as a circle,
made the "square" with straight sides, completed and connected the sides of the "triangle," and
drew the "X" with two straight lines. You
cleaned up, corrected, and connected the figures
to match your interpretation of them.

It seems then, that we exist within a loop formed by
selective perception, reflexive construction, and arbitrary interpretation.

Diagrams are not our only evidence for this cycle.
Maturana, in collaboration with Jerome Lettvin and
others, has demonstrated the highly selective nature of
a frog's visual perception (Lettvin, et. al. 1959). In their
experiments, microelectrodes were used to monitor
activity in the frog's visual cortex. Though an enormous variety of shapes, colors, and movements were
placed in the frog's visual field, only four types of information were transmitted to its brain: general outlines,
moving edges, small dark objects, and sudden decreases
in light.

These results indicate the species-specific nature of
the frog's perception—a perceptual structure geared for
survival. Moving up the evolutionary ladder, the recent
work of Edelman and Finkel, Merzenich and Kass and
others similarly indicates the actively reflexive constructions of species-specific perceptual apparatus in
primates (Finkel 1992, 398–403).

Where does this leave us with regard to the question of 'real' reality? We do, after all, seem to get on in the world, at least in terms of physical survival. And so does the frog, even though he/she perceives a world vastly different from our own. The catch seems to be that we perceive just enough of the activity in the world to allow us to navigate the environment with a minimum of mishaps. From this, we presume that our images *mirror* an objective exterior world. More likely, we are involved in a kind of dreaming, a connect-the-dots game that gives the appearance of stability and order. Lief Finkel, a neurophysiologist at the University of Pennsylvania, offers an evolutionary perspective:

> The elaboration of [an] internal reality gave rise, by and by, to the emergence of consciousness and the subjective perception that the internal world was, in fact, coextensive with the external. Yet this projection arose from a methodological fallacy. . . . The world, to a large extent, is a vision of our own creation. We inhabit a mixed realm of sensation and interpretation, and the boundary between them is never openly revealed to us. And amid this tenuous situation, our cortex makes up little stories about the world, and softly hums them to us to keep us from getting scared at night (Finkel 1992, 408).

These directions in neuroscience and philosophy pose fundamental questions for the cultural debate around the issue of cyberspace. The neo-Luddite must be asked, "What do you mean by holding to 'real' reality?" Without denying the existence of trees, rocks,

337

freeways, and airplanes, we must be wary of a reactionary insistence on a reality "as we always knew it." Things probably *aren't* only what they seem, and we are much akin to ostriches if we do not explore the very real implications of the reality-as-construct view.[5]

On the other hand, there are equally pressing questions for those who would uncritically embrace and propagate virtual domains. Characteristic of such advocacy is Kevin Kelly's suggestion that when a critical mass of humanity is digitally 'wired'—in distributed, egalitarian fashion—we will slip the bonds of industrial-era hierarchy and be 'out of control.' Through networked feedback systems, our collective consciousness will transform into a 'hive-mind', all to the benefit of mankind. The means by which this hive-mind is achieved is akin to the invisible hand in Adam Smith's proto-capitalism—it is in the nature of the thing to self-regulate (Kelly 1994, 126):

> As far as our lives allow us, we are equipping our constructed world to bootstrap itself into self-governance, self-reproduction, self-consciousness, and irrevocable self-hood. The story of automation is the story of a *one-way* shift from human control to automatic control. [emphasis in original]

I would argue that the merit of this view lies not in its intended heuristic, but in its token qualification: "as far as our lives allow us." I take the position that very specific factors in our lives will *not* allow us to perform such bootstrapping, as I will explain below.

Gregory Bateson's delineation of 'ecologies of mind' has had an enormous influence on socio-cybernetic theory since the 1960s; this influence is evident throughout Kelly's *Out of Control* and any number of other popular visions of a cybernetic future. But 'ecology of mind' has a theoretical nemesis in Bateson's world view; this he referred to as *pathologies of epistemology*. I contend that such pathologies are built into the very cybernetic systems that will supposedly lead us to self-governance, self-hood, and so on. Without our facing such pathologies directly, it is folly to think that technical systems can be relied on to address and resolve them spontaneously.

By 'pathologies of epistemology' Bateson meant systemic confusions in the way we come to know—and therefore act in—the world. Ironically, these pathologies are 'ecologies' in and of themselves, to the extent that they create and sustain psychological and social environments. Bateson suggested that such pathologies were due to the very sleight-of-hand pointed to by constructivists. He explored the implications, from the perceptual level into the inter-subjective psychological level, and finally to the global collective level. For instance, according to Bateson the simple notion, "I see you," generates epistemological pathology, because I do *not* see you: I see an image constructed in my brain in arbitrary fashion, and name it and believe it to be 'you' for convenience sake. For a culture to believe the premise "I see you"—to commit to an objectified world—leads to an endless multiplication of pathologies, resulting in endemic pollution, polarized world views, and the fomenting of hostilities.

Citing an Ames perceptual experiment which demonstrated to him the illusory, constructed nature of perception,[6] Bateson pointed to the immense difficulty of attempting, in one's daily life, to correct these pathologies (1987, 488):

> Since about 1943 when I saw the experiment, I have worked to practice living in the world of truth instead of the world of epistemological fantasy; but I don't think I've succeeded. Insanity, after all, takes psychotherapy to change it, or some other very great experience. Just one experience which ends in the laboratory is insufficient.

In spite of rhetorical claims to the contrary, I contend that cyberspace and its proponents have in no way sufficiently challenged an objectivist orientation to the world. Indeed, in lobbying for a dramatic acceleration of self-referencing digital systems, cyberists neglect the possibility that the systems they envision emerge from, are defined by, and propagate the very pathologies Bateson was concerned with.

To summarize: Any questions regarding the efficacy or dubiousness of digital realms should—but generally do not—take into account the representational processes of the human mind that fuse sense data with pre-established categories and meanings to produce the experience—or dream—of 'a world'. Given this failure, we are faced with a category mistake of great significance. This mistake resides in the assumption that either (a) an *elaboration* of our current mode of experiencing reality (embracing digital realms) or (b) an *entrenchment* of our current mode of experiencing reality (holding fast to 'unmediated' or concrete reality) are our primary options. For both views assume our current mode of experience is fundamentally given, and essentially 'true.'

It is a central premise of this essay that our basic, day-to-day experience is not necessarily 'true', as indicated by constructivist philosophy, current neocortical research, and (as we shall see) Tarthang Tulku and David Bohm. To engage in the current debate about the nature of reality—a debate with massive societal implications—without sustained consideration of the superstructural aspects of lived experience, is tantamount to debating what kind of windows to put in a house built on an active fault line. It fails, as Tarthang Tulku might say (LOK, 173–75), to address the 'founding story'—the underlying scheme of experience we tacitly agree to leave untouched.

What actually happens in cyberspace? As of 1996, cyberspace is primarily a text-based medium, supplemented by two-dimensional icons, sound, and video. Full-immersion virtual reality is some time away from mass consumption—the necessary economies of scale do not yet exist. Yet even in a text-based medium, as Turkle points out, plastic, multiple selves are already a ubiquitous fact. Referring to MUDs (Multi User Dungeons—electronic 'rooms' where people meet in cyberspace), Turkle notes (1995, 185):

> Traditional ideas about identity have been tied to a notion of authenticity that such virtual experiences actively subvert. When each player can create many characters and participate in

many games, the self is not only decentered, but multiplied without limit.

A MUD participant's comments illustrate this sense of cyberspatial *plasticity* (1995, 184):

> You can be whoever you want to be. You can completely redefine yourself if you want. You can be the opposite sex. You can be more talkative. Whatever. You can just be whoever you want, really, whoever you have the capacity to be. You don't have to worry about the slots other people put you in as much. It's easier to change the way people perceive you, because all they've got is what you show them. They don't look at your body and make assumptions. They don't hear your accent and make assumptions. All they see is your words.

The prospect here is for an endless 'fractalization' of self-images, a fractalization unilaterally controlled by the sender. In this version of the distributed self, the much-vaunted interactivity of cyberspace is conspicuously absent: "*. . . all they've got is what you show them.*" Equally relevant in this participant's experience is the theme of disembodiment: "*They don't look at your body and make assumptions.*"

As we shall see, the notion of disembodied intelligence is not simply one of many options available for the participant in cyberspace—it is a historical and metaphysical underpinning of the entire cyberspatial enterprise. First, however, it is useful to examine the manner in which the postmodern elements we have surveyed so far—the Derridean signifier/signified, the distributed self, and the disembodied self—have converged in a new aesthetic of cyberspace.

Mark Taylor and Esa Saarinen's *Imagologies* (1994), something of a field manual for emergent socio-digital realities, epitomizes this convergence, while alluding to the historical context from which the postmodern digital self emerges:[7]

> While marking the closure of the Western metaphysical tradition, deconstruction also signals the opening of post-print culture. Deconstruction remains bound to and by the world of print that it nonetheless calls into question. What comes after deconstruction? Imagology. To realize what deconstruction has made possible, it is necessary to move into the world of telecommunications technology. . . . Imagologies follow the lead of deconstruction by giving up the search for secure foundations. The disappearance of the signified in the endless field of signifiers is embraced as an unavoidable cultural condition. . . .
>
> In cyberspace I can change myself as easily as I change clothes. Identity becomes infinitely plastic in a play of images that knows no end. Consistency is no longer a virtue but becomes a vice; integration is limitation. With everything always shifting, everyone is no one. . . . In the global compu-telecommunications network, the real is digitalized and the digital is real. Along the channels of the fiber optic network, disem-

bodied minds travel at the speed of light. As speed increases, distance decreases. Space seems to collapse into a presence that knows no absence and time seems to be condensed in a present undisturbed by past or future. If ever achieved, such enjoyment of presence in the present would be the fulfillment of the deepest and most ancient dreams of the Western religio-philosophical imagination.

Michael Heim has traced the historical antecedents for such scenarios to seventeenth century Germany, where Gottfried Leibniz developed a pair of conceptual schemes which inform both the mechanics and the implicit metaphysics of cyberspace. The first was a notational system designed to remove ambiguity and contingency from vocalized language and thought, allowing a universal, deductive language for problem-solving. Central to this language was its binary, 'either/ or' logic. Heim notes that Leibniz' binary language

> can transform every significant statement into the terms of a logical calculus, a system for proving argumentative patterns valid or invalid, or at least for connecting them in a homogenous matrix. . . . Given the right motor, the Leibnizian symbolic logic—as developed later by George Boole, Bertrand Russell, and Alfred North Whitehead and then applied to electronic switching circuitry by [Claude] Shannon—can function at the speed of thought (1993, 93–94).

Heim further outlines the manner in which the work of the mind is 'streamlined' when the memory circuitry of the computer applies Boolean searches, based on purely symbolic logic:

> 'On the machine level, the computer's micro-switches in the central processing unit organize everything through a circuit based on symbolic logic, and Boolean searches simply apply that logic to text processing. Hardly noticing this spider-like, non-direct logic, we stand at a new remove from concretely embedded language. The computer absorbs our language so we can squirt symbols at lightning speeds or scan the whole range of human thought with Boolean searches. Because the computer, not the student, does the translating, the shift takes place subtly. The computer system slides us from a direct awareness of things to the detached world of logical distance. . . . Through minute logical apertures, we observe the world much like a robot rapidly surveying the surface of things. We cover an enormous amount of material in an incredibly short time, *but what we see comes through narrow thought channels*" (1993, 21–22; emphasis added).

Relevant here is the acclimatization to a mode of thought produced entirely outside the field of awareness. While the *content* that can be experienced through this system may be unlimited, the higher-order system *producing* that content (deductive binary logic, high-speed 'Venn diagrams', etc.) is based on very specific principles of limitation and elision—a sieve conceived precisely to eliminate ambiguity in the structure of the thought process. It is noteworthy that this process is similar to von Foerster's 'blind spot': a phenomenon (in this case a particular breadth of mind) is excluded from the field of awareness, *but we are not aware of its absence.*

Leibniz' second conceptual scheme is the *monadology.* Monads are irreducible mental substances—"the Atoms of the universe." The phenomenal world as we commonly think of it is merely a by-product of the monads' internal perceptions and representations. And though monads are intrinsically solitary entities— "incorporeal Automatons"—each is aware, hologram-like, of the representations held by other monads: "each Monad represents the whole universe." This awareness is achieved via a matrix of "primal regula-tion" controlled by none other than God himself. And while only God manifests perfection and limitlessness, monads are "small divinities," "imitations approach-ing him [God] in proportion to their perfection." Monads thus aspire to a God's-eye view of reality and an all-at-once-ness transcending space and time: "In a confused way they reach out to infinity or to the whole, but are limited and differentiated in the degree of their distinct perceptions" (Leibniz 1902, 251–72).

One need not look far for examples of essentially this view as a primary undercurrent in cyberspatial phi-losophy. From academic and technical discourse to the pop-culture proclamations of *Wired* magazine, the mon-adological aesthetic is ubiquitous. Meredith Bricken, a virtual reality engineer at the University of Wash-ington, posits "the experience of meta-observation, or

the timeless infinity of 'higher' levels of consciousness" (Bricken 1996, 68). Taylor and Saarinen (1994) are
even more explicit:

> Some of the most intelligent and articulate
> preachers of the electronic gospel proclaim a
> New Age in which not only omniscience and
> omnipotence but, more important, omnipres-
> ence becomes possible. In cyberspace, the limi-
> tations of temporality and spatiality seem to be
> overcome in an out-of-the-body experience that
> realizes the most ancient dreams of religion.
> Fleeting electronic images carry the hope of
> immortality. . . .
>
> One of the most fascinating aspects of the com-
> puter revolution is a surprising mixture of tech-
> nical sophistication and mystical aspiration. . . .
> [M]any of the outspoken evangelists of electron-
> ic technology have learned the lessons of Eastern
> religions. The goal of life, they insist, is the
> unity of consciousness, which becomes possible
> on the net. Computation replaces meditation."

It is possible, then, to begin to discern one primary
trajectory of the postmodern self, in both theory and
practice. Uprooted from restrictions imposed by the
narrow commitment to one specific, bound identity,
the self smoothly glides into a decentered 'relational'
existence, its cognitive capacities interfacing with a
high-speed filing machine. This lubricious, frictionless
self is then disembodied, elevated to the status of
omniscient/omnipresent seer via Net-worked information. Therein it achieves 'the unity of consciousness'.

Forgotten here, but not gone, is the 'meat machine'—that pesky lump of carbon, the body.

Michelle Kendrick has outlined the problematic aspects of assuming the evolution of a disembodied self, suggesting that cyberspatial aesthetics "invoke implicitly and explicitly a philosophical tradition that insistently devalues the material in order to create an idealized, ahistorical notion of the self" (1996, 151). She argues that a shift in philosophical stance is required to address the myopia of the Leibnizian model, to take into account the embodied nature of experience:

I suggest that it is precisely the Leibnizian erasure of the body—repressing its materiality into the form of the monad—that makes his philosophy problematic in theorizing the complications of computer technologies. . . . The bodiless entity that hypothetically exists in cyberspace depends, in myriad ways, on the referent of the corporeal body in front of the computer. The relationship between the embodied user, the creation of "alternate" subjectivities in cyberspace, and the technology of the computer, is tightly intermeshed; and evoking Leibniz can reduce the complexity by *bracketing the body*, allowing its displacement into the seemingly unencumbered, desiring intelligence. . . . I would . . . suggest an alternate history that factors embodiment into descriptions of subjectivity. (Kendrick 1996, 151–52; emphasis added)

Kendrick's perspective is useful, not simply as yet another way of emphasizing the body, but rather for the manner in which she begins to clarify why the body is so important in understanding the self. Drawing on David Hume's assessment of identity, Kendrick provides a basis for understanding the body as a *pivot into new terrain,* in the sense raised at the beginning of this essay (1996, 152–54):

> (Hume): However at one instant we may consider the related succession [of perceptions] as variable or interrupted, we are sure the next to ascribe to it a perfect identity, and regard it as invariable and uninterrupted. . . . Thus we feign the continu'd existence of the perceptions of our senses, to remove the interruption; and run into the notion of soul, and self, and substance, to disguise the variation.

> (Kendrick): The process of crafting the fiction of 'soul, and self, and substance,' Hume argues, is founded on memory. Memory is, in a very real sense, truly the process of re-membering— yoking the temporal sequence of distinct sensory impressions and the beliefs and ideas that they inspire through notions of *resemblance* and *causation.* . . . The subject exists through time, in memory, and by means of the 'habit' of connecting perceptions in such a manner that they continually reinscribe the fiction of a stable identity. The spaces of sensory impression, in contrast to the imaginary spaces behind the computer screen, are proprioceptive spaces. . . . There can be no dismissing the space of our bodies, which perceive and sense, *which gather*

the data on which to assemble our habitual fictions. [emphasis added]

We return to the notion of a groundless, chimerical self. Unlike Gergen's social chameleon, however, this self is groundless due to its *direct apprehension of the unbounded phenomenal world from which it derives its very being*—an apprehension that can only occur through the body. We find here a clue to the impulse to crystallize identity: The shock of the unknown, arising moment to moment, pervades the entire psychosomatic system, generating a perpetual existential crisis—a search for some reliable point of reference in a dizzying flux of events. The solution is the formation of an 'I', a point of remembered continuity that orders and makes sense of the flux.

Precisely because this shock arises again and again, its resolution—the image of a self—must be constructed again and again. This cycle, proceeding much faster than the speed of conscious thought, both derives from and feeds back into the body and the senses. Having been 'practiced' at the psychosomatic level throughout the course of one's life, it is coded at a much more fundamental level than language or social norms.

Tarthang Tulku offers a useful perspective here (LOK, 223):

A world in which the 'historical self' is no longer 'real' may seem inconceivable. But in moments of surprise or unusual intensity, when the self is taken off guard, such a possibility may for a moment seem to open up. The response on the part of the self is likely to be a profound fear, described by some writers as fear of the void: an existential anxiety that can paralyze the will and destroy all hope for joy in living.

Usually such an anxiety is not tolerated for long; instead, the prospect is thrust out of awareness. The intense fear that it generated is soon forgotten, but its effects remain, solidified into fixed 'boundaries' and mental patterns that exclude certain kinds of knowledge.

Such perspectives open the possibility for a truly radical exploration of the foundations of the self—an exploration that is *qualitatively different* from that offered in cyberspace. In the next section I will have more to say about such exploration, attempting to illustrate how 'proprioceptive spaces'—mind/body relationships—can reveal the substrate from which the 'primordial' self emerges. For now, I wish to emphasize that immersion in cyberspace moves in precisely the opposite direction. It subsumes and enfolds the primordial dynamic, thus leaving it fully intact and wholly unexplored.

We are left with a core insight. To casually pronounce the 'end of the subject' is to offer a miscue. Whether it leads us into the purely linguistic world of deconstruction or gestures toward the disembodied digital world of 'pure consciousness,' such a pronouncement leaves us with insufficient resources for directly encountering or challenging the primordial foundations of the self.

351

PART III: PIVOTS

Forming a picture of reality based on the 'reality as construct' insight is one thing; but inhabiting that picture is quite another.   *(VOK, 5)*

How do we move from an inferential theory of 'reality as a construct' to a living embodiment of that theory? How are we to understand the self in this context? In this final portion of the essay I will tentatively explore the manner in which the TSK vision and the work of David Bohm address these questions.

A close reading of both Tarthang Tulku and David Bohm reveals assessments of the self's groundlessness that echo the work of David Hume. From Tarthang Tulku's perspective (LOK, 173):

> The ongoing persistence of a unified self appears to the mind as a self-evident truth. It brings with it two corollaries: the flow of experience from past to future, and the objective existence of a surrounding world that is subject to that flow. . . . Such basic constructs . . . are set up and offered for interpretation before the mind knows it. Understandings, judgements, even the basic structure of consciousness itself, arise within this pre-existing matrix, which itself remains immune to inquiry. . . . Arguments may be advanced that undermine the logic of a unitary self; alternative stories may be told; but it all takes place within the founding story.

And from Bohm (1996a, 120–22):

> [T]he concept of the self must include the idea that the self has existed, and will exist: it includes time. If you say, 'I only exist at this moment', nobody would regard that as a concept of the self. . . . You also form an image of the world in which you live, because the self-image must have an image of the world in which it lives. . . . That image is sensed as reality. It's very vital, full of energy and it is sensed as reality—the supreme reality, the central reality, from the very beginning. . . . So everything is attributed to the self-world image: whatever you do, whatever you think, whatever you desire, whatever your intentions are—they are all attributed to the self-world image.

I propose that this 'self/world image'—usually immune from inquiry—has an Achilles heel: the body itself. From this perspective the body can be used as a *pivot*—a means of 're-turning' to a living matrix of energy and information not available when the body is bracketed in cyberspace, or when all meaning is attributed to a 'play of language'.

In the book, *Time, Space, and Knowledge*, a series of specific exercises involving both mind and body provide the foundation for such an inquiry. The first series of exercises and commentaries focuses specifically on the nature of embodiment. This focus is not used to glorify the body, nor to attribute any absolute qualities to it, but rather to emphasize its inescapable relevance in comprehending the nature of our existence. The 'giant body' exercises, for instance, seem designed in part to allow the mind's inner vision to become intimately familiar with the thought-emotion-feeling complex. Tarthang Tulku addresses the issue in Exercise 7 (TSK, 35):

> In each situation [in daily life], notice that its overall character and nature are reflected in your own psycho-physical embodiment. Observe the complex interrelationship between sensation, 'mind', thoughts, emotions, and body which constitutes 'you in that situation'. For instance, the mind receives input; it thinks thoughts; these thoughts bear an emotional dimension; and emotions are embodied in particular physical areas (the stomach, the throat, etc.). Such embodiment leads to sensations which again tie in with particular emotions, memories, thoughts, and so on.

In looking into the same issue, Bohm remarks:

> Movements are taking place inside of you—physical feelings—the heartbeat, the blood pressure, the way you breathe, the way your body feels tense; and also the kinds of thoughts that go along with these feelings. You can observe these things, be aware of them, and of their connection. . . . As you become aware of the connection, it becomes more clear that they are not independent of one another. (1996c, 74)

I understand these observations, and others like them, to be proposing a field of inquiry that encourages us to move beyond inferential understanding into the actual flow of living energy. The intention is not to pacify or manipulate the dynamic of the field, but to see it at work. To enter this field is to move closer to the shock described in Part II of this essay (see p. 350 above)—the shock of unbounded experience that bewilders the mind and (under ordinary circumstances) reflexively generates the self.

From within this field of inquiry, it becomes possible to experiment with a further—and crucial—aspect of the whole process: the emergence of a watching self, an 'I' that can watch 'me' as well as 'the world'. Tarthang Tulku (like Bohm) presents ways to encounter this 'watching self' in a non-inferential, embodied manner. Exercises 8 (The Translucent Body) and 9 (Participation as Observer; Participation as Embodied Person) in the first TSK book outline, among other things, the following process:

One attends to the field of body-mind-thought relations, aware of the patterns at work, while at the same time "try[ing] to remain aware of your own presence as the observer of all the patterns." One also attends to the partitioned nature of 'body', 'mind', and 'thought'—though they are interconnected, they still seem somewhat opaque and distinct. One can then perhaps allow a kind of 'translucence' to emerge, in which these distinctions (between body, mind, thought, as well as between the experience and the experience-er) begin to 'open up' or dissolve. Finally, close attention is paid to the tendency to 'come out' of the openness—to pull back as a separate watcher that examines the openness.

One is not encouraged to try to stop the emergence of the watcher, but simply to "watch that process very carefully". In this way, says Tarthang Tulku, *"it may be possible to see the emergence of objects and of the ordinary 'knower' as a tendency toward 'freezing' what is actually a completely open dimension"* (TSK, 36–37; emphasis added).

A related process is presented by Tarthang Tulku in his overview of Kum Nye (exercises developed by him for Westerners on the basis of Tibetan medicine and Buddhist teachings). Here is a summary of the threefold process he describes (1978, 12–13):

1) One attends to feelings which are "easy to identify and describe" and have a specific 'tone' "such as joy or sadness." Specific sensations—'surface feelings'—accompany these tones, and are felt in specific parts of the body. There is a distinct sense of the self being aware of these feelings and sensations.

2) Attending to these initial sensations enables one to penetrate to a deeper level in which feelings are characterized by "greater density and toughness" and "a holding quality which blocks energy flow." These denser aspects can, however, be 'gently melted'. *"[T]here may be a sense of the exercise doing itself*, though there is still an awareness of the 'self' feeling the sensation. The self may, however, be experienced as less solid." [emphasis added]

3) No particular feelings can be "separated out and identified;" "we approach pure energy or experience." The only approximation to a feeling is "a

kind of totally melting quality." Finally, "[a]t this level the individual ego no longer exists, for we become the feeling, totally one with it."

There seems to be a common theme in these two sequences: Beginning from an overt subject/object polarity, one moves into the sensory-cognitive realm, attending to the embodied dynamic of feelings and thoughts. In this way, the distinctness of a separate observer is diminished, and perhaps becomes translucent. By 'relaxing into' this translucence—a kind of transition zone—the sense of watcher may then disappear completely, albeit perhaps only for a brief period. With regard to the sense of being 'in' a feeling or thought, rather than standing apart from it, Tarthang Tulku alludes to a particular kind of "knowingness":

> Through such 'knowingness' which is 'in' all psychological energies, we can perform a kind of natural alchemy and transform emotions and trends which are ordinarily troublesome. Such a transformation *need effect no changes*, but is simply a matter of being *in* the energies which we are. . . . This approach to integration and balance is much more effective than therapies which take 'treatment' to mean 'change.' If we set out to *change* something, we are clearly not *in* it.

> Therapies which seek to relive or work through traumas succeed to the extent that they do because they involve a degree of contact with the knowingness that is *in* the traumatic feelings (TSK, 268; emphasis in original).

I understand what Tarthang Tulku has presented in these exercises and commentaries to be a 'living map' of the generating dynamic of the primordial self. Of course, the written description is not the living map. Moving *into* various somatic states, however, will take us to the living map—the active energy distributed throughout the mind/body complex.

David Bohm also puts forward suggestions regarding such a living map. Bohm's map has at its heart the notion of *proprioception*, which means literally 'self-perception'. This is not introspection, or the self looking at itself. The term is most commonly used in therapeutic physiology, and refers to the body's ability to immediately monitor its own activity. Proprioception is what allows us to walk up and down steps in a coherent manner, or to maintain a comfortable upright position in a chair, without exercising conscious control. Bohm proposes that while the body has proprioception, the thought process seems to lack it. (It should be noted that when employing the term 'thought,' Bohm is actually using it as shorthand for 'thought-feeling-emotion-body.')

Bohm suggests a series of experiments which might be used to extend physiological proprioception into the domain of thought. He offers what could again be understood as a three-fold process: suspension, proprioception, and the merging of the 'observer' and the 'observed':

1) The suggestion is to *suspend* any particular experience, such as being hurt and angry:

Normally when you are angry you start to react outwardly, and you may just say something nasty. Now suppose I try to suspend that reaction. Not only will I not insult that person outwardly, but I will suspend the insult that I make *inside* me. Even if I don't insult somebody outwardly, I am insulting him inside. So I will suspend that, too. I hold it back, I reflect it back. You may also think of it as suspended in front of you so that you can look at it—sort of reflected back as if you were in front of a mirror. In this way I can see things that I wouldn't have seen if I had carried out that anger, or if I had suppressed it and said, "I'm not angry" or "I shouldn't be angry" (1996c, 20; emphasis in original).

The point of suspension is to help make proprioception possible, to create a mirror so that you can see the result of your thought. You have it inside yourself because your body acts as a mirror and you can see tensions arising in the body (1996c, 25).

2) The next phase is to move more deeply into the thought-feeling nexus, rather than keeping a distance from it:

There is a difference between thinking *about* the hurt, and *thinking the hurt*. Thinking about the hurt is saying the hurt is 'out there,' and I form abstractions about it, like a table. Therefore I'm not doing anything, because the hurt isn't like a table—it's *me*. The other way is to *think the hurt*, which is to go through the thought and let it produce whatever it's going to do, which means to let it stand in the body and in consciousness without being suppressed and without being carried out (1996c, 77; emphasis in original).

The view here is that by merging with the hurt rather than standing at a distance, we can directly experience the interplay between words, thoughts, emotions, and physical reactions, very much as described in TSK's Exercise 8. A direct sensing of these dynamic tensions can further deepen awareness:

So we need the 'negative' sense of incoherence, which is the road to coherence. If a person is sensitive to incoherence, he begins acknowledging it, and finding out what its source is. . . . Coherence includes the entire process of the mind—which includes the tacit process of thought. Therefore, any change that really counts has to take place in the tacit, concrete process of thought itself. It cannot take place only in abstract thought.

The tacit, concrete process is *actual* knowledge, and it may be coherent or not. In the case of riding a bicycle, if you don't know how to ride, then the knowledge isn't right—the tacit knowledge is not coherent in the context of trying to ride the bike, and you don't get the intended result. The incoherence becomes clear— you fall when you want to ride . . . .

Therefore, changing the abstract thought is one step, but unless it also changes the way the body responds, it won't be enough. Someone could say, "You're not doing it right. . . . You should turn in the direction you're falling, but your instinct is making you turn the other way." All of that would help, but eventually it has to come into the tacit. You need the tacit knowledge *which you actually get by riding*, and then you are sort of correcting the previous knowledge. There is a movement in that tacit knowledge, which is that it is exploring possibilities. . . .

The question is, can we do this in thought as well as in bicycle riding? I am proposing that thought—to think—is actually a tacit process more subtle than riding the bicycle. The concrete process of thinking is very tacit. At the actual level where thinking emerges in the tacit process, it is a movement. In principle, that movement could be self-aware . . . without bringing in a 'self' who is aware of it. 'Proprioception' is a technical term—you could also say 'self-perception of thought,' 'self-awareness of thought,' or 'thought is aware of itself in action' (1996c, 78–79; emphasis in original).

This particular 'tacit knowledge'—or proprioception of thought—is, I would suggest, precisely what Tarthang Tulku refers to as the "'knowingness' which is 'in' all psychological energies."

3) The move 'into' the mind-body interplay can reveal a dynamic in which the observing self has no part to play:

The ordinary picture is that the only connection between thoughts, feelings, and actions is the central entity who does it all and experiences it all. That is one idea of how everything is connected up, and that's why the 'central entity' is felt to be so important: everything goes through him. But in fact you can get evidence that thoughts and feelings move as processes on their own; they are not being run by "me." They are not being produced by the me, and they are not being experienced by the me (1996c, 74–75).

We can see in these sequences that both Tarthang Tulku and David Bohm recommend a comprehension of the movement and interplay of embodied experience. To move 'into' this interplay is crucial, in that it allows access to the very terrain from which the self emerges. Indeed, to begin to move beyond the limitations imposed by the codings of the embodied self presents us with dramatically new possibilities. Tarthang Tulku states (LOK, 291–92):

There are so many ways of being—so many different worlds, each with its own patterns of arising and becoming. Beneath the world of daily existence vibrates the fantastic world of subatomic particles. In the depths of outer space black holes transform the nature of time and place. There are realms of higher energies, realms visible and invisible, realms existent and non-existent.

As conceptual analysis gives way to more direct forms of inquiry, and such alternative ways of being become newly accessible, we may tap a knowing difficult to put into words. Yet even as we struggle with the limitations of language and thought, we begin to notice that such knowledge is self-affirming, communicating itself not only in what we think or say, but in our actions and our way of being.

And Bohm remarks (1996b, 141–42):

I'm saying that all of us can change. We don't say it's going to be easy or hard (we don't know), but it opens up the way—like saying that once you see that uranium nuclei can disintegrate, it opens up a big perspective. . . . You see, there may be an infinity of worlds possible for us, according to how they're represented. That's why I said not to accept the notion of 'reality' too uncritically. This is a very subtle notion. . . . You can't do it too quickly. The notion that there is a unique world, a uniquely possible world, may not be right.

In closing this essay, I would like to suggest a further exercise which may be helpful in illustrating many of the issues raised to this point. I offer this exercise in the spirit suggested by Tarthang Tulku: "You are free to make your own commentaries, add your own insights, develop your own versions" (DTS, xxiii).

Imagine the impact of an experience, say embarrassment. Picture the initial embarrassment as a stone dropped in a still pond—it sends out concentric waves in every direction. In fact, the concrete experience of embarrassment is very much like this—waves of tense energy radiate through the body and mind. For a brief moment, there is a kind of shock, and nothing more—just the raw embarrassment. Quickly, of course, comes the observer, or watcher. This watcher is rarely, if ever, neutral or still. He has some business to conduct—to diminish the embarrassment, to cover it over, to alter it in some way.

Imagine now that *the energy generated by the watcher's activity* is like a second stone dropped into the pond—the pond, of course, being the body. The energy generated by this second stone will radiate throughout the mind and body much as with the first stone. But there are now two energy patterns, or wave patterns. The second pattern encounters the 'concentric waves' generated by the initial stone, creating an interference pattern and altering the very constitution of the first wave pattern. Correspondingly, when one experiences actual embarrassment, and then judges that embarrassment, a new level of tension—generally leading to a distinctly muddled and confused condition—arises. This confusion is not in the mind only, but is *directly perceptible throughout the entire body.*

Noticing this, one may have an impulse to stop the generation of the second pattern—to stop judging. Most likely, this will generate yet another energy pattern—a third stone being dropped. An infinite regress is thus set in motion. Some version of this infinite regress seems to be the very way we conduct our daily lives. The suggestion here, however, is that it may be possible to transform this impulse toward regress into the 'knowledge' Tarthang Tulku refers to, or the 'proprio-ception of thought' that Bohm describes.

First, we can envision any particular experience as the 'first stone.' When a second stone is then dropped, the important point is to *sense directly* the extra surge of tension/confusion that occurs when the two energy patterns (first stone plus second stone) encounter one another. For instance, I am angry, and I then tell myself I should not be angry. It is the *direct sensing* of these two energy patterns 'running into one another' that holds out the possibility for ending the cycle of infinite regress—the cycle of watcher watching watcher, then being watched by another watcher, and so on.

How might this work? When I touch a hot stove, an awareness faster than thought—faster than any watcher —immediately causes my hand to retract. This aware-ness is highly sensitive to *difference*—in the case of the stove, the difference in temperature indicates danger to the organism. In the same way, the body can be direct-ly, sensitively aware of the difference generated when the energy of judging is added to the energy of anger, or embarrassment, or whatever the case may be.

Inherent in this difference is a subtle but pervasive forcefulness or aggression. But because we do not nor-mally attend to the precise moment of difference when this force is generated, we become acclimatized to this dynamic—the watcher 'operating upon' the watched. The suggestion here is that directed attention—ini-tially at the conscious level—can allow the body's awareness of its own energy to 'read' and respond to the concrete activity of the observer upon the observed.

We can now envision a new prospect—one which moves in the opposite direction of endless regress. We can imagine the 'second stone' that is dropped to be of varying size. Narcissism or self-loathing would be a 'big stone'; mild agitation might be an 'average-sized stone'; casual noticing might be a 'small stone'. Each stone, of course, generates a correspondingly large or small energy wave. The larger or stronger the wave from the second stone, the greater the force with which it encounters the first wave. If, however, the body's mind is becoming increasingly sensitive to these differences in force, a new dynamic can come into play. Concretely realizing that the very act of observing is causing potentially confusing perturbations, the body's mind begins naturally to diminish the 'observing impulse.' We could thus envision 'second stones' of smaller and smaller size being dropped, causing less and less perturbation, and allowing the first stone, be it embarrassment, joy, or any other condition, to permeate the entire field of body and consciousness in relatively unobstructed fashion. Is it possible ultimately to have no second stone, no interference pattern, no separate observer? What would happen then? What kind of world would we be in?

CONCLUSION

Having inquired in a rudimentary way into aspects of the body-mind interplay put forward by Tarthang Tulku and David Bohm, we can return to the concerns raised at the beginning of this essay—total questioning and the exploration of new terrain as the basis for cultural wisdom. Based on the discussion here, I suggest that to question the self—concretely, not theoretically—is a genuine move toward total questioning.

As the self is a modeling of reality which subsumes all other modelings, questioning this self implicitly questions our entire world view, as well as the meanings it contains. Pursuing the implication that there may in fact be no actual 'self' (in the way we normally think of it) would then be a move into truly unknown territory. It has been my contention throughout this essay that the questioning of an *embodied* self is of a more fundamental order than to question the *idea* of a self, as posited by postmodern theory and practice.

The strange marriage of deconstructionist reductionism and digital transcendentalism may in fact prefigure the future of humanity, but I'm not sure it is a future I would want to inhabit, or that I would wish upon our children. Human *meaning* may yet be reduced to linguistic formulae, while human *being* is progressively attributed to mechanical prostheses. But this vision strikes me as bleak, and I would pay it little heed were it not for the fact that its stock is rising rather rapidly.

Fortunately, our options are not so slim as this. Human beings continue to sense the presence of extra-linguistic meaning and non-prosthetic being, rooted in a matrix of unknown origin. As long as these sensibilities remain alive, it is possible to tilt toward a culture of wisdom—an enlightened society, as Tarthang Tulku says—rather than a culture of algorithms.

In such a context, technologies will find their place, perhaps augmenting a deeper kind of knowing. But we cannot allow matters to work the other way around. To suggest that technologies—which are never anything more than the ornaments of one limited aspect of our own consciousness—can or should order the human, is a recipe for collective delusion, and perhaps disaster.

What an enlightened society might look like, we do not know. Surely, though, it must take into account the 'orderings' of reality, as best we can discern them. We seem to understand that oak trees bear oak trees, and not cats. Yet somehow we are coming to believe that the deeper imperatives of the 'self/world view' will do something other than regenerate in the postmodern world. We drift toward this belief because we have not examined it. And we do not examine it because we are increasingly encouraged to reconfigure the self so that it dovetails with what we are learning from our fragmented society.

To counter this trend, we must learn to give sustained attention to the concrete nature of this everemerging self. This may take an instant, or it may take a thousand years. Either way, the opportunity is always near at hand—as near as eyes, bone, and blood. And as we probe into this unknown terrain, we may begin to discern, from the outposts of embodied being, that indeed, *the mountains are moving like waves.*

NOTES

1. Derrida (1981) and Derrida (1991a) both present Derrida's theories in relatively concise form. See also Leitch (1983), a partisan yet excellent introduction to the foundational tenets of deconstructionism.

2. Doel's exposition of this issue is by way of insisting that Derrida himself is in no way concerned with the 'destruction' of the subject. He thus posits two modes of deconstruction: 'reactive' deconstruction (exemplified in the quote in the text) and 'affirmative' deconstruction (exemplified by Derrida, whose ostensible concern is to properly 'configure' the subject). As it is the 'reactive' mode that has most fully entered the culture at large, I focus on it here.

3. See, for instance, Smith (1988).

4. For the flavor of this debate, see "What Are We Doing On-Line?" *Harper's Magazine*, August 1995.

5. It may be useful at this point to clarify some potentially confusing terminology. The reader may suspect certain affinities between deconstruction and constructivism, and both views do posit a certain relativity and indeterminacy of experience. But while deconstruction equates experience with language, constructivism imposes no such limitation on its scope of inquiry. As constructivism is initially concerned with the bio-perceptual foundations of cognition, it explores the non-linguistic experience of various species, and leaves open questions concerning the nature and meaning of both human and non-human experience.

Hayles (1995) has used the term 'social constructivism' to denote an amalgam of deconstructionism and traditional constructivism. While useful in some contexts, this fusion of terms is not helpful for the purposes of this essay.

6.   Bateson leaves open the question of how much our reflexive perceptions are due to genetic factors, and how much due to learned habits.

7.   This book has no page numbers—perhaps to be in keeping with the space/time aesthetic of cyberspace?

REFERENCES

Bateson, G. 1987 [1972]. *Steps to an Ecology of Mind.* Northvale: Jason Aronson.

Bohm, D. 1996a. *Ojai Seminar Transcripts 1986–1989.* Ann Arbor: University Microfilms International. Section 1987.

_____. 1996b. *Ojai Seminar Transcripts, 1986–1989.* Ann Arbor: University Microfilms International. Section 1988.

_____. 1996c. *On Dialogue.* London: Routledge.

Bricken, M. Quoted in R. Markley. "The Metaphysics of Cyberspace."

Doel, M. 1995. "Bodies Without Organs: Schizoanalysis and Deconstruction." In S. Pile and N. Thrift, eds. *Mapping the Subject,* 228–29. London: Routledge.

Derrida, J. 1981. *Positions*. Chicago: Univ. of Chicago.

_____. 1991a. "Différence." In P. Kamuf, ed., *A Derrida Reader*. New York: Columbia Univ. Press.

_____. 1991b. "Speech and Phenomena." In P. Kamuf, ed. *A Derrida Reader*. New York: Columbia University Press.

Finkel, L. 1992. "The Construction of Perception." In J. Crary and S. Kwinter, eds. *Zone 6: Incorporations*, 398–403. New York: Urzone.

Gergen, K. 1991. *The Saturated Self*. USA: Basic Books.

Hayles, N.K. 1990. *Chaos Bound: Orderly Disorder in Contemporary Literature and Science*. Ithaca and London: Cornell University Press.

_____. 1993. "The Seductions of Cyberspace." In V.A. Conley, ed. *Rethinking Technologies*. Minneapolis: University of Minnesota Press.

_____. 1995. "Searching for Common Ground." In M. Soule and G. Lease, eds. *Reinventing Nature? Responses to Postmodern Deconstruction*. Washington D.C.: Island Press

Heim, M. 1993. *The Metaphysics of Virtual Reality*. New York: Oxford University Press.

Kelly, K. 1994. *Out of Control: The Rise of Neo-biological Civilization*. Reading, PA: Addison-Wesley.

Kendrick, M. 1996. "Cyberspace and the Technological Real." In Markley, *op. cit.*, p.151

Kozinski, J. 1970. *Being There*. NY: Harcourt Brace.

Leibniz, G.W. 1902. *Discourse on Metaphysics; Correspondence with Arnaud; Monadology.* G. Montgomery, trans. Peru, IL: Open Court.

Leitch, V. 1983. *Deconstructive Criticism.* New York: Columbia University Press.

Lettvin, J.Y., Maturana, H.R., McCulloch, W.S., and Pitts, W.H. 1959. "What the Frog's Eye Tells the Frog's Brain." *Proceedings of the Inst. of Radio Engineers* 47:11

Markley, R. 1996. "The Metaphysics of Cyberspace." In R. Markley, ed. *Virtual Realities and Their Discontents.* Baltimore and London: Johns Hopkins University Press.

Ornstein, R. 1991. *The Evolution of Consciousness.* New York: Touchstone.

Smith, P. 1988. *Discerning the Subject.* Minneapolis: University of Minnesota Press.

Stone, A.R. 1992. "Virtual Systems." In J. Crary and S. Kwinter, eds. *Zone 6: Incorporations.* New York: Urzone.

Tarthang Tulku. 1978. *Kum Nye Relaxation, Part 1.* Berkeley: Dharma Publishing.

Taylor, M. and Saarinen, E. 1994. *Imagologies: Media Philosophy.* London: Routledge.

Turkle, S. 1995. *Life on the Screen: Identity in the Age of the Internet.* New York: Simon and Schuster.

von Foerster, H. 1989. "On Constructing a Reality." In P. Watzlawick, *The Invented Reality.* NY: W.W. Norton.

'HARD KNOWLEDGE' AND THE TIME, SPACE, AND KNOWLEDGE VISION

Maxim Osinovsky

The Time, Space, and Knowledge vision ("TSK"), until now elaborated single-handedly by Tarthang Tulku, emerged as a system of thought supposed to provide "a visionary medium through which a common ground could be found in the pursuits of knowledge carried out by various sciences and religions" (TSK, xxxi); and "to communicate a way of understanding that does not depend on customary categories of explanation such as existence and non-existence or true and false" (DTS, xiv). As such, it is in tune with the ongoing humanistic reorientation of Western thought that departs from the still prevailing scientific and positivist methodologies.

My intention is to investigate whether TSK nonetheless is able to help deliver "hard knowledge," the kind of knowledge that is usually said to be firmly grounded in facts on one hand, and to be linked to the scientific method practiced in both the natural sciences (fundamental knowledge) and technology (applied knowledge) on the other.

The risk in such an undertaking has been noted by Tarthang Tulku, who writes:

> The interest in making connections between the TSK vision and other paths of inquiry, though natural, is evidence that a 'lower' form of knowledge is in operation. Knowledge is naturally free, but when it is claimed on behalf of a particular doctrine this unlimited freedom is easily lost. Labeling ideas and then comparing those labels does little to further a deeper knowing. In contrast, when inquiry 'takes place' *within* Space, Time, and Knowledge, it does not require adopting one position or rejecting another. As the activity of Knowledge itself, it reveals 'knowingness' and celebrates the independence of the human mind. (LOK, xviii)

It should be noted that Tarthang Tulku considers "hard knowledge" as I have described it to be precisely a "lower" form of knowledge. This makes the present essay even more suspect. Nevertheless, having noted these concerns, I hope that my efforts will help clarify certain issues related to TSK as a *workable* approach to knowledge in the stiff and difficult areas of science and technology.

In writing this essay, I have sought to stay within the spirit of TSK. My aim has been to make definite statements where I could, without taking sides, and to be ready to challenge everything, including the TSK vision itself.

PART ONE

1. An Overview of TSK

I will start by reviewing the TSK vision, highlighting certain features of the vision of potential importance to the subsequent discussion.

Although Tarthang Tulku warns that "it is not easy to trace the true source for the TSK vision" (DTS, xii), his motivation for presenting the vision seems easier to identify. He writes:

> Today we find ourselves in . . . confined circumstances. The sign is that our time is occupied, our space full, our conditions determined; the mark is that we miss the point. When such rhythms are in full swing, we live a life that is wholly burdensome. From the weary moment we wake in the morning to the dark hour when we collapse at night, we deal with routines of restriction. There is no time to feel or think or see. We stand on what has no value and repeat without understanding. We forget that we could test our purpose in being there (DTS, 226).

[In] our tumultuous era, from decade to decade and year to year, events are speeding up. Once we penetrate beneath the tremendous variety of things generated on the surface of experience, we realize that the choices available to us at a deeper level are steadily diminishing. The temporal momentum threatens to overwhelm us. A dark directionality is gathering force, and the lightness of life is losing its luster (DTS, 335).

However, these circumstances could change. "We are architects of our response" (DTS, 226). Available to us is a deeper and more abundant knowledge, creative beauty, a rich and fulfilling life, universal synthesis, 'eternal youth', and so on. "We have been seekers and shakers and talkers and owners too long. Now it is time for transformation" (DTS, 238).

With these possibilities in mind, Tarthang Tulku set about exploring causes of the present gloomy situation and charting a possible way toward transformation of both our personal lives and the life of society. The result is the TSK vision, which is offered freely as a record of his own thoughts and inquiries and an invitation to follow the same path to unlimited knowledge and fulfillment.

TSK eludes any definition. Tarthang Tulku prefers not to define it in any way, although he often says what TSK is not:

I have often been asked how TSK can be classified as a field of study. The question has no easy answer. It is not philosophy or psychology and not religion. Perhaps it can be seen as an adventure of the mind, with the potential to branch out in many directions. For someone knowledgeable in a particular field, TSK may be able to inspire new ideas related to that discipline. For others, TSK may stimulate clarity and a sense of value (DTS, xvi).

TSK is not a system to be learned, assimilated, and applied in a routine and mechanical manner to emerging situations or objects. It leads through various stages and views (including those unexplored by Tarthang Tulku) without clinging to them, so it cannot be identified with any of them. In this sense TSK is a way or a process rather than a doctrine. The search for a new knowledge is more important than taking possession of it. For "knowledge is not a matter of contents, but of an active knowing expressed in inquiry itself" (LOK, xvi). Therefore, TSK may be more accurately characterized as a non-stop path of free and open inquiry: "a symbol for creative freedom . . . *activated* through an inquiry that sets no limits in advance" (LOK, xxvi–xxvii). In this sense, it includes more conventional forms of knowledge, but goes beyond them:

The inquiry here investigates the fundamental process by which human beings turn perceptions into judgments, judgments into patterns, and patterns into fixed positions. It resonates with the central issues of philosophy, psychology, religion, education, and every other field of knowledge that takes the human situation as central (LOK, xxvii).

377

Free and open inquiry is no longer concerned
with answers in the usual way. We look at our
situation 'lightly'; observing in an equal, balanced, and inviting way, we make no special
effort to 'make sense' of what we see. We follow
images and thoughts without accepting their
authority, and make use of reason and observation without having to establish the truth of
what they present. We 'take' no position—not
even the position 'I am the observer'. Prepared
to question observation itself, we can observe
without friction, creating a boundless rhythm
and momentum within perception and awareness . . . . An all-accommodating inquiry can be
activated through analysis that turns from what
is known to the 'coming to be' of what is known
(LOK, 273–275).

Answers are not the purpose of our questioning.
When we learn how to ask fundamental questions in ways that are fresh and alive, we conduct into our lives an intelligence that applies
directly to our own immediate circumstances. . . .
My firm intention is for nothing to be fixed in
advance. The process of questioning itself always
stands at the center (VOK, ix–x).

Another important feature of TSK is that the process
of inquiry changes not only our knowledge but also
ourselves. To some extent this applies to ordinary
knowledge, too: Our knowledge influences our perceptions, judgments, and actions, and so shapes what we
are. But, beyond our formative years, those influences

in most cases mean slow incremental growth or drift rather than a transformation. TSK, however, insists on a most radical transformation. This is necessary for several reasons, the most important being that the structures of ordinary knowledge are ingrained and encoded in the very constitution of our selves. The self cannot understand reality "because it is precisely the *embodiment* of a lapse of such understanding" (TSK, 166).

To put it differently, the self and its knowledge are 'given together'; they are inseparable. Therefore, to be able to conduct a free and open inquiry one needs to get rid of one's self—to literally discard oneself, initiating a most sweeping change. Since ordinary reality, or what we ordinarily think to be reality, is given together with the self, challenging the self means also restructuring reality (DTS, 143); this point will be covered in more detail later. Hence the importance of the TSK "exercises," offered in all of the TSK books.

2. An Initial Critique

As TSK intends to be a major force of personal and social transformation, it will be questioned by others 'out there' from *their* own perspectives. And as there is no shortage of recipes for transformation, many of those questioners will be skeptical. That is, they may wish to evaluate the potential merits of TSK *before* setting their feet on the TSK path. What might they say, on the basis of what has just been presented? Before they even attempt to deal with the "substance" of the vision, they would be likely to raise several doubts.

The most materialistic skeptics probably will say something like this: "If TSK is such a wonderful thing, why are TSKers not among the most successful and influential people on this planet?" One might reply that TSKers do not care about such ordinary concerns as wealth, influence, and so on. But this response, even if it proved accurate on further inquiry, will be unsatisfying for such people, who will presumably decide that TSK does not address their immediate problems and move on.

A softer version of the same challenge might look to Tarthang Tulku's statement in the first TSK book:

> [I]t would seem that now is the time for a new venturing out, for a vision which would integrate and unite all aspects of being, thereby inspiring a broad, open-ended, and vigorous appreciation of life. Space and Time themselves have now presented such a vision . . . (TSK, xxxiv).

If this is so—if TSK has arrived at the "right" time, why has TSK not spread over the Western world like a forest fire? Why does one need to promote or encourage TSK, when one does not need to advertise the Internet, multiculturalism, environmentalism, and other popular ideas?

Let us look now at a different sort of challenge. A questioner interested in what would feed the soul might observe that TSK is nothing more than a school of thought within the Human Potential (HP) movement. Indeed, many features of TSK would fit well with the following typical description of the HP movement:

This is the potential of individuals for self-fulfilment, self-realization or self-actualization. Self-actualizing individuals are characterized by: capacity for acceptance, efficient perception of reality, spontaneity, transcendence of self-concern, detachment, independence of culture and environment, transcendence of environment, social feeling and compassion, deep but selective social relationships, tolerance and respect, ethical certainty, unhostile sense of humour, creativeness.

Realization of human potential is also characterized by expression and defence of values such as: truth, goodness, beauty, wholeness, aliveness, uniqueness, perfection, completion of growth and development, justice and order, simplicity, richness and variety, effortlessness and unstrained action, playful amusement, and self-sufficiency.

Achievement of full human potential is also characterized by higher or transcendent states of consciousness, giving an awareness of undifferentiated inner unity, a sense of underlying oneness behind the empirical multiplicity of external sense impressions, a sense of transcendence of space and time, a deeply felt positive mood of joy and peace, a sense of sacredness, a heightened sense of objectivity and insight into reality and a transcendence of self (Leonard, 1969).

One might reply that TSK goes beyond the question of self-fulfillment to address fundamental issues of philosophy, science, and so on; however, it is also undeniable that those issues are tangential to such invariant core themes of TSK as ultimate reality (called Great Space, Great Time, and Great Knowledge), Being, Great Love, freedom, wholeness, inspiration, ecstasy, enjoyment, creativity, and so on, all of which fit very well into the description of HP above.

Nevertheless, there *is* a fundamental distinction between TSK and the HP movement. Although the quotation given speaks of transcendence of self, HP remains devoted to building on or beautifying the self: making it more open, more creative, more compassionate, etc. TSK, on the other hand, depends on getting rid of the self. This is a first approximation only; a more exact statement would be to say that TSK uses the self as a springboard to jump off into self-less Being. So in TSK the self performs the double function of being a hindrance and an opportunity:

> Beyond the knowledge that the temporal order conducts, there is the knowledge through which the structures that we conduct into being take form. If we are to find a point of access to such knowledge, it can only be in the presentations of the present temporal order: the stories we tell and the structures we conduct. Here, within the ordinary, is where the unknown prior will make itself available.

> Let us be more specific. The knowledge that gives conducting form cannot belong to a self, for the self is a creature of conducted time, and its world is a conducted world. Yet if we reject

the self, with its emotions, its claims of identity, and the pain it inflicts in deceiving itself and others, we will close the only gateway through which a founding and conducting knowledge can emerge. To arrive at the prior, we must first inhabit fully our presenting world, whatever its content and obscuring patterns. . . .

Restructuring reality by challenging the self seems an effective way to bring about change. Something like this seems to happen at various levels in psychotherapy or certain kinds of spiritual experience (DTS, 142–43).

This dual role is deeply problematic, for (as the text just cited goes on to note), a subtle residue of the self persists through multiple insights and illuminations. The Western seeker cannot overcome this problem through Eastern methods for cutting off the self, such as unconditional devotion to a guru or a chosen ideal. In addition, the problem is compounded by the fact that such a seeker usually possesses a well developed intellect (in fact, as should be clear by now, following the TSK path requires a considerable degree of intellectual development). Again, this circumstance both creates a difficulty and offers a potential advantage.

3. The Threefold Path of TSK

One easily notices that any short description of TSK, such as the one given in the previous section, will be vague and superficial. It is easy to talk about such things as understanding the true nature of reality, attaining knowledge free of presuppositions, etc., but it is not that easy or immediately clear how to do it. In other words, a detailed path must be charted and tested. Here Tarthang Tulku has been remarkably successful, outlining such a path with great clarity and care. The TSK books contain detailed and precise theoretical analyses on a wide range of related issues, as well as numerous carefully selected exercises, whose importance has already been suggested.

Presenting the TSK vision in ordinary language was a major challenge, as the terms needed to express many facets of the new vision were nonexistent. Tarthang Tulku has chosen a mixed way of proceeding. He uses familiar terms in new ways, and he also coins new terms (such as 'ness', 'ness-ness', 'zero-structure', and 'bias-stander'). A clue to the way he uses familiar words in non-standard ways can be found in DTS (xxii–xxiii): "In the case of certain technical terms, my own usage may not accurately reflect the conventional meaning, so the reader should look carefully at the context to see what is intended. Often I have relied on the evocative power of the words and on their play and interplay rather than their usual associations."

Given this use of language, reading the TSK texts requires great attentiveness and sensitivity if the transforming power of what is written is to be preserved:

Ordinarily we organize words into stories, definitions, explanations, and interpretations. Constructs give rise to structures that conceal the clear and open interplay of time and space with knowledge rather than revealing them. A

TSK telling must operate differently. It must find a way for language to hold meaning that does not depend on structure or directly support structure. Otherwise the presentation of the vision will be self-defeating, contradicting what it says in the act of saying it.

. . . We must evoke a different way of using words, a telling that remains a questioning and a questioning that is also an imagining. The reader must join in the telling, like a musician who brings a score alive by playing it instead of simply settling back to listen (VOK, 61–62).

With these background comments on the style in which the TSK books are written, let us look at the structure of the presentation of the vision in the published works.

First, the vision is presented under the three interlocking aspects of Time, Space, and Knowledge. Although these three facets are each clearly defined individually, they also serve to comprehend and merge into the unity of Being. It could be said that they embody the triune nature of reality. Inversely, Being, appreciated in an appropriate way, reveals its threefold aspect and so justifies the tripartite structure.

Each of the three aspects in turn may be considered on three different levels. Tarthang Tulku emphasizes that this threefold division, unlike the previous one, is not natural. Instead, it is used (in the first three books of the TSK series) as a convenient device, "a useful way to introduce a way of understanding that departed quite sharply from more conventional kinds of analysis" (DTS, xiv). The first level of Time, Space, and Knowledge is an ordinary level. The second level overcomes all rigid limitations of the first level and reflects the more fluid aspects of reality, which still possess something resembling subtle name and form. The third level transcends all limitations of name and form. Although fundamental to the vision, it does not overly concern us here, since it has little to do with the 'hard' knowledge on which we are presently focusing. This makes a total of nine levels of reality, which may be analyzed in their interplay both horizontally and vertically.[1]

Let us now consider these nine levels in more detail.

Space, 1st level   This is our ordinary space perceived as an empty background filled with well defined things having more or less sharp boundaries, but seen in the light of further possibilities for human fulfillment (cf. TSK, 111). Closer investigation shows that the appearance of objects is due to a special 'focal setting' or perspective. By maintaining this limited focal setting, we perpetuate our way of seeing the world (in its spatial aspect) as an empty space populated with separate things. This way of seeing extends to the psychological and sociological domains. It creates such notions as our sense of inner space or spaces, populated with thoughts, sensations, and emotions; or a social space, populated with separate nations, races, groups, etc.

Space, 2nd level   As soon as we realize that our familiar vision of the world depends on a particular focal setting and learn to 'open' the setting, we find ourselves in a second-level relationship to Great Space (reality or

Being in its spatial aspect). This is an infinite realm to explore, and the new relationship can manifest in infinitely many ways: an increase of personal freedom, greater physical relaxation, a heightening of the senses, and so on (TSK, 112–13).

On this level it becomes clear how the first-level vision emerges. If we adopt a particular restricted perspective, that perspective shapes our feelings, images, and interpretations in a certain way, and triggers a process of consolidation giving rise to coherent complex patterns. These patterns then become 'frozen' and further consolidate our sensations, etc., in accordance with the original perspective, via a process of feedback. Thus a kind of screen between us and reality (or, more exactly, within reality) is formed. What we see is what is transmitted by and through the screen. "Thus there arises the conventional view. . . . The person 'sees things', locates them in space, traverses the intervening distance, and touches them" (TSK, 32–33).

The same process also gives rise to a sense of oneself as a separate being. The notion of solid, stable objects out there necessitates the structure of "an independent self or mind as the source or basis of" the first-level "experience" (TSK, 49). "In order to preserve its status as a continuous being in a stable, meaningful world, the self assumes a position. It must then freeze this position by considering it as an absolutely stable or motionless platform from which the changes and affairs of the world can be viewed. As a result, this viewing discovers a strictly external space which is no more than 'room', regions, or locations" (TSK, 49–50).

The self and its objects thus emerge together. "[T]he mind is a sign of a specific focal setting being taken on Great Space" (TSK, 64). They are likewise to be transcended together. We cannot change our world-view in a radical way without changing ourselves. We need to work on both the subject-pole and the object-pole of experience. The first step on this path is to challenge, transparentize, and open up the output of a setting, thus deactivating it. After that we may be able to change the focal setting itself. The change in setting may open beyond ordinary appearance to Great Space, or there may be a more subtle shift, through which we perceive the initial output as already a manifestation of Great Space.

Space, 3rd level (Great Space)   As we proceed in this way, everything that was previously seen as subject-object encounters or various focal settings (including philosophy, art, science, etc.) is eventually perceived as a play of Great Space. The strategy of opening a focal setting is not needed anymore; the picture of levels breaks down. Great Space is a great equalizer: "[F]inally, it becomes clear that Great Space is not higher than something else and that the Great Space experience is the 'same' as the narrow 'setting' experience" (TSK, 113).

Time, 1st level   This is ordinary time as an index for states and events. On the first level of experience, and in terms of physical events, the flow of time cannot be modified (except for certain exotic relativistic effects), stopped, or reversed. In psychological terms, this is 'lived time'—more flexible than "physical" time (for example, it may shrink or become more prolonged), but often perceived as a hidden, autonomous force that relentlessly pushes us about.

Time, 2nd level   An encounter with time on the second level brings a direct experience of time and reveals its hidden dynamics. "'Time' at this second stage can be seen to be the essential force that lets moment give way to moment, *and* the factor which permits items *within* a situation or moment to have their own identities" (TSK, 146). "Once we see that the glue linking moments—and also 'things' within moments—is 'time', and that 'time' shows Great Space, we may also see that 'time' provides a third sort of link. It is a bridge to other realms entirely different than our usual one" (148).

At this stage we realize that all kinds of unusual experiences that may arise are transitional appearances, given with time. Rather than stopping our inquiry at this point, we need to "*[feed] everything that is given with 'time' back into 'time', . . . stimulating and accelerating it,* getting more resultant energy and again putting that back into 'time'. All understandings and realizations which we have can be fed back in this manner, rather than holding on to them and taking them as 'the truth'." (TSK, 149).

"This acceleration process has a tremendous transmuting and lifting effect" (TSK, 150–51). "Solid things, places, and directed processes seen on the first level become appreciated—in their second-level 'time' aspect —as being very fluid. This fluid quality is a central feature of 'time', which [on the first level] has been rendered more dry and friction-filled in order for us to play in a first-level way" (161). Further second-level insights include a breakdown of ordinary space-time laws ("happenings cease to follow a standard coherence or ordering principle" [150]); and seeing "all serial 'timing' to be occuring in the same place, rather than establishing an extended 'world out there'." (151).

However, this stage is still fraught with subtle obstacles. "Perhaps the most seductive trap and the pinnacle of second stage experiences is the feeling of intimacy or mutual interpenetration on a cosmic scale—a kind of all-embracing field phenomenon. 'Thing' perspectives are replaced in this case by a field perspective. . . . However, such ideas regarding Space, Time, and what is fundamentally real are only applicable on a second stage view of time. . . . [T]here remains the idea that *there is something*. . . . There is also still a sense of 'occuring' or 'happening'. Both of these characteristics, oddly enough, vitiate a fully 'intimate' way of being. Interaction itself . . . is a dimming of a full 'being together'." (TSK, 158).

Time, 3rd level (Great Time)   This is best described in negative terms: It is neither a thing, nor a process, nor a happening. Fluidity on the third level attains the utmost degree and may be likened (my comparison) to the phenomenon of superfluidity observed in some quantum liquids:

> When fully appreciated, Great Time is seen to be a kind of perfectly fluid, lubricious dimension—it is quintessentially 'slippery'. For this reason—although there seems to be movement and separate places to move to on the first level, and still more open, fluid possibilities of move-

ment on the second level—on the third level there is no 'going' and no separate places. It is as though all the friction in the world were removed —nothing can then walk away from anything else. So, from a third level view, an eternity of 'straying' still leaves us very much 'at home', intimately united (TSK, 161–62).

Knowledge, 1st level (ordinary knowledge)   Because it relies on the self as a knower, ordinary knowledge employs the subject-object orientation. It consistently interprets reality in terms of separate interacting objects embedded in the spatio-temporal environment. This perpetuates the gap between the knower and the known, and forces the knower to fabricate theories and models to reconstruct reality. In this way knowledge becomes limited, distorted, trapped, or even inaccessible:

> Although there may be nothing wrong with beliefs and concepts in themselves, if they constitute the only way we know of being, they become a trap. They proliferate and interlock until no alternative to them is even visible. They amount to massive solicitations of our attention, keeping us 'tuned in' in a very constrictive way (TSK, 233).

> There is very little depth or sensitivity to 'lower knowledge', and little fluidity as well. Everything is forced into conformity with a certain implicit logic of how knowing occurs and of how the known world is structured. 'Lower knowledge' acts like a kind of magnet, attracting experiences and presuppositions that obscure

understanding of the nature of appearance. It tracks only the merest surface of Space and Time. . . . It creates a kind of local gravitational field, and in trying to find our way out of it through using 'lower knowledge' itself, we are actually carrying it along with us (TSK, 237–38).

Since lower knowledge and the self are inseparable ('given together'), the self needs to guard lower knowledge in order to protect and perpetuate itself:

We have remained unconcerned about the problems caused by 'lower knowledge' *because we are actually afraid to question them.* . . . The self does not want to know at the cost of losing its primacy in the overall scheme of things. It will not let itself acknowledge such 'knowings'; it would rather keep on playing with belief systems. . . (TSK, 238–39).

The role of the self in relation to knowledge is complex, and Tarthang Tulku explores in considerable detail a variety of specific roles the self plays in this regard. For us, the most interesting of these roles is the self as narrator, for it is the narrator who engages in what we ordinarily consider acts that involve knowing: oral communication, writing newspaper articles, TV broadcasting, creating historical texts, scientific theories and technical manuals, exchanging information on the Internet, and so on. "The self as narrator actively links successive moments of knowing, wanting, and interpreting" (LOK, 171) and weaves them into stories. The aim of the narrator's stories is twofold: to give coherence to the flow of events and to impart a meaning to the self's doings, thoughts, and imaginings.

The self's stories are immensely varied and reflect its needs, desires, feelings, experiences, projects, naming, explanations, and interpretations. They generate subsidiary stories, stories about stories, and even "stories (such as this one) about how the story-telling mechanism operates" (LOK, 172). This extremely complicated web of stories rests on a so-called founding story (a metastory):

> The narrator's stories unite owner, actor, and objective self, bearing witness to their existence and persistence 'over' time. The central narrative structures —"I am; I feel; I experience; I want; I act"—are the self-authenticating truth of every story. . . . The narrator thus asserts the self by telling another story —a founding story that makes possible all other stories. . . . This founding story is intended as its own witness: presented as the basis for self and world alike. . . . Such basic constructs . . . are set up and offered for interpretation before the mind knows it. Understanding, judgments, even the basic structure of consciousness itself, arise within this preexisting matrix, which itself remains immune to inquiry. . . .

> These consensus constructs, which center on the self, are the 'founding story'. Established prior to all questioning, the founding story is 'self-perpetuating'. Arguments may be advanced that undermine the logic of a unitary self; alternative

stories may be told; but it all takes place within the founding story. . . . Universal assent to the founding story means unbridled power for the narratives that the founding story unfolds, for in terms of the claims of the self, apart from such narratives *there is no reality*: The world of historical time and of events bound together in meaningful patterns unfolds as a dynamic to which no countervailing force can be opposed (LOK, 172–74).

Knowledge, 2nd and 3rd levels The above quotes, extracted from what is a much more complete description, offer an awesome account of an all-powerful and self-consistent force, a gigantic illusion keeping a tight grip on our minds. It is so powerful that it can absorb any project intended to deactivate it, for any project will still be "mine." Eventually it will find its place within the founding story or in the superstructure of derivative stories (it is to be remembered that internal conflicts fit into the web of stories, too).

No finite solution to the problem will work. However, an infinite solution is possible—turning a theory of freedom into a path to freedom. By always moving on, never stopping to settle down in an absolute or ultimate truth, we can thread the way of open and free inquiry. In doing so we eventually see that the path is synonymous with Time, so it is seen not as a path but actually as *life*. One becomes the path itself:

What is being suggested is not an absolute position describing the truth about a world order, but rather a way of growing without ever falling into a stagnant orientation. Space, Time, and Knowledge are not a fixed set of terms, or a determinate system, but a kind of vehicle to infinite opening. . . . Great Space and Time are 'here'. Great Knowledge can appreciate the opportunities and value they offer. The rest is just a matter of living out this unfolding vision in everything that we do. This is truly an 'all positive', *life oriented* path (TSK, 215–16).

Suppose that instead of *possessing* knowledge, we could successfully *embody* it. Our new inseparability from knowledge might reveal a universal knowledgeability, active throughout space and time. The result would be a true transformation in our being (DTS, xxvii).

It may at first seem impossible to start a truly open and free inquiry. "The idea that this Knowledge cannot be gained or utilized by a self, might seem at first to thwart ordinary progress and achievement" (TSK, 219). This is not quite so, according to Tarthang Tulku: even fabrications of the self *are* Great Knowledge, though greatly distorted (from the point of view of a lower knowledge). In that sense, Great Knowledge has always been available to us. The first step is to realize that "the only thing preventing us from utilizing Great Knowledge is our unwillingness to leave aside our ordinary feelings about ourselves and our world, and to work with these on a new basis. And this willingness evolves naturally through a 'thawing' process which begins with an intuitive insight, a change of habit, or even with a critique of ordinary views" (TSK, 220).

Next one may launch a systematic process of criticizing conventional assumptions about reality, knowledge, etc. The TSK books offer many examples of such philosophical analyses, which could be viewed as "blueprint[s] for 'acquiring' Great Knowledge" (TSK, 221). Together with the guided exercises found in the books, such analyses

> can combine to press the notion of the 'mind' to its limits, to 'open it up' without damaging anything. In the process, a different picture of reality arises. Rather than being an extended field of separate knowables, acts of 'knowing', and confusion, the picture which emerges is more balanced. . . . [P]ervasive clarity . . . begins to be exposed as a balancing factor or common denominator. . . .

> [O]pen-ended clarity can be found even within the obstructing presence of ordinary knowledge —and in ordinary 'not-knowing' and confusion as well. By working with appearance, refining this quality of clarity in everything, it becomes possible to use this clarity itself rather than 'mind' and 'things' as our orienting guide. As a result, our view of reality changes still further. . . . There is no longer a 'looker', but instead, only a 'knowingness' which can see more broadly, from all sides and points of view at once" (TSK, 281–82).

This knowing reflects a "multidimensional understanding" (LOK, xlv).

4. A More Substantive Critique

I offer now some comments on what may be considered weak spots in the TSK vision as presented above.

1. Social aspects of the acquisition and use of knowledge are virtually ignored in TSK. Although Tarthang Tulku tells us that personal change will result in social transformation, this seems inadequate. Social life is not just an extension and amplification of personal lives, but a phenomenon of a different order that may require separate attention. For instance, in these days of far-reaching division of labor, the true holders of knowledge are communities of knowledge professionals, rather than individuals. These communities live in a different space (social space) and different time (historical time).

Seen from this perspective, the situation does not seem to be as gloomy as TSK suggests. Individual people may fail, get frustrated, and abandon their quest for knowledge, or else trade it for more comfortable reproduction of patterns of the known. Yet humanity as a whole continues to make a steady progress in exactly the same direction as TSK suggests, that is, toward free and open inquiry. Perhaps the full implications of this development, unique to our culture, will escape the attention of those (like Tarthang Tulku) who have come to the West from traditional societies.

On a related point, many people in the Western world may find that their social activities present better opportunities for personal transformation than such individual pursuits as study, exercises, meditation, and the like. The way of selfless service to our fellow men is well regarded in our society, and may be an excellent means to get rid of the self and break the narrow confines of our personal space and time. After all, this is a potentially infinite path, one that need not be turned into a goal-oriented activity.

2. Tarthang Tulku is perhaps right in saying that people—meaning *most* people—are found on the first, or ordinary level of existence. This, however, does not mean that humanity as a whole stagnates at this level. It is a commonplace that progress is mostly due to a few creative people whose ideas benefit the rest of us. It is as if in addition to the multiple cocoons of our selves (individual constructs), we are trapped in a collective veil (the social construction of pseudo-reality). A rent made at any place in this veil lets in a fresh inflow of Great Knowledge. The vast bulk of humanity feeds on this Knowledge. While they certainly weave it into their cocoons, the net result is still less illusion and more light.

This model, if correct, returns us to a point raised above. Why has the "materialization" of the TSK vision twenty years ago not led to a flood of Great Knowledge? Why has TSK not become a major visible force in the world? One reason may be a not quite adequate presentation of the vision in the books published up to now. Another may be that the written presentation is insufficient to anchor the vision in the ordinary realm. If TSK is to be a way of life, or even life itself, then the best teacher of TSK would be a public life lived out in accordance with the vision. Remember that Socrates, the guiding light of Western thought, exerted his decisive influence on his disciples and friends through his way of life. He wrote nothing.

PART TWO

1. The TSK Critique of Science

Tarthang Tulku recognizes the progress made by science and technology (see, e.g., TSK, xxxvii). He also sees a possibility for using TSK as "a visionary medium" to provide a ground for the pursuit of sciences and religions (see Part One, Section 1 above). Inversely, he thinks that science, along with religion, might be of some help on the path of TSK:

> Because opening the focal setting to the Great Space dimension is essential to a complete grasp of the factors involved in appearance, the techniques offered by religions for relaxing the strictures imposed by obscuring focal settings can be viewed as a contribution to the physical sciences' quest for knowledge. And the observations of these sciences need not merely reinforce the ordinary world-view and preoccupation with causal connections between particular items. Scientific discoveries can serve as guiding insights which assist in opening the focal setting and thus indirectly complement the religious endeavor (TSK, 77).

However, in TSK, and especially in later books, Tarthang Tulku's view of science and technology is in general more negative than positive. It may safely be said that Tarthang Tulku has a clear case to make against both science and technology. Here are some of his main points, together with my responses where I have any:

1. Proliferation of Western science and technology has resulted in extinction of many non-Western cultures or their abandoning valuable insights that might be necessary for more balanced living "and even necessary for the success of the scientific solutions to life's problems" (TSK, xxxvii).

A possible answer: Perhaps correct. An inevitable evil, the law of survival of the fittest in action. Very little can be done about it, for there is yet no mechanism to manage cultures on a global scale.

2. Reliance of scientific models on the 'cause and sequence' orientation anchors our knowledge in first-level space and time and prevents us from appreciating the higher levels (TSK, 75).

Answer: There is no serious alternative to the 'cause and sequence' orientation insight. Some people cite in this connection C. G. Jung and W. Pauli's principle of acausal synchronicity; however, that principle was never recognized by mainstream science.[2] Others refer to the breakdown of the deterministic picture in quantum mechanics, but this consideration is misguided, as the time-dependent Schrödinger equation is as deterministic as the Newtonian equations of motion.

3. Since we are not able to control time, we instead control the body, the mind, and the environment through technological means. We yield to lower time and try to adapt to it rather than aiming to transcend it, and thus cut off our opportunities for personal freedom and fulfillment (TSK, 138).

4. Science is inherently restricted from knowing anything beyond phenomena and their common ground. "No ordinary 'knowing', or observation, however amplified by instrumentation, amounts to more than [knowledge of the phenomenal world]. . . . Nowhere in such investigations can a door to greater knowledge (or a transcendent ground for observed phenomena) be discovered" (TSK, 247).

5. Despite all their successes, science and technology fail to meet our deeper needs, such as achieving more individual freedom, full understanding of the consequences of our actions and meaning of our lives, complete fulfillment, and so on.

6. Technology (and also technological knowledge) are obsessed with getting results, and fail to address the issue of the meaning and value of those results (LOK, 33).

7. Ordinary knowledge is built up through 'models': "explanations or descriptions of how things work within a specified domain" (LOK, 130). Models establish fixed patterns and thus freeze out the possibility of fundamental change; they miss knowledge that does not fit within the basic structure of ordinary knowledge. Model-based knowledge "is distanced from direct experience in favor of conceptual structures;" "models turn

our attention away from a direct inquiry into the unfounded assumptions of the models themselves" (LOK, 132–33).

Answers 3 to 7: Probably correct, at least in part. Once again, however, there seems to be no better alternative for the time being.

2. Applying TSK to Science

Given all of this, science and technology as we now know them are inherently flawed. However, Tarthang Tulku appears to think that scientific and technological knowledge may benefit if raised to the second level (the third level is out of the question here). To explore what this might mean, let us start with two important facts that science has established.

First, the scientific picture of the world—and perhaps the world itself—possess a complicated hierarchical structure permeated with numerous horizontal and vertical links and correspondences. It is not so easy to untangle this underlying structure on the macroscopic level, but take a small segment of the entire structure on the microscopic level and it reveals what initially appears to be a clear linear order: fundamental particles (quarks, electrons, neutrinos, photons, gluons, and so on), composite nuclear particles (protons, neutrons, etc.), leading on to nuclei, atoms, and molecules. After that the linear character is lost: The chain branches off to give macromolecules, atomic and molecular clusters, exotic atoms, electron gas, plasmas, crystals, and so forth.

Every level builds up its own "vertical" substructure, which may resemble phenomena on other levels. For example, quarks and gluons may form a sort of plasma, or nuclei may possess hydrodynamic properties resembling those of conventional fluids. So it turns out that the emerging structure is really nonlinear, and the levels may intermingle.

Second, a principle of correspondence holds as well: If two levels are in a hierarchical relationship, the laws that operate at the more complex level can be reduced to the laws of the more basic level in areas where the latter apply. For example, the laws of thermodynamics can be reduced in part to the laws of mechanics, but also differ from the latter (especially with regard to the "arrow of time" and irreversible processes). In the same way it is assumed that biology may somehow derive from physics and chemistry, and consciousness from brain processes.

This does not mean, however, that the laws of the more complex realm should be seen as poorer in their content just because they derive from more basic laws. Deeper laws do not abolish less fundamental laws, but rather complement them.

Now, according to TSK, 1) the first level of reality is an incomplete and distorted reflection of more basic levels, while 2) from the perspective of Great Space, Great Time, and Great Knowledge, there is no such thing as a separate first level; that is, Great Space, etc., are everything that is. Accordingly, general features of the first level (where hard science operates) should in some form present themselves when more basic levels are in operation. In effect, then, the principle of correspondence or interacting hierarchies that science reveals holds among or between levels.

Tarthang Tulku has recognized such a law, calling it "a reversibility factor—anything [on the lowest level] can be traced back to the realization of perfection" (TSK, 276). As he explains:

> 'Reversibility' preserves the notion that we have 'strayed' from perfection, but indicates that the possibility of 'return' remains somehow available within the 'flawed' ordinary level. . . . These distortions are not deceptive in any final sense. They can be taken as symbols which can point back to the higher order (TSK, 278–79).

Such symbolic 'pointings back' can be seen as correlations. Here are some of the correlations indicated by Tarthang Tulku. They may be read in either direction: higher-level features as expressed in the corresponding lower-level features, or lower-level features as pointing to the corresponding higher-level features:

Higher-Level Features	Ordinary-Level Features
Openness of Great Space	Space as a 'container' of things
Unity of Great Space	Space as a continuum, a unified field of units
Great Time's timeless Being	Law-like regularities of linear time
Great Time's vitality	Energy as the basis for technology

Great Time's expressiveness or ability to evoke Great Space's openness	Speech
Great Knowledge	The subject Thinking and knowing acts, cast in "*x* knows *y*" fashion

Tarthang Tulku notes that more correlations could be mapped, but writes, "[S]een from the transitional standpoint of the [higher levels,] the important thing is to make the journey from the first [level to the higher levels] as directly as possible" (TSK, 279). He therefore leaves this approach undeveloped.

Just here, however, an opening presents itself for exploring the ways that hard science can contribute to TSK and vice-versa. If we trace such correlations, could they not offer a possible way in which scientific ways of looking can lead to higher knowledge?

When we begin to make this effort, we quickly find that some aspects of Western science have more credibility than Tarthang Tulku seems inclined to think. For example, science does attempt to identify the "law-like regularities" that pertain to the temporal aspect of the ordinary knowledge, which is where TSK is content to leave the matter. But it also provides alternative ways of looking at reality. Two of the most important are a systems-theory perspective (related to the spatial aspect of ordinary knowledge)[3] and an information-science approach (the knowledge aspect of ordinary knowledge). Taken together, these approaches present an intricate *grid*, woven into both ordinary knowledge and the hidden structures of our mind; that is, implicit in the unitary 'field' of ordinary knowledge, ordinary reality, and selves. By the same token, there is more to technological advances than doomed attempts to harness the energy of time—they point to the vitality of Great Time itself!

Pursuing such deeper correlations across and between different levels may offer Western science and technology a way beyond conventional knowledge, a way of making progress without breaking away from the great tradition that has fed science for so many centuries. This would be the way of least resistance. It offers an attractive alternative for scientists drawn to TSK. Instead of feeling compelled to switch from doing science and technology in favor of searching their souls as to the legitimacy and epistemological foundations of the scientific enterprise, they can investigate the idea of correlation between and across TSK levels, drawing on their unique knowledge of the first-level realms to do so.[4]

3. TSK and Model-Based Science

If correlations between levels in the TSK sense are to be established, the vehicle will be various scientific models. Yet the use of models is problematic from a TSK perspective, and deserves further comment.

The reliance of science on models has increased greatly in modern times, for the important reason that modern scientific and technological knowledge has moved farther and farther away from what is immediately given by the senses. In physical sciences, this move occured in the second half of the nineteenth century. Before that time, the major physical sciences were structured more or less according to whatever prevailing sensory or motor channels were used to collect observational data and respond to stimuli. Key areas for scientific research included optics (data acquired via seeing), acoustics (hearing and speech), thermodynamics (feeling), and mechanics (cf. mechanical devices imitating limbs).

In this century all that has changed. We take it for granted that the physical sciences should be organized in accordance with the structural levels of matter being studied.[5] Partly as a result, there are now many more intermediate stages between observational data and the objects being studied. The previously thin man-made veil separating the self from reality has acquired some depth, becoming a thick (though perhaps porous—see the discussion above on correspondence) interface. To an increasing degree, scientific knowledge has actually become a knowledge of models.

This agrees perfectly with what Tarthang Tulku has to say about models, discussed above. However, there is another way of looking at models that sees them, not as substitutes for reality, but as *symbols* or *signs* of reality.[6] Quite paradoxically, they may be very definite without having any form at all—formless identities. Seen in this way, models can be a gateway to knowledge rather than a limitation.

A few examples may help to clarify this important point. The first comes from the field of mathematics. Modern abstract mathematics no longer takes as its objects such relatively 'concrete' entities as numbers and geometrical figures. Instead, it deals with more abstract objects, such as groups, or with mathematical space. For instance, mathematicians may speak of a "topological space" without ever considering its points or giving its constructive description.

Another remarkable example is quantum theory. Ordinary quantum mechanics needs to specify the exact particle composition of a quantum system and all interparticle interactions, but nothing beyond that. All further information about the system is hidden in a mysterious 'thing' called a "state vector," which exists, but has no specific content.

A state vector is truly a thing in itself ('*Ding an sich*'), existing but hermetically sealed from everything else (as suggested by the symbol "ı>", often used to designate it). To get concrete information about it we need to ask a specific question. If the question is asked in terms of numbers, we receive an exact arithmetic answer, but we are free to ask other, more qualitative questions that bring other kinds of answers.

In quantum field theory, which is considered the most advanced known form of quantum theory, the model becomes even less defined. Now one does not need to specify either system or its content. The state vector ı> is also not specified. Instead, basic equations say what happens to ı> in space and time. ı> in fact represents the whole spectrum of all possible states of the universe: all pure one-particle states, all pure two-particle states, etc., as well as various mixtures of pure states. Thus ı> implicitly holds information about all possible universes.

Of course, we cannot go into such matters here. However, it would be interesting to investigate from a TSK perspective the thinking processes of researchers working in abstract mathematics and quantum physics by means of such models. Do they conform to the models for the acquisition of lower knowledge offered by Tarthang Tulku? Or do they go beyond such models toward a second-level knowledge?

Having said this much, perhaps I can offer a more general critique of the TSK critique of model-based thinking. Any working scientist cares very much whether his or her models work. Tarthang Tulku realizes and acknolwedges this fact, but seems to downplay its significance:

> As long as models can be said to 'work', perhaps it does not matter very much if they remain unfounded. Even if in the end we can rely only on 'blind faith', our reliance may be justified in terms of what it accomplishes, or on the basis of other, less immediately obvious criteria. Whatever the specific reasons we advance, however, there are good grounds for investigating further, for it seems that reliance on models limits knowledge in fundamental ways (LOK, 131).

One immediately feels a fundamental weakness in this argument. Yes, it is absolutely true that models are terribly flawed, but . . . Are there better, more workable models available? Or better, more workable non-models, for that matter? Is not the scientist who pursues that question on the path to knowledge? In the quote just given, Tarthang Tulku turns from models with the suggestion that it is necessary to investigate further. But it seems to me that researchers do exactly that.

IMPLEMENTATION AND TRANSFORMATION

Implementation of TSK in the hard sciences faces the difficulty that TSK by its nature resists implementation—it requires instead transformation. Since, however, this transformation will not happen instantly (though TSK would challenge this statement, too), it might be quite possible for a practitioner of TSK interested in the hard sciences to make use of its implementable elements for quite a long time. Since the cycles of humanity are even longer than individual cycles, humanity might be implementing TSK for centuries.

The implementable elements of TSK include everything on the first level and some (the less bizarre) elements on the second level. Since TSK on the first level explores areas that have also been dealt with in depth by many critics of conventional knowledge, let us concentrate on the second level. To clarify what this would mean in practice, let us consider the following rough characterization of the three levels:

1st level: multiplicity; little freedom

2nd level: multiplicity; a plentitude of freedom (and creativity)

3rd level: unity plus unrestricted freedom

The second level is thus one where one enjoys relative freedom within the confines of multiplicity. According to Tarthang Tulku, this is a vast field, extending from the first experiences of fluidity and thawing to the greatest intellectual and spiritual revelations.

In my opinion, these three second-level ideas: multiplicity (the allowing power of Space), freedom (the emancipating power of Time), and creativity (the freely acting power of Knowledge) are also applicable to scientific and technological knowledge, understood not as accumulation of information but as *gnosis*—a faculty (and a way of thinking) that combines rationality and precise imagination. Here, then, is a place where TSK and hard science could conceivably interact.

The postmodernist thinker Ihab Hassan wrote:

Advanced scientific work is an imaginative act; on this almost everyone agrees. The axiomatic basis of scientific theories cannot be extracted from sensory data; it must be freely invented. . . . Dream, play, poesis are complicitous in the scientist's work as in the artist's, for neither really is satisfied merely to confirm. . . .

[Ernst Cassirer] believed that in the symbolic universe, science held a special place, and could be regarded as "the highest and most characteristic attainment of human culture," precisely because it was theoretical, metaphorical, because it possessed, together with language and art, that "spontaneity and productivity" which animate "the very center of all human activities" (Hassan, 1982).

This seems to me a most sound perspective on hard knowledge, one that provides the necessary ground for the meeting, mutual understanding, and fruitful cooperation of TSK and scientific and technological knowledge. Such a meeting ground immediately removes many of the problems and contradictions discussed above. It calls for creating—that is doing—rather than critiquing and reasoning. However, creating may express itself in rational forms without betraying its own nature. The interplay that this approach suggests might throw some light on the TSK vision as a way of free and open inquiry. And it might allows us to temper some of the harsh statements made in the TSK books about technological knowledge, models, and the like. For if one arrives at a piece of technological knowledge or a model in an act of creative activity or uses it in a creative manner, it should be good and appropriate.

To be creative in this sense requires that one not rely on TSK as a source of understanding as such. Instead (as Tarthang Tulku would surely agree), one should go directly to the source of all inspiration. We might call that source Time, Space, and Knowledge. What remains then, is the eternal movement of creative energy manifesting itself—in the TSK vision as it does in science and technology, and in forms too numerous to name.

Further Possibilities for Science and Technology

We have discussed two possible areas of contact between the TSK vision and science and technology:

the use of levels, and creative activity. Contact at either of these points might make the production of scientific knowledge more efficient, and in this sense would have to count as a successful implementation of the TSK vision in the hard sciences.

However, this certainly does not exhaust the potential relationship between TSK and hard knowledge. Even a cursory look at the contents of the TSK books shows that the range of the vision goes far beyond creativity, the feature on which I relied in suggesting a basis for reconciling TSK with science and technology at the close of the last section. Among these essential ingredients are freedom, intimacy, beauty, and so forth. Can some of those additional ingredients be used in the pursuits of hard sciences and technology; for instance, as possible shortcuts to knowledge? It is well known that considerations based on beauty, symmetry, and so forth often serve as important principles leading to the discovery of truth in science, especially in the fundamental sciences. Can TSK contribute to this approach?

To explore this question, we must ask what it is about the sense of beauty, etc. that distinguishes these faculties from our knowing faculty. In my opinion, such non-cognitive capacities are distinguished by several features. First, they seem to be innate in human beings; it is as if they were in our genes. Even if they are learned rather than awakened, they seem in some way to be natural. Second, and in direct relationship to the first feature, they are rooted in the individual rather than in a group, although, of course, they are further developed and perfected in a group environment. One may experience feelings of beauty, etc. in solitude. Third, they are immediate: we feel beauty, etc. directly. Fourth, they survive through all the stages of our personal growth; although they may be modified, previous experience is refined and purified rather than discarded and replaced. That is why, for example, we still enjoy great literary works of the distant past, some of them remaining unsurpassed masterpieces of their respective genres (e.g., Homer's poems).

Not so with conventional knowledge, as practiced by the hard sciences. True, the will to know seems to be innate in us. But while in earlier periods of history, knowledge seems to have possessed the four features I have just listed, in modern societies that is no longer the case. In the course of human history a gap began to form between humanity and its knowledge on one side, and (ordinary) knowledge and reality on the other. For modern science, these features have either already been lost, or are on the way to dissolution.

Let us look at this more carefully. First, scientific knowledge no longer seems to be innate in us, or to grow out of our nature. While it remains quite possible for a layman to create a masterpiece of art without being an artist, or to perform a feat of freedom without being a politician (e.g., Martin Luther King, Jr.), or to display great love, it is now virtually impossible for a layman to make an unexpected discovery in quantum mechanics or molecular biology. What is worse, it is unclear why a layman should even be motivated to decipher the genetic code, or to understand involved rotational-vibrational spectra of molecules, or to become interested in something called "classification of all compact semisimple Lie groups." Despite certain exceptions (certain branches of observational astronomy, ecology) modern "ordinary" knowledge as developed by science has tended to become alienated from humanity as a whole and to become the possession of a few knowledge professionals.

Second, due to growing specialization, knowledge cannot be practiced in private, but must rely on transfer and communication between knowledge professionals via reasoning and language (including the language of mathematics). Thus it becomes heavily invested in scientific and technological models, and often in groups of scientists rather than in the individual scientist. It is as if knowledge resides in a space between scientists, rather than in scientists themselves.

Third, modern knowledge is far from being immediate. In many cases (e.g., relativity theory and quantum mechanics) it is manifestly counterintuitive. And fourth, science today proceeds by first feeding on the past, but then breaking with it, instead of refining it.

Thus modern science, like Janus, is a two-sided enterprise. In its essence it becomes an ever closer approximation of reality, but in its shape it leads us farther and farther away from reality.

Now, one way of understanding this is as a kind of conspiracy. Robins and Ross (1996) and other scholars engaged in what is called the "social studies of science and technology" choose to interpret the trends I have described as evidence of a conspiracy on the part of privileged natural scientists, supported by the military-industrial complex in particular and the entire structure of capitalist societies in general. These views were summarized by Alan Sokal, in his well-known parody of postmodern attitudes toward science and technology, in the following terms:

> [S]cientific "knowledge," far from being objective, reflects and encodes the dominant ideologies and power relations of the culture that produced it . . . (Sokal 1996, 218).

> [T]he fundamental goal of any emancipatory movement must be to demystify and democratize the production of scientific knowledge, to break down the artificial barriers that separate "scientists" from "the public" (*Ibid.*, 230).

However, this analysis, even if accurate, does not go far enough. If science is relieved from its supposed role as the handmaiden of the bourgeoisie, there will still remain the above-mentioned epistemic gap between its essence (approximation of reality) and the shape it takes (models).

Why is this so? Why should science be forced to use models at all? In my opinion, the reason is that we do not possess any organ to directly acquire and appreciate knowledge that lies under the surface of things. We are able to feel beauty directly; we can have an unmistakable feeling of intimacy that needs no model to support it; we can instantly tell freedom from slavery. But we are not equipped to see knowledge directly, at least beyond some immediate surface features.

Let us take an example. When we look at a beautiful rose, we can enjoy it apart from any theory of aesthetics, but we cannot directly read out from it the laws underlying the morphogenesis of plants. In the same way, we look at a falling apple and we cannot read out directly from this event Newton's laws of motion and the law of gravity. To arrive at such laws we need to observe a lot, to compare, and to build models and test them, looking for a model that correctly explains the observed phenomena.

The same is true of technology. In modern industrial societies relying on division of labor and multi-step technological processes, there is a gap between the worker and the object that the work helps to shape or process. Consider the worker who presses a button that initiates a production process (pressing the button → electric current in the control circuit → activating a microprocessor or a switch → and so forth), until finally a cutting tool contacts a piece of metal or a feeder injects certain substances into a chemical reactor. This is a far cry from the potter who directly applies muscular force to shape a clay ball. In addition, unlike the potter, the worker is not supposed to understand all the details of the production process, and certainly is not free to adjust it at his pleasure.

This alienation and dehumanization of the workforce is in part an alienation from knowledge. It is more fundamental than the economic and political alienation discovered by Marx, for even if the means of production are taken from capitalists and given to workers, workers will still work in the same way. This is one example of why science and technology generate such ambiguous feelings. They feed the scientist's pride in their astonishing successes, and at the same time provoke the scholar's amazement at their apparent inadequacy to reality.

Of course, if we only judge science by its fruits in this way, we miss something of essential importance. For the act of creating and shaping a model—as opposed to the finished product, the model itself—may require great creativity and appreciation for beauty, as well as a sense of wonder. Unfortunately, TSK sometimes seems to fall into this trap, which means that its critiques become an obstacle to communication rather than a source of new insight. Similar concerns were raised by van de Hulst (1993).

Still, I do not believe we should let this difficulty cut off the potential for dialogue. Fortunately, scientists themselves also are not quite happy about the way science works: the unending stream of models, the lack of agreement about where science is headed, the lack of understanding of why science works at all, etc. (Horgan, 1996). So there is ample room for criticizing science and technology. The TSK vision could certainly be one perspective for such criticism.

For now, as some of the best modern scientists are in a state of confusion and cannot provide reliable alternatives (Horgan, 1996), it may be permissible to offer some TSK-inspired speculation. If we are lacking the organs that let us respond directly to deeper forms of knowledge, would it perhaps be possible to "grow" such organs, developing the capacity for direct mental perception and direct action that we presently seem to lack? There has long been a dream of knowledge not mediated by concepts and models, and of direct action in the world of matter not mediated by hands or tools. There are suggestions in TSK that this is possible. There is even the sense Tarthang Tulku may have already implemented this possibility, as is evidenced by his direct vision (especially in KTS) of the structure of matter and the structures of ordinary knowledge. To give some examples:

> At the base of matter, mind, and energy alike, a constant motion whirls. Since each 'measured-out' point contributes to this motion anew, generates it anew, motion accelerates exponentially. And since 'within' any point there are more points (for it seems there can be no gaps), motion builds on motion.

> Motion gives to each point a strength and stability—an ability to uphold itself—without establishing anything solid. In a sequence that challenges all ordinary assumptions, rhythm intensifies, acceleration becomes infinite—form arises (KTS, 85).

> From this perspective, substance could be understood as a kind of 'holding pattern' against the force of momentum, a way of using momentum to support what persists. But acceleration continues even when held in check, proliferating the constructs of lower-level knowledge. As thoughts acceptable within the 'logic' of the 'logos' are piled atop one another, existence

becomes opaque, so that we can see only surfaces. Bound to the position of the 'bystander',
we struggle to satisfy our needs and concerns,
but end up feeding the same patterns of acceleration. In the end we can sustain the gathering
momentum only with our own substance. Not
attuned to the 'aliveness' of rhythm, we find
ourselves aligned with a momentum that moves
steadily toward death (KTS, 97).

If such descriptions really do grow out of direct
vision, and if such vision is a fruit of the TSK vision,
our problem—the gap between ordinary knowledge and
other human faculties—would in principle be solved.
Yet such direct vision may go farther than scientists
would like. If we agree that it could reveal the inner
mechanisms of the universe, it could also reveal the
limitations of scientific models. Scientists perhaps
would prefer to stop at the point of seeing the laws of
nature directly, exploiting this ability in order to discover better, preferably ultimate laws.

That, however, would constitute a half-measure,
based on an undue fondness for the models that till
now have served us as crutches. What is fundamental,
and what science would have to face to derive the full
benefit of TSK, is the idea that with our present mind
as an organ of knowledge there are sharply-drawn limits on how far we can go. This is true for fundamental
science, but similar statements may be made about the
conventional processes of technology.

From the standpoint of TSK, the idea of complete
transformation is inevitable and natural. From the

standpoint of the hard sciences, however, this is a revolutionary approach. It implies a change much more radical than simply replacing imperfect methodologies with better ones, or stuffing the mind with right information. Still, perhaps this alternative can be explored in a way that does not depend on giving up the beauty, the creativity, and the inspiration, as well as the highly effective methodologies, that have characterized science in our modern world. Only if some such approach is developed and adopted by the hard sciences will a fruitful contact between hard knowledge and the full range of the TSK vision become possible.[7]

NOTES

1. In LOK (xxiii) Tarthang Tulku goes even farther, suggesting (evidently for pedagogical purposes): "As investigation deepens, these nine levels can each be understood as embracing nine more levels, and so forth."

2. See Jung and Pauli (1955). Many authors have speculated on the issue of synchronicity (e.g., Progoff [1973], Peat [1987], Mansfield [1995]), but it still remains just that—a speculative idea. Note that according to Tarthang Tulku, in second-level time the "causal continuity" picture breaks down, and discontinuities, gaps, and synchronicities may occur (TSK, 148–53).

3. Ronald Purser (1993) has written about the spatio-temporal texture and dynamics of organizations, "the space of open systems theory," structures based on the standard first-level spatial characteristics of separation

421

and distance, organizations in relation to the environment, and so on. All this, and especially the very term "open systems," resonates well with the spatial aspects of first-level knowledge.

4. The idea of correlations between the higher and the lower figures prominently in some schools of esoteric thought (e.g., the Hermetic axiom, "As above, so below'). More mainstream thinkers have sometimes approached it as a variant on the analogy between microcosm and macrocosm (e.g., Conger [1922], Allers [1943], Wayman [1982]). This idea conceives man as mirroring the universe as regards his composition and operating principles. It follows that man (1) is seen as embedded 'in the fabric of the universe'; (2) reproduces in his small world the workings of the universe; and (3) holds in himself keys to understanding the entire world. This understanding closely resembles Tarthang Tulku's insistence that the knower and the outer world are 'given together', as well as its higher analog, the unity of Being.

5. A typical description of the structural levels of matter based on atomic and molecular physics may be found in Alexander (1944). The idea was foreseen, formulated, and elaborated by Friedrich Engels in the context of Marxist philosophy in his *Dialectics of Nature* well before the emergence of atomic physics. For a contemporary discussion of this issue and the relevance of Engels' views, see Masulli (1990).

6. Compare what Tarthang Tulku says about the twofold role of symbols: "Attuned in a new way to the patterns of our lives, we may be ready to see that our

words and stories are not names for a fixed reality, but symbols of a deeper knowing" (LOK, 372). On the other hand, "the seeming success of the move to the symbolic level in allowing us to sidestep assertion is somewhat illusory. In the realm of first-level meanings, the symbol must have meaning as a pointer. If the zero-point points nowhere, it is meaningless. We might just as well say nothing, or say 'Boo!'" (LOK, 346–47).

7.   I am grateful to Jack Petranker for useful discussions and help in shaping this article into its final form.

REFERENCES

Alexander, J. 1944. "Successive Levels of Material Structure." *Etc.: A Review of General Semantics* 1, 133–47.

Allers, R. 1943. "Microcosmus from Anaximandros to Paracelsus." *Traditio* 1, 319–407.

Conger, G.P. 1922. *Theories of Macrocosms and Microcosms in the History of Philosophy.* New York: Columbia Univ. Press.

Hassan, I. 1982. Joyce and the Gnosis of Modern Science. In *The Seventh of Joyce,* ed. B. Benstock. Bloomington, IN: Indiana Univ. Press.

Horgan, J. 1996. *The End of Science? Facing the Limits of Knowledge in the Twilight of the Scientific Age.* Reading, MA: Addison-Wesley.

Jung, C.G. and W. Pauli. 1955. *The Interpretation of Nature and Psyche/Synchronicity: An Acausal Connecting Principle, by C.G. Jung. The Influence of Archetypal Ideas on the Scientific Theories of Kepler, by W. Pauli.* New York: Pantheon Books.

Leonard, G.B. 1969. "The Human Potential." http://www.uia.org/uiademo/hum/h0461.htm.

Mansfield, V. 1995. *Synchronicity, Science, and Soul-Making: Understanding Jungian Synchronicity Through Physics, Buddhism, and Philosophy.* Chicago: Open Court.

Masulli, I. 1990. *Nature and History: The Evolutionary Approach for Social Scientists.* NY: Gordon and Breach.

Peat, F.D. 1987. *Synchronicity: The Bridge between Matter and Mind.* New York: Bantam Books.

Progoff, I. 1973. *Jung, Synchronicity, and Human Destiny: Noncausal Dimensions of Human Experience.* New York: Julian Press.

Purser, R. 1993. "'Opening Up' Open Systems Theory: Towards a Socio-Ecological Understanding of Organizational Environments." In MOM.

Robins, B. and A. Ross, issue editors. 1996. *Science Wars: A Special Issue of Social Text.* No. 46–47:1–252.

Sokal, A. 1996. "Transgressing the Boundaries: Toward a Transformative Hermeneutics of Quantum Gravity." In Robins, B. and A. Ross, issue editors. *Science Wars: A Special Issue of Social Text.* No. 46–47:1–252.

Tarthang Tulku. 1977. "A New Vision of Reality." In *Buddhist Thought and Asian Civilization: Essays in Honor of Herbert Guenther on His Sixtieth Birthday.* L. S. Kawamura and K. Scott, eds. Berkeley: Dharma Publishing.

van de Hulst, H.C. 1993. "Pleasure in the Consistency of the World: A Test Case to Explore the Obstacles a Scientist May Meet in Studying the TSK Vision." In MOM.

Wayman, A. 1982. "The Human Body as Microcosm in India, Greek Cosmology, and Sixteenth-Century Europe." *History of Religions* 22, 172-90.

DIMENSIONALITY AS A CULTURAL/HISTORICAL APPROACH

John Smyrl

Unlocking Forms of Knowledge in Western Civilization

When I first began to explore the Time, Space and Knowledge vision, one of the exciting discoveries was the way in which certain "boundaries" of my conceptual world seemed to open, as if they were doors to unexpected vistas. Initially, however, I inserted some boundaries of my own in my expectation of the "fields" to which the exploration of TSK could reasonably "apply." Of course, the vision suggests that the range of what can be explored is boundless, touching every area of life. Yet I have opened to this invitation only gradually.

One area that has begun to attract me from a TSK perspective is cultural and historical studies. Tarthang Tulku has offered a few suggestions in these areas: in *Knowledge of Freedom*, LOK, and KTS (see especially the section entitled "Rhythm of Allowing" [KTS, 59]). He has directed our attention to the way that society and civilization appear as primary carriers of knowledge within a particular 'order', developing "in accord with a basic pattern that brings different ways of knowing to the fore in different eras."

Western civilization recognizes historical development over time in the idea of progress: a growing availability of knowledge over time. Often this progression is understood to be marked out by transitions that happen at certain pivotal moments. Recently, these shifts have been increasingly referred to as "paradigm shifts," thought of as changes in the fundamental ways that knowledge is structured, with revolutionary consequences for the approach taken to basic fields of study.[1]

However radical these shifts in knowledge, they have usually been conceived as occurring 'within' the ways of knowing which are part of the Western tradition. In this sense, the West has conceived of its knowledge as 'universal'. This is sometimes expressed by saying that Western knowledge aims at being objective and encompassing, beyond all cultural and temporal biases (hence the "university" as the repository for such knowledge). However, this claim to objectivity and universality has recently been questioned, particularly in fields such as philosophy and literary theory, once considered in the vanguard among the universalizing fields of knowledge.

If the pattern that has guided the unfolding of the Western tradition of knowledge now appears to be splitting apart, the very cracks in the pattern seem to have potential for letting light through. Put differently, exploration of the pattern itself, *in light of* its limits and uncertain future, can take us beyond the 'order' to which it belongs. Ultimately, we can see how the standard embodiments of knowledge themselves live in space and time.

To take up the patterns of knowledge in this way, focusing directly on space and time, seems highly appropriate to the culture and history of Western civilization. Perhaps inescapably, this culture embodies the knowledge it relies on in the forms of art, literature and music, all of which must stand in a particular and direct relationship to time and space in order to 'appear' at all. Explored as appearances of knowledge and expressions of the time-space interplay, these cultural artifacts seem to me to offer us the possibility for new insight into Western culture and history. At the same time, this exploration may open a fruitful field of investigation for the further study of the TSK vision. What I wish to do here is present some launching points and sources for such an exploration. Of particular interest to me are sources that deal with the concept of "dimensionality."

Jean Gebser and the Dimensions of Cultural Worlds

One of the leading twentieth-century thinkers to undertake the study of cultural forms with a view to their presence in space and time is Jean Gebser (1905–1973), a German scholar of many disciplines. Gebser appears to have started as a social historian with an interest in ethnography, psychology, and philosophy, but he also demonstrated incisive insights into painting, literature, music, and architecture. His magnum opus, *Ursprung und Gegenwart* (published in English as *The Ever-Present Origin* [1985]) presents his analysis of Western cultural history in general, with a special focus on the Modern Period (that is, the early twentieth century). In the course of this analysis, he hypothesized a series of major shifts in Western culture's way of knowing.

Of particular interest in Gebser's work is the way that he demonstrates how—for each of the temporal stages of Western culture—cultural consciousness and its related perceptual fields manifest within the forms of the culture. The temporal stages he identifies and then maps out in this way reflect structural change at a deep level within the culture. He argues that this can be seen in terms of both perceptual and conceptual development.

While Gebser demonstrates many correspondences among various cultural phenomena for each temporal stage of Western history, he uses as symbolic key for each stage the concept of "dimension." However, the role of dimensionality is more than symbolic. The perception of dimensional space in each historical era or stage turns out to correspond in very specific ways to conceptual cultural structures (what I would call "psycho-epistemologies)", as shown in the following chart:

STRUCTURE	SPACE AND TIME RELATIONSHIP		
	DIMENSIONING	PERSPECTIVITY	EMPHASIS
Archaic	Zero-Dimensional	None	Prespatial Pretemporal
Magic	One-Dimensional	Preperspectival	Spaceless Timeless
Mythical	Two-Dimensional	Unperspectival	Spaceless Natural Temporicity
Mental	Three-Dimensional	Perspectival	Spatial Abstractly Temporal
Integral	Four-Dimensional	Aperspectival	Space-free Time-free

At the most basic level, Gebser's scheme of development presents three European "worlds" or developmental stages, each organized around dimensionality. They are the Unperspectival (or pre-perspectival), the Perspectival and the Aperspectival (or trans-perspectival) worlds.

The Unperspectival world describes the stage of European cultural history prior to the Renaissance development of representational perspective in painting.[2] This epoch, and the ones preceding it, are marked precisely by the lack of such a representational perspective. They present space as somewhat undifferentiated. Gebser draws parallels between architectural/artistic structures that reflect this understanding of space on the one hand, and the dominant consciousness on the other. He sees this consciousness as one of a "mythic/group identification," lacking ego in the sense of individual assertion of consciousness as the cultural norm. In Gebser's words (1985, 10):

Man's lack of spatial awareness is attended by a lack of ego-consciousness, since in order to objectify and quantify space, a self-conscious "I" is required that is able to stand opposite or confront space as well as to depict or represent it by projecting it out of his soul or psyche.

The Unperspectival world is further divided into substages, for which Gebser's work should be consulted.

In the shift from the Unperspectival to the Perspectival, space becomes objectified. Now it is available as perspective. It is related to the "viewpoint" of the individual "self" at the "moment" of rational clock time (which replaces the temporal rhythm of mythic narrative). Perspective begins with paintings by Giotto, and is mirrored by other cultural elements:

> But in the work of Giotto, the latent space hitherto dormant in the night of collective man's unconscious is visualized; the first renderings of space begin to appear in painting, signaling an incipient perspectivity. A new psychic awareness of space, objectified or externalized from the psyche out into the world, begins—a consciousness of space whose element of depth becomes visible in perspective. This psychic inner-space breaks forth at the very moment that the troubadors are writing the first lyric "I" poems, the first personal poetry that suddenly opens an abyss between man as poet, and the world or nature (1250 A.D.). Concurrently at the University of Paris, Thomas Aquinas, following the thought of his teacher Albertus Magnus,

asserts the validity of Aristotle, thereby initiating the rational displacement of the predominantly psychic-bound Platonic world. . . . And the world (which amounted to a virtual timelessness) gave way to the visualization of, and openness to, time with a quantifiable spatial character. This was exemplified by the erection of the first public clock in the courtyard of Westminister Palace in 1283. (Gebser 1985, 11–12)

The perspectival dynamic is also shown to influence other cultural areas such as theology, science, and economics. Theology, for example, is seen as developing along similar lines, moving from a Scholastic to a Reformation perspective, in which the individual, following his or her own reason and interpretations, develops his or her own "view." This view attempts to comprehensively survey the conceptual "geography," with the transcendent aspect of the view represented by the perspectival "vanishing point."[3]

The Perspectival world brings an added dimension of freedom, but it also creates some new problems. The fragmentation of self and world brings pain and fear, and the clash of finite individual "views" creates ongoing social conflict, much of which continues to our day. The combination of rationality and objective nature allows science to arise and give birth to technology, but human beings, inhabiting a world of objective surfaces, frequently experience being trapped as "ghosts in the machine."[4]

While Gebser sheds light on the nature of the Unperspectival and Perspectival worlds, his main focus is on the emergence of the Aperspectival world. Gebser believed that a new structure of consciousness was emerging during his lifetime, a way of seeing and knowing that transcended Perspectivity, adding yet another degree of freedom. This movement is symbolized by the shift from three to four dimensions in painting, which mirrors profound developments in physics, and a corresponding shift in our understanding of time as relative (e.g. Einstein's Relativity and the subsequent development of the "New Physics").

Gebser was a contemporary and friend of Picasso, and it is his work, and that of other Cubists, which provide for Gebser the greatest examples of Aperspectivism in painting. Looking at a typical Picasso cubist drawing, Gebser observes (1985, 24–25):

In this drawing, however, space and body have become *transparent*. In this sense the drawing is neither unperspectival, i.e., a two-dimensional rendering of a surface in which the body is imprisoned, nor is it perspectival, i.e., a three-dimensional visual sector cut out of reality that surrounds the figure with breathing space. The drawing is "aperspectival" in our sense of the term; time is no longer spatialized but integrated and concretized as a fourth dimension. By this means it renders the whole visible to insight, a whole which becomes visible only because the previously missing component, time, is expressed in an intensified and valid form as the present. It is no longer the moment, or the "twinkling of the eye"—time viewed through the organ of sight as spatialized time—but the pure present, the *quintessence* of time, that radiates from this drawing."

Most of Gebser's work, including his later writings, develops the idea of the "Aperspectival world." In *The Everpresent Origin* he goes on to explore four-dimensionality and aperspectivity in other art forms and in literature, architecture, philosophy, and religion. In the course of this work, he conjectures with remarkable accuracy on the future course of Western civilization. Had he lived longer, he would have seen many of these conjectures validated, especially with regard to the arising of new religious, psychological, and philosophical movements.

The Aperspectival World as a 'Read-Out' in Time, Space, and Knowledge

The shifts between "worlds" in Gebser's work offers interesting material for students of the TSK vision, precisely because the observations that mark the characteristics of the shift themselves manifest Time, Space, and Knowledge in action. Several implications of Gebser's work are particularly worth exploring.

Firstly, in looking at major shifts in culture and history in the way Gebser proposes, one discovers that the interplay of time, space, and knowledge in very immediate terms is inseparable from complex conceptual developments and ideas. What is breathtaking about Gebser's work is not only that he is able to synthesize seemingly unrelated cultural phenomena into a holistic vision, but that he does so on the ground of intrinsically simple and concrete manifestations. Gebser finds a true universality among the disciplines, not based on a particular cultural order, but on the fields in which they appear—modes of knowing that unfold according to the aspects of space and time which allow the unfolding to occur. Looking for space and time to be present within knowledge in this way preserves an openness to inquiry that allows for new directions and cross-disciplinary insights, without rejecting either traditional modes of knowing or academic rigor.

Secondly, the observation of dimensionality as a cultural and conceptual phenomenon illustrates how the range of possibilities related to specific ways of knowing may open, based on simple shifts in the field of space or the rhythm of time. Entire new ranges of meanings and perceptions become available through an added dimension or "degree of freedom." By observing this, it is possible to see how this dynamic works to reveal or conceal knowledge which is already present, but may not be available because of a limited "view" of the situation. In turn, when we understand that the knowledge we lack may already be present, we are further encouraged to look at the 'order' and corresponding pattern to which our way of knowing belongs, and to see the ways in which our knowing has become "limited in advance."

Perhaps the most revealing implication of Gebser's work for exploration within the TSK vision comes through a focus on the shift from the Perspectival world to the Aperspectival world. In this context, we discover the historical "self" to be a source of limitation.

This is particularly apparent if we use the illustration of perspective in painting. In a painting that uses three-dimensional perspective as its mode of representation, the "view" of space is tied to the field of vision held by the immediate viewer. From this vantage point, space opens outwardly, revealing the surfaces of objects in three dimensions, with objects growing smaller and diminshing in clarity, based on how far away they are located from the "position" of the viewer. If, for example, a road is located in the center of the "view", then the road will diminish in size and clarity until it disappears at the horizon of the "view," at what is referred to as the "vanishing point". View, perspective, horizon, and vanishing point define the entire world of the "viewer" in advance. Since my "view" and "perspective" do not match yours, we will not agree as to the true nature of the immediate landscape, and can only speculate as to "what" lies over the horizon.

Of course, this description holds true not only for a perspectival painting, but for the way of knowing that pertained in Western culture until quite recently, and in many ways still does. The priorities assigned objects by the viewing self are given in advance, based on proximity (which is not only spatial, but involves the priorities set by the self's concerns). The historic self in this context is defined by the "photographic" perspective: a view which is frozen in an instant of time. The artist David Hockney, lecturing on this phenomenon, pointed out (1990, 30–31):

The photograph is the ultimate perspective picture. The viewer is outside the picture and there is a vanishing point, and the vanishing point can theoretically be called infinity. If the infinite were God, the viewer and the infinite could have no connection whatsoever, and never have any connection, so I assume that is the God that died at the end of the nineteenth century. When you reverse perspective, which is what Picasso did with Cubism, the viewer can see all sides of an object, has movement in space, and is everywhere at the same time. Infinity is therefore everywhere, including within the viewer. That actually sounds better to me, theologically.

When the possibility of adding a new dimension to our view becomes available, the first thing to shift is the way the self is related to time. No longer frozen in an "instant," time becomes available as what Gebser refers to as "time-freedom." Not trapped in the instant, the viewer is also not limited to a single temporal "rhythm" or pattern. This allows for the possibility of "simultaneity," transforming the infinite nature of time from an endless succession of instants, which are not truly available, to time as available and present. This new "presence" of time, as well as space, becomes available without becoming an "object" to be possessed by the self. Objects, in fact, which from the perspectival view were merely hierarchical surfaces in space, now have transparency and interiority, and are no longer dependent on their location. In fact, they are not necessarily objects apart from the "field" or "landscape." For that matter, neither is the self!

As distinct from the limited possibilities of a photographic frozen instant, the richness of simultaneity allows multiple perspectives and views in the same "field" of space. This is initially difficult to see, whether in the "view" of a cubist painting or in the conceptual "view" which is no longer limited by a single position or "perspective," as explored in TSK. In both cases, the first glimpse of the added dimension creates an experience of freedom, which in turn deepens our appreciation and allows us to "move" with greater flexibility.

The renewed sense of vision that comes with seeing the landscape in a new way leads to the realization that we can exhaust neither the range of dimensional "worlds" nor the lines of inquiry that we can trace into cultural and historical backgrounds. Not only is it possible to find new ways of knowing "just around the corner," but the corner itself is known with new meaning!

Compare the above with the notion of emerging transparency (VOK, 133):

Time, space, and knowledge open the beginning, middle, and end implicit in every structure. They go to the beginning of the beginning and the ending of the end, where any starting point points to what is prior, and any ending point points toward what follows. As beginning and ending point toward the middle, points lose their distinctive definition, and structure becomes transparent. 'Possible' points toward 'impossible', with no felt need for definitive statements

> to separate the two. . . . Living closely in time, we merge with coemergent experience.

See also the discussion of 'no source from' in TSK and the parallel discussion in DTS (e.g., 189).

Launching Points for Further Study: An Initial Syllabus on Aperspectivism

In this limited space, I have only been able to introduce these rich new areas for inquiry. Below are some sources and ideas for further exploration.

In addition to Gebser's works, which offer enough to keep most students of culture and history busy for a long time, here are some references, presented as threads of inquiry to follow. Some proceed rather directly from Gebser's work, while others do not.

THE VISUAL ARTS

Picasso, by David Hockney. 1990. NY: Hanuman Books.

A good discussion on the Aperspectival aspect of Picasso by a prominent artist who himself creates paintings and stage scenery with an aperspectival slant.

The Fourth Dimension and Non-Euclidean Geometry in Modern Art, by Linda Dalrymple Henderson. 1983. Princeton, NJ: Princeton University Press.

A more general survey, with a fairly technical discussion of the fourth dimension.

Fourfield: Computers, Art, and the Fourth Dimension, by Tony Robbin. 1992. Boston: Bulfinch Press.

A book by an artist of four-dimensional work that includes discussions of four-dimensional art history and gives some samples of the artist's work. Of particular interest is the material discussing the use of computers and virtual reality to assist with visualizing the fourth dimension. The book comes with special glasses, a print, and a free software offer.

Art and Physics: Parallel Visions in Space, Time, and Light, by Leonard Shlain. 1993. NY: Quill/Morrow.

This work is useful for finding parallels between representational time/space and time/space as it is described by science.

LITERATURE

Flatland: A Romance of Many Dimensions, with illustrations by the author, a square, by Edwin A. Abbott. 1963. New York: Barnes & Noble.

Abbot's classic tale of higher dimensional spaces was one of the first popularizations to explain the fourth dimension by analogy.

Modern Writers

The first real appearance of an Aperspectival literature was among the Modern writers; in particular, T.S. Eliot in poetry and James Joyce and William Faulkner in the novel. Especially famous is Joyce's *Ulysses*, which not only presents a series of events and places from three different perspectives, but creates an interesting interiority through a pathbreaking stream-of-consciousness presentation of the character's thoughts.

The Dismantling of Time in Contemporary Poetry, by R. Jackson. 1988. Tuscaloosa: Univ. of Alabama Press.

An excellent introduction to "time-freedom" in the work of several Postmodern poets.

Gebser himself offers several interesting discussions on literature. In particular, I want to call attention to his "Notes on Etymology," a section in *The Everpresent Origin*, which offers a tantalizing sample of a whole potential field of study that I am certain deserves much greater exploration. One of the threads I would like to follow is the ways in which complex, conceptual words of Greek origin often have as their roots prepositional compounds that imply a spatial orientation.

MUSIC

A proper discussion of the sources in music would go beyond the scope of this list. Gebser, as well as some of the other sources mentioned above, introduce some threads that would be worth following. One topic I would like to pursue: elements of polyrhythmic music (especially modern jazz) as "time-freedom."

Goedel, Escher, Bach: An Eternal Golden Braid, by Douglass R. Hofstadter. 1979. New York: Basic Books.

Intriguing explorations of the interconnections among logic, space, and music.

GENERAL SOURCES

Living in the New Consciousness by Hugo Enomiya-Lassalle. 1988. Boston: Shambhala.

Enomiya-Lassalle presents certain aspects of Gebser's work within the context of what he sees as a new religious consciousness. He himself represents an interesting example of Aperspectival religion, being both a Jesuit Priest and confirmed Zen master. He helped build the Church of World Peace in Hiroshima, Japan.

A Brief History of Everything by Ken Wilber. 1996. Boston: Shambhala.

Wilber is a pioneer in Transpersonal thought. The particular value of this work is his reading of Gebser and discussion of subsequent developments which fall in line with Gebser's ideas.

The Fourth Dimension: Toward a Geometry of Higher Reality by Rudy von Bitter Rucker. 1984. Boston: Houghton Mifflin.

This is the second book on the fourth dimension by Rucker, a mathematician who presents the technical, mathematical aspect of dimensionality for the general reader. Rucker also writes science-fiction set in multi-dimensional worlds.

NOTES

1. The term "paradigm shift" entered into popular use through Thomas Kuhn's *The Structure of Scientific Revolutions*. Kuhn, a historian of science, used it to refer to occasions when the deeper presuppositions and methodological structures of a scientific discipline change, having an almost "revolutionary" effect on the discipline in question. Kuhn's work provoked much controversy within his own discipline, but his ideas were readily taken up by academics in a variety of different fields. The term has since undergone several transformations in popular use, and today is even part of popular business vocabulary. It has been parodied as a trendy "buzzword" by a popular syndicated comic strip.

2. Gebser actually demonstrated that the Perspectival world begins to develop in the late Classical period, but indicates that all of the elements which create a cultural differentiation were not in place until just prior to the Renaissance.

3. Gebser discusses the "vanishing point" as the obvious limitation of the rational stage of cultural development, but did not actually apply it to theology except as a "point of view," to be defended from other erroneous points of view. But it is not a great leap to so extend the idea, as the quote by David Hockney in the text below implies.

4. For an excellent discussion of the consequences of these developments, see the work by Ken Wilber listed in the syllabus at the end of this essay.

REFERENCES

Gebser, Jean. 1985. *The Ever-present Origin (Foundations and Manifestations of the Aperspectival World)*. tr. N. Barstad with Algis Mickunas. Athens, OH: Ohio University Press.

Hockney, David. 1990. *Picasso*. NY: Hanuman Books.

Kuhn, Thomas. 1970. *The Structure of Scientific Revolutions*. 2nd edition. Chicago: Univ. of Chicago Press.

Tarthang Tulku. 1984. *Knowledge of Freedom: Time to Change*. Berkeley: Dharma Publishing.

CONTRIBUTORS

DON BEERE earned his Ph.D. from Michigan State University in 1971, and has been a practicing clinical psychologist since that time. He is currently a professor in the Department of Psychology and Director of Clinical Training for the Psy.D. in clinical psychology at Central Michigan University. He has been awarded a Diplomate in Clinical Psychology by the American Board of Professional Psychology, the highest award the profession gives to practitioners. His orientation is experiential, integrating the interpersonal and the phenomenological, and is firmly grounded in philosophical phenomenology. For the past ten years, he has researched Dissociative Disorders, such as Multiple Personality Disorder (Dissociative Identity Disorder), and has presented and published frequently on topics related to dissociation.

HAL GURISH, MSW, has over forty years experience as a therapist and meditation teacher. In 1973 he participated in the first Human Development Training Program led by Tarthang Tulku at the Nyingma Institute, and in 1977 was a member of the first and only TSK Training Program to be led by Tarthang

Tulku. In the 1980s he completed a five-year intensive retreat at Odiyan Buddhist Center in northern California. He has studied and taught TSK for twenty years.

ALAN MALACHOWSKI, M.Phil, is Honorary Lecturer in Philosophy, University of East Anglia, Part-Time Lecturer in Philosophy, University of Reading, and editor of the *Journal of Philosophical Cosmology*. He was editor of *Reading Rorty* (Blackwell, 1990) and is author of *Business Ethics: A Textbook Approach* (forthcoming, Routledge), and *Living in a Universe: An Introduction to Philosophical Cosmology* (forthcoming).

ALFONSO MONTUORI, Ph.D., is Associate Professor at the California Institute for Integral Studies. He is the author of several books and numerous articles on creativity, social change, systems and complexity theories, and the role of culture in public and personal discourse. He is also the Associate Editor of *World Futures, The Journal of General Evolution*, Series Editor for *Advances in Systems Theory, Complexity and the Human Sciences* at Hampton Press, and on the editorial board of *Pluriverso* (Italy). An international consultant and a musician, he lives in San Francisco with his wife, jazz singer Kitty Margolis.

LEE NICHOL is a freelance writer, editor, and tour guide in northern New Mexico. After studying under Chogyam Trungpa Rinpoche in the 1970s, he spent fifteen years participating in the educational projects of J. Krishnamurti. He is currently general editor of David Bohm's philosophical works, including *Thought as a System, On Dialogue*, and the forthcoming *On Creativity* (all published by Routledge).

MAXIM OSINOVSKY, Ph.D. holds a degree in Theoretical Physics from the Institute of Metal Physics, Academy of Sciences of Ukraine, Former Soviet Union. He spent much of his professional life as a research physicist in the area of condensed matter physics and theoretical physics, and also taught physics at Kiev Polytechnic Institute. He is currently a project manager in the Conservation Department of the Main Library, University of California, Berkeley, and a freelance consultant to the American Institute of Physics.

JACK PETRANKER received an M.A. in Political Theory from the University of California, Berkeley and a J.D. from Yale Law School. He is an editor for Dharma Publishing, has for many years been on the faculty of the Nyingma Institute, and is an active member of the State Bar of California. He has been principal editor of the books in the TSK and Perspectives on TSK series since 1985.

RON PURSER, Ph.D. is a father, husband, teacher, researcher, consultant, nature lover, jazz enthusiast, and book addict. Currently an Associate Professor in the Loyola University School of Organizational Development, he recently accepted new positions as an Associate Professor of Management at San Francisco State University and adjunct faculty member at Saybrook Institute and Benedictine University. He is co-author (with Merrelyn Emery) of *The Search Conference* (Jossey-Bass, 1996), and co-editor (with Alfonso Montuori) of *Social Creativity*, a four-volume series (Hampton Press, 1997). His most recent book, *The Self-Managing Organization*, will be published by

The Free Press in 1998. Dr. Purser's research interests focus on workplace democracy and the participative design of organizations, the theory of ecologically sustainable organizations, social dimensions of creativity and creative collaboration, and critical organization theory. He has published over forty articles and book chapters and consulted with numerous private and public sector organizations. In 1983 he was a student in the Nine-Month TSK Program at the Nyingma Institute in Berkeley, California.

STEVE RANDALL holds a Ph.D. in East-West psychology. He is a trainer, business consultant, and editor of the TSK newsletter, *Reports from the Field*. He was co-editor of *Dimensions of Thought* (1980), the first book in the Perspectives on TSK Series, and is author of *Results in No Time: Timeless Peak Performance in the Workplace* (forthcoming: Amber Lotus). He has been exploring the TSK vision for twenty years, and is one of the founders of the recently formed Time, Space, and Knowledge Association.

JOHN SMYRL is a San Francisco poet and coffee-house philosopher, who supports his habits by working at a large computer company in the nearby Silicon Valley, hacking web pages. He has been an occasional student of the TSK vision for many years. One of his primary interests of late has been Benedictine spirituality. Some of his poems and other musings will soon be available on the World Wide Web at http://www.strannik.com/.

TARTHANG TULKU received an intensive education in Buddhism in his native Tibet before going into exile in 1958. After six years on the faculty of Sanskrit University in India, he came to America in 1968. He completed *Time, Space, and Knowledge* in 1977, and has published four more TSK-related books since that time, as well as seven other titles. The hallmark of Tarthang Tulku's career has been his focus on achieving valuable results. Having arrived in the West bearing the knowledge of a whole civilization, he has been tireless in communicating that accumulated insight and preserving it for future generations. His books have nourished people at countless levels, and the many organizations he has founded and directed have in common a record of accomplishment far beyond their size. His dedication to preserving the Buddhist literature of Tibet has resulted in publication of over 700 archival volumes, containing more than 80,000 works by 1,500 authors: possibly the largest publishing project in history. By uniting vision, leadership, and management skills with energy and perseverance, Tarthang Tulku has demonstrated that knowledge can manifest as a dynamic force, shaping time and space toward significant action.